MANAGEMENT, WORK
AND ORGANISATIONS

Series editors: **Gibson Burrell**, The Management Centre, University of Leicester
Mick Marchington, Manchester Business School
Paul Thompson, Department of Human Resource Management,
University of Strathclyde

This series of new textbooks covers the areas of human resource management, employee relations, organisational behaviour and related business and management fields. Each text has been specially commissioned to be written by leading experts in a clear and accessible way. The books contain serious and challenging material, take an analytical rather than prescriptive approach and are particularly suitable for use by students with no prior specialist knowledge.

The series is relevant for many business and management courses, including MBA and post-experience courses, specialist masters and postgraduate diplomas, professional courses and final-year undergraduate courses. These texts have become essential reading at business and management schools worldwide.

Published

Emma Bell **Reading Management and Organization in Film**
Paul Blyton and Peter Turnbull **The Dynamics of Employee Relations** (3rd edn)
Sharon C. Bolton **Emotion Management in the Workplace**
Sharon Bolton and Maeve Houlihan **Searching for the Human in Human Resource Management**
Peter Boxall and John Purcell **Strategy and Human Resource Management**
J. Martin Corbett **Critical Cases in Organisational Behaviour**
Susan Corby, Steve Palmer and Esmond Lindop (eds) **Rethinking Reward**
Keith Grint **Leadership**
Irena Grugulis **Skills, Training and Human Resource Development**
Damian Hodgson and Svetlana Cicmil **Making Projects Critical**
Marek Korczynski **Human Resource Management in Service Work**
Karen Legge **Human Resource Management:** anniversary edition
Patricia Lewis and Ruth Simpson (eds) **Gendering Emotions in Organizations**
Stephen Procter and Frank Mueller (eds) **Teamworking**
Alison Pullen, Nic Beech and David Sims **Exploring Identity**
Helen Rainbird (ed.) **Training in the Workplace**
Jill Rubery and Damian Grimshaw **The Organisation of Employment**
Harry Scarbrough (ed.) **The Management of Expertise**
Hugh Scullion and Margaret Linehan **International Human Resource Management**
Ruth Simpson and Patricia Lewis **Voice, Visibility and the Gendering of Organizations**
Adrian Wilkinson, Mick Marchington, Tom Redman and Ed Snape **Managing with Total Quality Management**
Colin C. Williams **Rethinking the Future of Work**
Diana Winstanley and Jean Woodall (eds) **Ethical Issues in Contemporary Human Resource Management**

For more information on titles in the Series please go to www.palgrave.com/business/mwo

Invitation to authors

The Series Editors welcome proposals for new books within the Management, Work and Organisations series. These should be sent to Paul Thompson (p.thompson@strath.ac.uk) at the Dept of HRM, Strathclyde Business School, University of Strathclyde, 50 Richmond St Glasgow G1 1XT

Rethinking Reward

Edited by

Susan Corby
Professor of Employment Relations,
University of Greenwich Business School, UK

Steve Palmer
Remuneration Specialist,
Office of Manpower Economics, UK

Esmond Lindop
Independent Consultant

palgrave
macmillan

First published 2009 by
PALGRAVE MACMILLAN

Palgrave Macmillan in the UK is an imprint of Macmillan Publishers Limited,
registered in England, company number 785998, of Houndmills, Basingstoke,
Hampshire RG21 6XS.

Palgrave Macmillan in the US is a division of St Martin's Press LLC,
175 Fifth Avenue, New York, NY 10010.

Palgrave Macmillan is the global academic imprint of the above companies
and has companies and representatives throughout the world.

Palgrave® and Macmillan® are registered trademarks in the United States,
the United Kingdom, Europe and other countries.

ISBN-13: 978–0–230–53723–1 paperback
ISBN-10: 0–230–53723–5 paperback

This book is printed on paper suitable for recycling and made from fully
managed and sustained forest sources. Logging, pulping and manufacturing
processes are expected to conform to the environmental regulations of the
country of origin.

A catalogue record for this book is available from the British Library.

A catalog record for this book is available from the Library of Congress.

10 9 8 7 6 5 4 3 2 1
18 17 16 15 14 13 12 11 10 09

Printed in China

Contents

Figures

Tables

Abbreviations

AfC	Agenda for Change
AEI	Average Earnings Index
APT&C	Administrative Professional Technical and Clerical
ASHE	Annual Survey of Hours and Earnings
CEO	Chief Executive Officers
CIPD	Chartered Institute of Personnel and Development
COED	*Compact Oxford English Dictionary*
DGB	German Trade Union Confederation
DWP	Department of Work and Pensions
ECJ	European Court of Justice
EHRC	Equality and Human Rights Commission
EqPA	Equal Pay Act
ESRC	Economic and Social Research Council
ET	Employment Tribunal
FCPE	Fonds Communs de Placement d'Entreprise
FTSE	Financial Times (London) Stock Exchange
GLA	Greater London Authority
HMRC	HM Revenue and Customs
HPP	High Performance Paradigm
HRM	Human Resource Management
ICE	Information and Consultation of Employees
IDS	Incomes Data Services
IPM	Institute of Personnel Management
IRS	Industrial Relations Services
IT	Information Technology
JCC	Joint Consultative Committee
JNCHES	Joint Negotiating Committee for Higher Education Staff
LAD	Local Authority Districts
LFS	Labour Force Survey

LPC	Low Pay Commission
LTIP	Long-Term Incentive Plans
NHS	National Health Service
NES	New Earnings Survey
NI	National Insurance
NMW	National Minimum Wage
OME	Office of Manpower Economics
ONS	Office for National Statistics
PAT	Profit After Tax
PBR	Payments-by Result
PEE	Plan d'Epargne d'Entreprise
PERCO	Plan d'Epargne Retraite Colectif
PPF	Pension Protection Fund
PPS	Performance Pay Systems
PRB	Pay Review Body
PRP	Performance Related Pay
RPI	Retail Price Index
SAYE	Save As You Earn
SIP	Share Incentive Plan
SLPZ	Specified Location Pay Zones
SME	Small and Medium-Sized Enterprises
SPP	Stock Purchase Plans
SSWD	Standardised Spatial Wage Differentials
STRB	School Teachers' Review Body
TELCO	The East London Communities Organisation
TGWU	Transport and General Workers Union
TMT	Top Management Team
TSR	Total Shareholder Return
TTWAs	Travel To Work Areas
TUC	Trades Union Congress
UNICE	Union of Industrial and Employers' Confederations
WERS	Workplace Employment Relations Survey
WWW	Women Working Worldwide

The editors and the contributors

The Editors

Susan Corby is a Professor of Employment Relations at the University of Greenwich. She was formerly a senior trade union official. She has led several funded research projects including pay and grading in the National Health Service (for Department of Health), gender and the labour market (for the South East of England Development Agency/European Social Fund), and gender and age in employment tribunal claims (for Department of Trade and Industry). She has published in a range of journals and is an Independent Expert under the equal value legislation, a member of the Employment Appeal Tribunal, the Central Arbitration Committee, and an Acas arbitrator and mediator.

Esmond Lindop is an independent consultant, advising on pay and conditions and skills issues for a variety of clients. He is currently a member of the School Teachers' Review Body. He was general manager and then managing director of Incomes Data Services (IDS) from 1989 to 2005. Previously he was deputy director of employment affairs at the Confederation of British Industry (CBI) and editor of Industrial Relations Services' (IRS) *Pay & Benefits Bulletin*. He produced a large number of publications in the course of his work with IDS, the CBI, and IRS. Other publications include articles for *Pensions World, Personnel Management,* and the *Industrial Relations Journal.*

Steve Palmer began his industrial relations career as assistant research officer at the National Union of Seamen. After taking a master's degree at the London School of Economics, he joined Incomes Data Services as a senior researcher in pay and conditions. In 1979 he started at the (then) Institute of Personnel Management as policy advisor on remuneration issues, a post he held for 11 years before becoming Director of Information and Development. In 1992, he was appointed deputy director of employment affairs at the Confederation of British Industry. He is now remuneration advisor at the Office of Manpower Economics which provides the secretariats to the six independent pay review bodies. He has also worked on secondment to the Low Pay Commission. He is a Chartered Member of the Chartered Institute of Personnel and Development and a visiting professor at London Metropolitan University.

The Contributors

James Arrowsmith is Senior Lecturer in Industrial Relations and Personnel Management at Warwick Business School, University of Warwick. He has worked on a number of ESRC-funded research projects. Those specifically focused on pay include: changing pay and working time in large UK organisations (1996–1999); pay, working time, and performance in small firms (2000–2001); and the relationship between variable pay and collective bargaining (2004–2007). He has also conducted research for the European Commission; the European Foundation for the Improvement of Living and Working Conditions; the International Labour Organisation; and the UK Department of Trade and Industry. Publications in the area of pay include: 'Pay bargaining in the UK' International Labor Brief (2005), 'Small Firms and the National Minimum Wage' in Marlow, S., Patton, D., and Ram, M. (eds) *Managing Labour in Small Firms* (2004, Routledge).

Jon Dymond MA (Cantab) is a Managing Consultant at Hay Group. Jon works with main boards, remuneration committees, HR directors, and compensation and benefits directors on all areas of executive and strategic reward. He has particular expertise in corporate governance and on specific business issue-related projects involving strategic or cultural change, such as those that relate to merger and acquisition activity, flotation, and delisting. Previously he was principal consultant at Halliwell Consulting and his background is as a strategy consultant.

Bob Elliott is a Professor of Economics and Director of the Health Economics Research Unit at the University of Aberdeen. He has been a visiting Professor at universities in the United States, Australia, and Europe, an adviser to national and international organisations including HM Treasury, the OECD, and European Commission, a member of the ESRC Training Board, President of the Scottish Economic Society, and currently is a Fellow of the Royal Society of Edinburgh. He chaired the 'Elliott Review' of local government finance in 1996 and was a member of the McCrone Committee of Inquiry into Scottish teachers' pay. He is a member of the UK's Low Pay Commission. He has published articles in a wide range of journals and his books include: *Labour Economics: A Comparative Text* (McGraw-Hill 1991); *Public Sector Pay Determination in the European Union* (with D Meurs and C Lucifora, eds) (Macmillan, 1999); and *Decentralised Pay Setting: A Study of*

Collective Bargaining Reform in the Civil Service in Australia, Sweden and the UK (with K Bender) (Ashgate, 2004).

Sue Field specialises in pensions consultancy with a wide ranging portfolio of private and public sector clients of various sizes. She is the Scheme Actuary for a number of occupational pension schemes advising trustees and advises a number of corporate clients. Her projects include advising on funding and accounting issues, pension plan design, and communication and risk management work. Sue joined Watson Wyatt in 1988 after graduating in mathematics from Oxford University and qualified as an actuary in 1991.

Paul Marginson is Professor of Industrial Relations, University of Warwick and Director of the Industrial Relations Research Unit. He was previously Professor of HRM at the University of Leeds. Recent ESRC funded research includes a study of variable payment systems and collective bargaining, a large-scale survey of employment practice in multinational companies in the United Kingdom, employment practices in German and US companies in central eastern Europe and the emerging boundaries of European collective bargaining. His many publications include: *European Integration and Industrial Relations: Multi-level Governance in the Making* (with K Sisson) (2004, Palgrave) and 'The Management of Pay as the Influence of Collective Bargaining Diminishes' in Edwards, P. (ed.) *Industrial Relations: Theory and Practice in Britain,* (with Brown, W. and Walsh, J.) (2003, Blackwell).

Helen Murlis is a Director of Hay Group internationally and has been with the firm since1990. She works with a wide range of clients in the public and private sectors on reward and performance management and practises as an executive coach. She is a past Chartered Institute of Personnel and Development (CIPD) Vice-President of pay and employment conditions and a past chair of the CIPD's Reward Forum. Previously she was a Managing Consultant at KPMG, Head of the Top Pay Unit at Incomes Data Services and Executive Remuneration Adviser at the British Institute of Management. She has written and lectured widely on reward issues and is co-author (with Michael Armstrong) of *Reward Management: A Handbook of Remuneration Strategy and Practice*, a key textbook now in its 5th edition (Kogan Page, 2004).

Christian Olsen is a consultant with Watson Wyatt and has been based in the United Kingdom since 2003. He joined Watson Wyatt's Melbourne office in 1998 after graduating from the University of Melbourne with a master's degree majoring in economics and actuarial science. He is a Fellow of the Institute of Actuaries of Australia and is a past winner of the Institute's Prescott Prize for overall achievement in Fellowship examinations. He has also acted as a tutor and examiner for the Institute's Superannuation subject. Christian has provided advice to a wide range of defined benefit and defined contribution funds in both Australia and the United Kingdom, assisting funds with restructuring and developing Internet tools for member communications.

Andrew Pendleton is Professor of Human Resources Management in The York Management School at York University. He has degrees from the universities of Bath and Oxford, and has previously held academic posts at the universities of Bath, Bradford, Kent, and Manchester Metropolitan. He has worked extensively on employee ownership and on employee share ownership plans in large listed companies, with financial support from the ESRC and the Nuffield Foundation. He has also conducted studies on employee share ownership in Europe, financed by the European Foundation and European Commission. He is the author of *Employee Ownership, Participation, and Governance* (Routledge, 2001) and the joint editor of *Corporate Governance and Labour Management: International and Comparative Perspectives* (Oxford University Press, 2004).

Jonathan Trevor is a senior researcher in the human resources and organisational behaviour group at Judge Business School, University of Cambridge. His doctoral research involved international case-study research into pay strategies in seven leading multinational firms. More recently, he has been a lead researcher at Cambridge on the *Global HR Research Alliance* project, reviewing leading and innovative human capital management practices of global organisations in collaboration with the Rotterdam School of Management, Cornell University and INSEAD. Previously he was a consultant with Mercer Human Resource Consulting and now continues to consult and speak regularly at academic and practitioner conferences, as well as teaching on MBA and executive education courses.

Richard Williams is a senior consultant at Watson Wyatt specialising in pensions: advising pension fund clients, advising on the pension aspects of privatisations and transfers of undertakings and reporting to the Armed Forces Review Body on a wide range of comparator pension schemes. He joined Watson Wyatt in 1973 and worked for the organisation in the West Indies, Africa, and Zimbabwe. He has a degree from the University of Cambridge (MA in Mathematics) and is a Fellow of the Institute of Actuaries.

Angela Wright is Senior Lecturer in Human Resource Management at Westminster University Business School. She has research interests in several aspects of pay and reward including employee benefits, as well as in diversity and equal opportunities. She teaches reward management on a CIPD programme and supervises Masters' dissertations in this field. Among her extensive career experience researching and advising on pay/remuneration issues, she worked for the public sector pay review bodies as their Remuneration Specialist/Adviser; and she led the pay research team at Industrial Relations Services, following a research role at Incomes Data Services. She is the author of *Reward Management in Context* (CIPD, 2004).

Part I
Introduction

1

Trends and tensions: an overview

Susan Corby, Steve Palmer, and Esmond Lindop

Trends

From salary administration to reward strategy

In 1978, recruitment consultants MSL advertised on behalf of a client for a 'Manager, Salary Administration'. The role was identified as incorporating 'a wide range of personnel activities' including salary and wage administration, job evaluation, liaison with line managers and trade unions, and remuneration policy formation. The successful candidate needed 'a salary administration background' (Institute of Personnel Management, 1978). The emphasis on administration is revealing. Indeed, the key texts for budding pay specialists at the time took *Salary Administration* as their titles (see, for instance, Armstrong and Murlis 1980; Rock, 1984). Not only that, but jobs purely in the pay field were in any event few and far between. A search through advertisements in the monthly *Digest* of the then Institute of Personnel Management (IPM) reveals considerable emphasis on general personnel, industrial relations or training and development jobs, with only a smattering of posts in salary administration and a few advertisers looking for specialists to run a job-evaluation scheme.

Compare this with a recent advertisement placed by Macmillan Davies Hodes in *People Management* in June 2007. Here the client considered the post of 'Compensation and Benefits Manager' as 'essential' for the development and transformation of its reward strategy. The incumbent would take 'full responsibility' for designing and implementing the strategy, including its interpretation and development, and would need 'a broad background in reward at strategic and operational level' (People Management, 2007, p. 61).

Clearly, the role of pay specialist represented by these advertisements has been transformed over the intervening years, in terms of both content and its associated expertise. Pay has moved from a largely administrative role to a much-more strategic one, with an emphasis on acquiring and developing talent and delivering broader business objectives. Moreover, the significance attached to reward management within organisations has greatly increased. It has simultaneously become both more the province of the strategic expert and a key responsibility of the line manager (a theme to which we return below). Writing in 1989, McBeath and Rands state that 'in little more than two decades, salary administration has developed from a relatively primitive activity carried out by specialists in progressive organisations to a universal process' (McBeath and Rands, 1989, p. vi).

The language of the advertisements also points to an intriguing change in the job titles given to pay specialists. These have gone through something of a cycle from salary administrator to remuneration specialist, compensation specialist, and reward specialist. Whilst the latter titles can be used interchangeably (the advertisement above, for example, uses both 'reward' and 'compensation'), they are not purely semantic.

The *Compact Oxford English Dictionary* (COED, 2007) refers to *pay* as 'money paid for work', a rather passive response based solely on meeting the bill for a certain activity. *Compensation* on the other hand, carries the connotation of recompense for an employee's lost opportunity of doing something else, whether work for another employer, development, or recreation. The *COED* notes its use to mean salary or wages, but considers this chiefly a North American definition. Finally, *reward* comes down to something given 'in recognition of service, effort or achievement'. It looks beyond employees' output to include their input. Reward would also include benefits alongside pay to reflect the entire package available to employees. (There is no clear trend in the use of titles in the pay field, although reward has probably become more popular, and pay and compensation less so, at least on this side of the Atlantic ocean. Perhaps revealing is the decision of the Chartered Institute of Personnel and Development (CIPD) to change the name of its forum for pay specialists from its original Compensation Forum to its current Reward Forum.)

This changing emphasis has also gone hand-in-hand with an upward shift in the relative pay of salary specialists themselves. In 1977, the median basic salary of managers in salary administration was £7,811 per annum (Computer Economics, 1977). The most recent survey, covering 2006–2007, puts the median basic pay for compensation and benefit managers at £47,700, and the average bonus at £6,210 (Croner Reward, 2007). This represents a rate of earnings increase of 570 per cent over 30 years. Compare this to the rate of increase in the economy as a whole where the median earnings of men and women have risen between 420 per cent and 440 per cent respectively over the same period (Department of Employment, 1977; Office for National Statistics, 2006). Reporting on its 2006–2007 personnel salary survey, Croner Reward notes that it 'shows again Compensation and Benefits Specialists are the highest paid specialism, receiving as much as 21 per cent more than the average salary for a senior manager' – figures, incidentally, that are even higher for those with an international dimension to their jobs (Croner Reward, 2007, p. xv).

A recent analysis from Incomes Data Services (IDS) supports the contention. 'Businesses and organisations ... are finding it difficult to recruit compensation and benefits specialists at all levels', IDS wrote in 2005. '[M]oreover, high demand is likely to continue into the near future ... with the prospect that the job market will become even tighter' (Incomes Data Services 2005a, p. 17). Why has there been such a change in the profile of the pay specialism resulting in a strong sellers' market today for people with these skills?

Incomes Data Services offers at least part of the answer, noting that reward strategies are becoming more sophisticated as they seek specifically to influence employee attitudes, behaviours, and performance. Another factor is the internationalisation of business, which brings with it a demand for knowledge and skills extending across national boundaries. Complications around taxation of pay and benefits, and the need to be comfortable with large pay databases, are also skills in demand as pay becomes both more individualised and market driven.

The changing context of reward

If the role of the salary administrator was more circumscribed in the past, we must take account of the context of the times. Pay specialists in the 1970s operated in a framework far removed from that of today: for example, for seven years of the decade there had been incomes policies of varying intensity which severely restricted the scope for innovation in pay policy (Chater et al., 1981). Alongside that, management freedoms of manoeuvre were also limited by employee relations structures. Well over 50 per cent of the workforce had their pay and conditions determined by collective bargaining, trade union density was high (as was trade union militancy) and under-pinned in many sectors by agreements making membership a condition of employ-ment; inflation ran at figures unrecognisable today, peaking at over 25 per cent in 1975. A third of the workforce worked in manufacturing, and for some income from piece-work systems accounted for 40 per cent or more of earnings (Cannell and Wood, 1992). White-collar workers in the public sector and many in the private sector were covered by incremental payment systems with automatic pay progres-sion based on service (Office of Manpower Economics, 1973). Benefit provision was rudimentary, with most benefits limited to white collar and/or senior staff (Reid and Robertson, 1965). In addition, there was comparatively little pay and benefits data available about practice in other organisations (Incomes Data Services, 1966).

The move away from 'administration' to 'strategy' undoubtedly picked up follow-ing the election of a Conservative government in 1979 wedded to a monetarist eco-nomic policy to drive down inflation, alongside a neoclassical economic philosophy based on freeing up markets – product as well as labour – to greater competition. The government's approach included the weakening of trade union power, the reduction of inflation and the abolition of minimum wage provisions. Trade union power was weakened by a raft of legislation, for instance ending the closed shop, restricting industrial action, and abolishing trade union rights to claim recognition from employers.

The union base was further eroded by privatisations, which moved highly unionised public sector organisations into the private sector, and contracting out of some public service activities, which saw typically lower paid ancillary posts moved from the public sector to private sector suppliers. Post-1980 inflation was indeed driven down (although not initially to the levels of more recent years) accompanied by recession that saw unemployment rise to three million, with the brunt borne particularly by the up-to-then highly unionised manufacturing sector (Kessler and Bayliss, 1998). As to minimum wage setting, this essentially ended when Wages Councils were abolished in 1993 (see Chapter 7).

At the same time, the composition of the workforce changed. Manufacturing employment, where unionisation had traditionally been high, almost halved from 1979 to 1996, whilst service sector jobs, where unions found it often difficult to organise and where unionisation had anyway traditionally been weak, grew in number (Kessler and Bayliss, 1998, p. 45). At the risk of caricature, if the typical trade unionist of the 1970s was a man working full time in manufacturing, today the typical trade union member is a woman, quite possibly a part-timer, employed in the public services (see Grainger and Crowther, 2007).

In the face of these combined pressures, trade union membership fell significantly. According to the annual reports of the Certification Officer, it fell from 13.2 million in 1979, some 53 per cent of the workforce, to ten million in 1989, to 7.6 million today, about a quarter of the workforce. The reduction in the influence of trade unions within most organisations where they are still recognised has been almost as precipitate (Brown et al., 1998). As we will see in Chapter 3, this rapid decline in traditional collective bargaining arrangements and in the role of trade unions as a channel of communication over pay has led to the development of other processes aimed at more direct engagement with employees.

Union decline has freed up the scope for management discretion over a range of personnel practices including reward practice. We are of the view that changes of this kind have been a necessary condition for development of the new practices of recent years, but the reduction in trade union influence has not been the driver of change. A series of other factors have played that role, most notably the growing competitive pressures on the private sector caused both by reform of domestic markets and international competition, topics too large to explore in detail here. What no observer can doubt is that the pressure on business generally to perform has focused minds on the acquisition and retention of talent at the most senior levels, and on how key employees might best be rewarded to align their interests with those of their employers (see Roberts (2001) for further discussion).

Therefore, since the early 1980s both the pressures and the opportunities have been there for organisations to use pay as a tool to deliver their objectives. The questions now centre on the shape that the wished-for-pay strategies should take.

The 'new pay' paradigm

The answer to these questions seemed to lie in the 'new pay' paradigm emerging from the United States of America (USA) (see, for instance, Lawler (1990) and Schuster and Zingheim (1992)). This paradigm was transported to the United Kingdom by multinational companies and cross-border management consultancies.

The key to new pay, its proponents argued, lay in moving away from the certainties of the past – such as job evaluation, rigid grading structures, service-based progression, annual cost of living adjustments, and paternalistic benefit packages – to pay systems focussed on the individual's market worth, performance, and flexibility. It is hard to imagine now what a revolution in thinking this turned out to be. It involved a fresh mindset, moving from pay for inputs – turn up and you'll get paid, turn up for several years you'll get paid more – to pay for outputs – turn up and perform to a satisfactory standard and you'll get paid, turn up and perform to a highly satisfactory standard and you'll get paid more. It has subsequently developed beyond rewarding *what* people do in their jobs to rewarding *how* people do their jobs, with jobs now being described in terms of the expected competencies and behaviours required to carry them out successfully.

One objective of the new pay agenda is therefore the individualisation of reward packages, an objective that fits with a wider social decline in collectivism. Partly this centres on recognizing individual contribution and skills, but other influences, particularly in the area of benefits, are more to do with giving individuals choice and at the same time enabling organisations to target and/or reduce their expenditure on benefits (see Chapters 10 and 11).

While the drive for a 'new pay' agenda certainly caught the zeitgeist, it has not been free from criticism. For instance, performance related pay awards have been criticised as nothing more than 'inflation in drag' (Incomes Data Services, 2005b) and conclusive evidence that incentive pay correlates with performance remains remarkably hard to find.

Moreover, new pay has not been universally applied across organisations. According to the Workplace Employment Relations Survey 2004, only two-fifths of workplaces had performance-related pay schemes for some employees (Kersley et al., 2006). Furthermore, research carried out by the Office of Manpower Economics and the Chartered Institute of Personnel and Development (CIPD, 2006) showed marked differences between the public and private sectors in respect of pay progression systems, with the former still very much reliant on service as the determinant. Indeed, the difference in pay practice between the public and private sectors will frequently emerge in the ensuing chapters, but there are also differences in pay approaches within sectors by size of organisation and by occupation (CIPD, 2007).

As to other aspects of new pay, there is some evidence of 'rowing back'. For example, broad banded pay structures appear more and more to represent broad graded structures or even *de facto* traditional salary structures, while reports of the death of job evaluation seem premature. It is alive and kicking in the public sector, driven in large part by concern about equal pay for work of equal value. There has been some pick up in use in the private sector too, though it tends to be less rigidly applied and is often used primarily to aid market comparisons (CIPD, 2007).

The role of line managers

In practice, things are a little more structured and centralised than might have been thought given the hype around 'new pay'. One example of this is the interrelationship between the pay specialist and other managers. The McBeath's and Rands's quotation referred to above continues 'salary administration has developed [into] a universal process, *participated in and operated as much by line managers as by remuneration specialists and other personnel staff*' (emphasis added; McBeath and Rands 1989, p. vi). A decade later Brown and Armstrong asserted:

> Reward is no longer an isolated function; it is part of the strategic business process. This contrasts with the traditional 'salary administration' approach in which pay specialists lived an isolated life as technical designers, running bureaucratic systems and dealing on a day-to-day or annual pay review basis with the immediate job grading or pay level issues…. The tendency now is to devolve pay decisions to line managers as part of a broader policy of empowerment and decentralisation of decision-making and responsibility within an organisation. (Brown and Armstrong, 2001, pp. 9, 15)

How much do these views shape up with reality? One could conclude that if pay specialists had truly empowered other managers to take pay decisions, and had equipped them with the skills to do so, they would not perhaps be able to command such a pay premium in the market. Survey evidence suggests that the specialists themselves do not consider that pay literacy has moved much beyond the reward department. Thus in its 2006 survey, the CIPD found that respondent HR managers cited line managers 'as a major inhibitor to the successful implementation of a reward strategy'. The only significant responsibility line managers had was over training, development, and flexible working. Not only were line managers not trusted to make pay decisions, they were also not trusted to communicate the rationale behind reward strategies (CIPD, 2006).

The CIPD concluded at the time that organisations considered line managers to be the biggest barriers to turning the rhetoric of reward strategies into reality, as line managers were not deemed by HR managers to have either the appropriate skills or abilities. This in turn means pay decision-making and communication are not delegated, training not given, and a vicious circle is created.

This perception was researched in greater detail by Purcell and Hutchinson, who collected the views of line managers themselves. In the context of financial rewards, they noted the importance of line managers in setting and explaining standards of performance and behaviours required, the aims of reward schemes, carrying out assessments, and communicating and defending judgements. However, line managers told them that they

- found it difficult to differentiate between employees,
- lacked ownership of outcomes,
- found it time-consuming and bureaucratic (especially when most schemes use forced distributions and the vast majority of staff get average performance), and
- lacked training/skills in appraisals which led to a lack of scheme transparency and employee concerns around bias in the results.

The authors concluded:

> [I]n spite of the evidence of line managers' increasing involvement in people management, the role of the HR function in the design of reward policies and practices that are delivered by line managers, monitoring and managing the effectiveness of practice delivery and providing support has been largely ignored. This is surprising, given that it is reported that HR professionals have concerns about line manager competence in many aspects of people management, including reward. (Purcell and Hutchinson, 2007, p. 11)

The CIPD has summed up the situation succinctly:, 'one issue that has been a constant refrain for the past number of years is concerns over front-line managers'; pay professionals do not believe that they have the skills, attitudes, and knowledge to manage performance-based rewards. However, what front-line managers themselves have problems with 'is that the performance management and reward process is often developed in splendid isolation by the HR department ... [and] the process of rewarding performance is something that is "done to" rather than "done with" line managers' (CIPD, 2007, pp. 35–36). If that is the view of line managers, what must it be like for the staff who report to them and are the ultimate recipients of organisational pay strategies?

Clearly, in many areas there remain limits to the individualisation of reward, with central control still very much alive. Ultimately, line manager's discretion over pay is circumscribed. There is much less to individualisation and targeting than meets the eye.

Tensions

The tensions between line managers on the one hand and reward specialists on the other, discussed above, are just one example of the conflicting pressures and personal tensions around the management of pay today. Other pressures and tensions at a personal level are between employees (and their representatives) and the employer. In addition, there are tensions at a theoretical level.

These tensions stem from the fact that reward policies and practices have a number of sometimes-conflicting functions. At its simplest, for employers, pay is a cost of

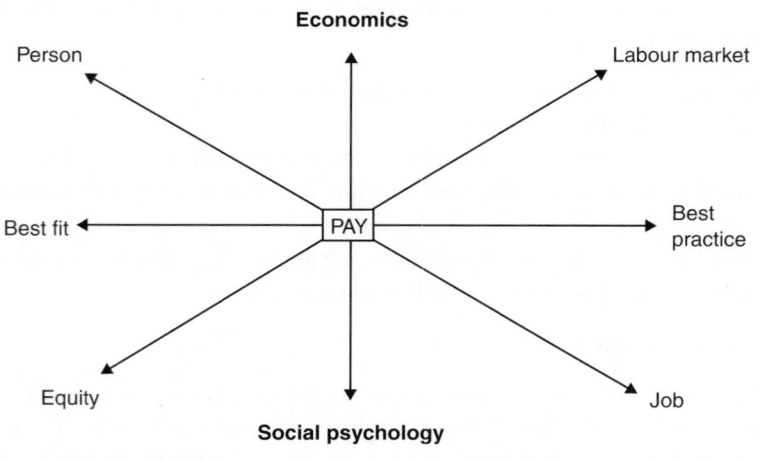

Figure 1.1 Tensions in pay

production, a signal to recruit and retain staff, and a tool for motivating staff. For employees, it is their main, and often only, source of livelihood and a reflection of their social identity. Thus, the level and form of pay and benefits are the outcome of implicit or explicit distributional conflict between employers and workers reflecting the balance of power and custom and practice and this conflict is institutionalised where there is employer/union bargaining (Grimshaw and Rubery, 2007). These tensions are encapsulated in Figure 1.1, whose resolution may vary by organisation, may change over time and location, and may not be the same for all employees.

Economics/social psychology

The overarching tension is between economic theories and social psychological theories and we will see these tensions surfacing in many of the following chapters. Classical economic thinking emphasises the forces of supply and demand with labour as a factor in production. It thus takes as its starting point the competitive labour market, together with the assumption that both employer and workers are rational economic maximisers, the assumption that workers have full information, and the assumption that workers have unimpeded mobility (hefty assumptions). For a given type of labour, the firm will hire increasing numbers of workers up to the point where their wage is equal to the value of their marginal product.

Building on the foundations laid by Adam Smith's seminal study the *Wealth of Nations* in 1776 (Seligman, 1910), other economists have elaborated and critiqued the application of classical economics to pay determination. For instance, workers are not like peas in a pod. Organisations pay some workers more than others because their experience, education, and training add to their value (human capital theory).

One of the key conundrums of employment relations is how to get employees to work productively, rather than merely to attend work. Economists argue that financial incentives can fulfil that role and, as we noted above, so do proponents of new pay. Accordingly, they say, some organisations pay some or all workers at a level above the market rate because they want to obtain superior performance and diligence (efficiency wage theory). Alternatively or additionally, organisations will offer selected key managers big bonuses if they achieve certain targets, believing that employees who have the opportunity to gain large bonuses will go the extra mile. The analogy is with large cash prizes in golf tournaments which, it is said, act as a spur to achievement (tournament theory).

Economic theorists recognise that the interests of shareholders and managers, or managers and employees, often differ. How can they be aligned? For economists, the answer, unsurprisingly, is financial rewards. Shareholders can shape managers' financial rewards and managers can shape employees' financial rewards to ensure that their interests coincide (principal/agent theory).

Against this background, employers are wage fixers, not wage takers. For a fuller discussion of these and other economic theories see Bryson and Forth, 2006; Claydon, 2001; Milkovich and Newman, 1996.

Social psychology takes the very different starting point of the long-term nature of the employment relationship. It argues that economists' theories do not match the real world, a view adopted in Chapter 7 on the UK's National Minimum Wage. Group norms develop among workers and these, rather than financial rewards, have a major influence on the extent that workers are productive (Claydon, 2001). Furthermore, social psychology emphasises social and institutional factors such as custom and practice both in the organisation and the sector, employers' strategies, pay determination methods and the values of the organisation, for instance on pay secrecy/openness and on risk taking/ avoidance, and an appreciation of these factors is essential when considering the effort-reward bargain. This approach, which is at one with much industrial relations writing, incorporates the classic, seminal studies on group limitations of output such as those by Lupton, Roethlisberger and Dickson, and Roy; see selected readings in Lupton, 1972.

Social psychology also emphasises the range of the individual worker's needs: these are not just money. Indeed money is not a motivator, though its insufficiency can lead to dissatisfaction, according to Herzberg's well-known (but arguably less than robust) work on the motivator-hygiene theory. There are higher needs such as esteem and self-actualisation, as Maslow's equally well-known (and equally less than robust) hierarchy of needs posits. In today's parlance not only is the legal contract, which specifies terms and conditions of employment, important but the psychological contract is important too (Rousseau, 1995). The latter refers to the implicit, unwritten understandings that employees and employers have of what each can expect to give or receive. See Bryson and Forth (2006) and Gerhart and Rynes

(2003) for a fuller discussion of these theories and the evidence supporting them. 'Total rewards', which we discuss in our last chapter, aims to meld economics and social psychology.

Labour market/equity

We now turn to the other tensions shown in Figure 1.1, starting with the tension between the labour market and equity. To what extent are pay and benefits a response to supply and demand in the labour market and to what extent are they a response to considerations of equity? For instance, should finance lecturers at a university receive higher pay in response to external labour market factors than HR lecturers, even though both groups of lecturers perform the same educational tasks? Should a firefighter receive more or less pay than an ambulance paramedic; after all they both work in the emergency services? Even within the same occupation, should pay vary if the worker is in London or in Cornwall? Chapter 5, on local pay, suggests that whereas some occupations have a national or international labour market, others have a local one, but defining the labour market can be problematic.

On the one hand, pay systems that give primacy to labour market considerations essentially disregard the fact that individuals are influenced by relative, not absolute rewards and compare their pay with that of 'referent others'. These are typically their fellow employees (internal equity) but may extend to those in other organisations (external equity). If employees are of the view that others are paid more for the same effort and that their pay is not fair, they will react negatively (for example, shirk) to correct their effort to their reward.

Equity and fairness, however, are not simple constructs: for instance, who are referent others and how is fairness perceived? Furthermore, equity and fairness embrace not only distributional justice, that is pay outcomes, but also procedural justice, the way the pay system operates, and interactional justice, how employees are dealt with by those responsible for administering pay such as their line managers, whose deficiencies in respect of reward have been noted above (see also Kessler, 2005). A full discussion of the role of equity and social comparisons is given in Adams (1963).

On the other hand, pay systems that give primacy to equity considerations essentially disregard the fact that the labour market for the same or similar jobs may vary significantly in different parts of the country (see Chapter 5 for a fuller discussion). Equally, there may be major market variations between different jobs at the same level, for instance between the pay for a marketing manager and a production manager.

Equal pay and value legislation, whereby men and women are paid the same where the demands of the job are the same in terms of such factors as effort, skill and decision, seeks to achieve gender pay equity (for instance, between a female cleaner and a male porter) and basically ignores labour market considerations. For further discussion of these issues, see Chapter 8.

Person/job

A further tension, which again stems from the overarching tension between economics and social psychology, concerns whether to reward the person or the job.

Trade unions have traditionally sought to establish standard rates of pay that reduce management's scope to award differential payments to workers based on their evaluation of a person's contribution where such workers are in the same or similar jobs (Heery, 2000) (Unions' responses to person-based pay are discussed in Chapter 6). Typically, a process of rewarding the job, not the person, is founded on a job-evaluation scheme to ensure a systematic approach, so that pay is felt fair.

Payment for the person rather than the job can be achieved either by recognition of length of service, on the assumption that the longer the person does the job, the more skills and knowledge is acquired, and/or in some form of performance pay. The latter can be either a mechanistic link between pay and output and/or after evaluation of behavioural characteristics (i.e., measurement of the individual's inputs). (Progression systems are discussed in Chapter 4).

Lawler (1990), a new pay proponent, argues that rewarding the job, not the person, sends a message to individuals about what is *not* included in their responsibilities, discouraging employees from being flexible and doing anything additional to their job description. Furthermore, he argues, job-based payment systems provide individuals who have been promoted with higher pay, *before* they have demonstrated that they can do their new jobs, while job evaluation reinforces hierarchy and bureaucracy. Yet those in favour of performance-related pay take little or no account of the problems of implementation: whether or not to use forced distributions, how to ensure that bias is eliminated, and how individual performance-related pay is consonant with team-working (see, for instance, Cannell and Wood, 1992; Makinson, 2000; Marsden and French, 1998).

Best fit/best practice

A further tension is the best fit/best practice debate. The basic premise of best fit is that pay structures should be tailored to support the way that the organisation is structured and how work gets done and to fit the organisation's business strategy. If the reward system is so matched, then pay can become a strategic lever to improve business performance. As Gomez-Mejia and Balkin (1992, p. 4) put it:

> The emerging paradigm of the field is based on a strategic orientation where issues of internal equity and external equity are viewed as secondary to the firm's need to use pay as an essential integrating and signalling mechanism to achieve overarching business objectives.

New pay theorists essentially argue for this best fit approach. Thus Lawler (1990), for instance, argues that the pay structure should fit the organisational structure in terms of how centralised or decentralised it is, how cohesive or disparate the various departments/functions/levels are, and what the organisation's business goals are.

Milkovich and Newman (1996) give as examples Wal-Mart's low-cost business objective, which is best fitted to a pay structure that generates low labour costs, and Hewlett-Packard's product innovation business objective, which requires a pay structure that rewards risk, initiative, and cross-functional flexibility. This issue of best fit, that is pay fitting the organisation's business strategy, also known as strategic pay, is discussed in much more detail in the next chapter.

The basic premise of best practice is that certain personnel and pay practices should be followed, irrespective of the organisation's structure and business objectives as those practices are correlated with business success. What is best practice, however, also known as high performance paradigms (HPPs), is open to question, although typically it entails bundles of HR policies and practices relating to selection and training, performance appraisal, single status policies, and contingent pay systems, such as individual performance-related pay, group bonuses, and profit sharing. Success can be defined in various ways, for instance economic performance such as sales per employee and worker commitment and satisfaction as measured by labour turnover.

A number of studies cast doubt on both the link between best practice and business performance and the link between best fit and business performance. Thus, Godard (2004, p. 355), reviewing the evidence on the best practice approach, suggests that 'we should treat broad-brush claims about the performance effects of HPPs, and about research findings claiming to observe them, with a healthy degree of scepticism', as support is at best limited. Similarly, Gerhart and Rynes (2003, pp. 260–261) point out that 'without measuring intervening variables, it is difficult to identify characteristics of either the pay design or context that contribute to [performance] variance'.

To sum up, as (Bryson and Forth (2006), p. 41) say:

> In truth, a reliance on any one theoretical position is likely to overstate the coherence and functionality of wages, and those working in the field of industrial relations have long recognised that no single theory of pay setting has an over-riding claim to virtue.

The forthcoming chapters

We will return to these tensions in the final chapter, but now we explain the book's overall approach and outline its contents.

The book's approach

When perusing this book, readers should bear in mind a number of factors. First, while we recognise that Reward can be both financial and non-financial, this book focuses on financial rewards only (apart from the last chapter). Second, it reflects the fact that Reward is both a theoretical field of study with an empirical underpinning and a management issue with a practical and operational impact. Accordingly, there are contributions not only from academic researchers but also from expert practitioners including management consultants, as the notes on contributors make clear. This, of course, means that some chapters are more theoretical than others.

Third, Reward draws on various academic disciplines: particularly industrial relations, law, and economics and these are reflected in the book. For instance, a legal perspective is to the fore in two chapters (one on the National Minimum Wage, the other on pay equity); an economics perspective is employed in Chapter 5 (local pay) while Chapter 3 (employee voice) employs an industrial relations perspective. Fourth, this book is not country specific. Although the majority of the chapters are UK-centred, three chapters (Chapter 2 on pay strategy, Chapter 6 on variable pay and collective bargaining and Chapter 12 on employee share ownership) have a cross-national focus. The choice of a cross-national focus in these chapters and not others, however, is unashamedly opportunistic – the reflection of current research.

This book, therefore, makes no claim to homogeneity or analytical or conceptual integration; its strength lies in diversity and eclecticism: of the background of contributors, of the field of study, and of country focus. Nonetheless, all the contributors adopt a critical perspective, going behind any rhetoric and challenging conventional thinking on Reward (with the final chapter pulling together cross-cutting themes in the individual chapters). Moreover, all the contributors have written in an accessible style, aiming to identify and then answer, with full supporting material, specific questions, while avoiding prescriptions.

Readers should also note that this book does not claim to be yet another textbook on Reward. Instead, it aims to identify the most significant areas of change in practice and this has governed the choice of chapters. For example, while a textbook typically has a chapter on employee benefits, of which only a small part is devoted to flexible benefits, this book has a whole chapter on flexible benefits, as that is the area of change. Similarly, the book has a chapter on pensions, because pensions provision is an area currently of major concern, while other benefits providing security when an employee does not work, such as sick pay, where change is currently minimal, are ignored.

Moreover, a textbook typically will have one or more chapters on performance pay (also known as contingent or variable pay) rehearsing theory and practice, but this book looks at new angles on this issue: how collective bargaining and variable pay interrelate (Chapter 6) and at performance pay in the context of progression systems (Chapter 4).

Another factor that has governed the choice of chapters is the decision to incorporate new research: several chapters contain research findings that are yet to be published elsewhere. On the one hand, whether or not there is new research on a topic is largely fortuitous. On the other hand, there is some theoretical validity as the incorporation of new research ensures that the book is at the cutting edge.

The book's outline

The book is divided into four parts:

- Introduction
- Pay issues
- Benefit issues
- Conclusions

The first part, the Introduction, contains this chapter and covers two other overarching issues: pay strategies and employee voice. In Chapter 2, Jonathan Trevor considers the pay strategies of multinational corporations and asks whether strategic pay is just rhetoric or whether a strategy can be rationally determined. Drawing on his research, he concludes that the aim of a pay strategy should not be to maximise value, given the constraints on the ability of companies to do so, but to minimise the inherent risks associated with pay, whether used strategically or not.

Chapter 3, by Esmond Lindop, looks at how employee voice on pay is articulated. Accordingly, Lindop considers not just collective bargaining, which has declined markedly from 1980 to 1996, but also newer forms of institutional and non-institutional employee voice such as consultation with non-union employee representatives, visits by pay review bodies to their 'constituencies', pressure groups, employee attitude surveys, and focus groups. He argues that these new mechanisms for employee input into pay decisions have been underestimated and are not necessarily inferior to collective bargaining.

Chapters 4 to 9 look at pay issues. In Chapter 4, Steve Palmer looks at grading structures and pay progression. Service-based increments and relatively narrow graded structures for many UK non-manual workers and spot rates or piece-work rates for UK manual workers have been replaced by broad banded and more amorphous pay structures, particularly in the private sector. At the same time, there has been a sharp increase in the use of performance-linked progression, though in the public sector this has often been tempered by some service related element. Indeed Palmer finds that there is a growing divergence between the public and private sectors in terms of pay, but both sectors face challenges including the management of employee expectations and the problems of implementing variable pay.

Chapter 5, by Bob Elliot considers local/regional pay, exploring both the arguments for it and its limits. Given the variations in the levels of unemployment and the cost of living between regions and between localities within regions, classical economic theory predicts that pay rates will vary between locally based establishments in national organisations. Yet although market forces may result in geographically based pay variations in the private sector, this is not the case in the public sector, where pay is less responsive to underlying labour market conditions. Against that background, Elliott reports evidence to support a move to greater localisation for some public sector workers, but also shows that it is not appropriate for all.

Chapter 6, by Paul Marginson, looks at performance pay and its impact on collective bargaining with its traditional emphasis on the rate for the job. Drawing on the author's research in retail banking and machinery and equipment in the United Kingdom, Marginson examines performance pay, both consolidated and unconsolidated, in its many forms, for example individual, team and organisation-wide, and challenges the received wisdom that performance pay necessarily undermines collective bargaining, arguing that under some circumstances collective bargaining has been reframed. He then looks at research in the same sub-sectors in Austria and Norway where collective bargaining arrangements differ from those in the United Kingdom. He argues that differences in the institutional arrangements have an effect on the relationship between collective bargaining and performance pay.

In Chapter 7, James Arrowsmith evaluates the impact of the UK's National Minimum Wage (NMW). Introduced in 1999, the NMW represented a defeat for the dominant paradigm of free market pay policies and classical economic theory. This predicted that the NMW would lead to increased wage costs, which in turn would lead to employers reducing the number of jobs. Arrowsmith, however, drawing on his and other published research, finds that the NMW's effect has essentially been benign. While significantly increasing the pay of the lowest paid (disproportionately women), the NMW has resulted in few job losses or changes in employment practices. Moreover, the NMW now seems firmly established and accepted by erstwhile political and business opponents.

Chapter 8, by Susan Corby, focuses on gender equality and pay and on age equality and pay. After discussing reasons for gender pay inequality and competing definitions of equality, it outlines the gender pay equity laws and their weaknesses. Then drawing on the author's research, it examines the practical problems faced by working women in claiming equal pay with men. It next turns to the legislation on age equality and pay, noting the numerous exemptions and loopholes. Corby argues that change is needed, not just a strengthening of the current laws, but a more root and branch approach to include new enforcement measures.

Chapter 9, by Jon Dymond and Helen Murlis, examines executive pay, considering why executive reward is such an emotive subject and the factors that have contributed to its growth. Next, the components of executive reward are analysed, including annual bonuses, long-term incentive plans and top-hat pensions. Finally, the authors ask whether executive reward will change.

Chapters 10 to 12 look at benefit issues. Chapter 10 by Sue Field, Christian Olsen, and Richard Williams examines the pensions revolution in the United Kingdom. Against a background of demographic change, successive waves of legislation and financial pressures, many employers have closed private sector final salary defined benefit schemes to new entrants, replacing them with either defined contribution or career average defined benefits. The public sector too is now starting to see major changes in provision. Field and her colleagues discuss what has happened and why. They then consider the balance between individual responsibility and collective provision and the type of employment related pension arrangements there are likely to be in the United Kingdom in ten to twenty years time.

In Chapter 11, Angela Wright examines flexible benefit schemes (also called cafeteria benefits), where individual employees are given a choice on the make-up of their benefit package. Such schemes, which have been made feasible by computer software programmes, have become popular in the United States largely because of the tax regime. Wright considers whether such flexibility is the future shape of UK benefits (and reward) and employers' objectives in introducing them. Are their objectives, such as greater cost-control or greater perceived value by employees, realised? Wright draws on her research into UK organisations which have introduced flexible benefits to answer these and other questions. She argues that the prospects for further growth of flexible benefits schemes does not seem likely in view of the potentially high transaction costs needed to make a scheme succeed both in terms of communication as well as other administrative requirements.

In Chapter 12, Andrew Pendleton considers employee share ownership plans in a number of European countries. In the context of a growing interest in such plans essentially from the 1990s,, the chapter examines the policy objectives of the European Commission, and governments of European Union member states, as well as employer and union perspectives. Furthermore, drawing on the author's research, the chapter examines the incidence of share plans by European member states and discusses whether employee share ownership goes hand-in-hand with employee participation and whether union presence influences employee orientations to share ownership plans.

The fourth part is the conclusion: Chapter 13, the final chapter, draws together the themes in the individual chapters and considers the role of a total rewards approach in unifying all the elements of the employment experience.

References

Adams, J. S. (1963) 'Towards an Understanding of Inequity', *Journal of Abnormal and Social Psychology*, 67, 422–436.

Armstrong, M. and Brown, D. (2001) *New Dimensions in Pay Management,* London, UK: Chartered Institute of Personnel and Development.

Armstrong, M. and Murlis, H. (1980) *A Handbook of Salary Administration*, London, UK: Kogan Page.

Brown, W., Deakin, S., Hudson, M., Pratten, C., and Ryan, P. (1998) *The Individualisation of the Employment Contract in Britain*, Employment Relations Series 5, London, UK: Department of Trade and Industry.

Bryson, A. and Forth, J. (2006) *The Theory and Practice of Pay Setting*, London, UK: Centre for Economic Performance, London School of Economics.

Cannell, M. and Wood, S. (1992) *Incentive Pay: Impact and Evolution*, London, UK: Institute of Personnel Management.

Chater, R., Dean, A., and Elliott, R. (1981) *Incomes Policy*, Oxford, UK: Clarendon Press.

CIPD (2006) *Reward Management Annual Survey Report 2006,* London, UK: Chartered Institute of Personnel and Development.

CIPD (2007) *Reward Management Annual Survey Report 2007,* London, UK: Chartered Institute of Personnel and Development.

Claydon, T. (2001) 'Human Resource Management and the Labour Market' in Beardwell, I. and Holden, L. (eds) *Human Resource Management: A Contemporary Approach,* 3rd ed., Essex, UK: Prentice-Hall.

Compact Oxford English Dictionary (2007), Oxford, UK: Oxford University Press.

Computer Economics Ltd. (1977) *Salary Survey of Personnel and Financial Functions,* London, UK: CEL.

Croner Reward (2007) *Personnel Rewards 2006–2007,* Stone, Staffordshire, UK: Croner Reward.

Department of Employment (1977) *New Earnings Survey 1979,* London, UK: HMSO.

Gerhart, B. and Rynes, S. (2003) *Compensation, Theory, Evidence and Strategic Implications,* Thousand Oaks, USA: Sage.

Godard, J. (2004) 'A Critical Assessment of the High-Performance Paradigm', *British Journal of Industrial Relations,* 42, 2, 349–378.

Gomez-Mejia, L. and Balkin, D. (1992) *Compensation, Organisational Strategy and Firm Performance,* Cincinnati, USA: South Western.

Grainger, H. and Crowther, M. (2007) *Trade Union Membership 2006,* London, UK: Department of Trade and Industry.

Grimshaw, D. and Rubery, J. (2007) 'Undervaluing Women's Work', *Working Paper Series No 53,* Manchester, UK: Equal Opportunities Commission.

Heery, E. (2000) 'Trade Unions and the Management of Reward' in White, G. and Druker, J. (eds) *Reward Management: A Critical Text,* London, UK: Routledge.

Incomes Data Services (1966) 'Looking Forward', *Report,* 1, April, 3.

Incomes Data Services (2005a) 'Compensation and Benefits Specialists', *Executive Compensation Review,* 17 August.

Incomes Data Services (2005b) Organisation Practice on Pay Progression – A Scoping Study for the OME and CIPD, Unpublished.

Institute of Personnel Management (1978) *Digest 156,* July, xiii.

Kersley, B., Alpin, C., Forth, J., Bryson, A., Bewley, H., Dix, G., and Oxenbridge, S. (2006) *Inside the Workplace: Findings from the 2004 Workplace Employment Relations Survey,* London, UK: Routledge.

Kessler, I. (2005) 'Remuneration Systems' in Bach, S. (ed.) *Managing Human Resources,* 4th ed., Oxford, UK: Blackwell.

Kessler, S. and Bayliss, F. (1998) *Contemporary British Industrial Relations,* 3rd ed., Basingstoke, UK: Macmillan.

Lawler, E. E. (1990) *Strategic Pay,* San Francisco, USA: Jossey-Bass.

Lupton, T. (1972) *Payment Systems: Selected Readings,* Harmondsworth, UK: Penguin.

Makinson, J. (2000) *Incentives for Change,* London, UK: HM Treasury.

Marsden, D. and French, S. (1998) *What a Performance: Performance Related Pay in the Public Services,* London, UK: London School of Economics.

McBeath, G. and Rands, N. (1989) *Salary Administration,* 4th ed., London, UK: Gower.

Milkovich, G. and Newman, J. (1996) *Compensation,* 5th ed., Boston, USA: Irwin/McGraw-Hill.

Office for National Statistics (2006) *Annual Survey of Hours and Earnings 2006,* London, UK: ONS.

Office of Manpower Economics (1973) *Incremental Payment Systems,* London, UK: HMSO.

Personnel Publications (2007) *People Management,* 13, 12, June, 61.

Purcell, J. and Hutchinson, S. (2007) *Rewarding Work – The Vital Role of Line Managers*, London, UK: CIPD.

Reid, G. and Robertson, J. (1965) *Fringe Benefits, Labour Costs and Social Security*, London, UK: George Allen & Unwin.

Roberts, I. (2001) 'Reward and Performance Management' in Beardwell, I. and Holden, L. (eds) *Human Resource Management: a Contemporary Approach*, 3rd ed., Essex, UK: Prentice-Hall.

Rock, M. (1984) *Handbook of Wage and Salary Administration*, 2nd ed., New York, USA: McGraw-Hill.

Rousseau, D. (1995) *Psychological Contracts in Organizations*, London, UK: Sage.

Schuster, J. and Zingheim, P. (1992) *The New Pay: Linking Employee and Organizational Performance*, New York, USA: Lexington.

Seligman, E. (1910) *An Inquiry into the Nature and Causes of the Wealth of Nations by Adam Smith*, Volume 1, with an Introduction by Prof. Seligman, London, UK: Dent.

2

Can pay be strategic?

Jonathan Trevor

Contemporary approaches to pay emphasise the importance of aligning employee behaviours to the strategic direction of the organisation, an approach often labelled 'strategic pay'. In reality, however, many organisations experience profound difficulties when attempting to execute pay strategies. Is strategic pay, therefore, mere rhetoric?

This chapter explores the theory and practice of strategic pay. It starts by defining strategic pay. In the second section, the theory of strategic pay, which is based on a rationalist approach to strategic *choice*, is examined and critiqued. Concepts of contingency and isomorphism are discussed as alternatives to the hegemony of the rationalist approach and worthy of greater attention within contemporary human resource management (HRM) and pay literature. In the third section, some findings of the author's own research are discussed providing an empirical basis for the final section. The chapter concludes by suggesting that sights should be lowered: contrary to prescriptions, strategic pay cannot and does not necessarily or automatically provide competitive advantage through value-added outcomes. Those responsible for determining an organisation's pay strategy should, therefore, focus on risk management and not on economic value maximisation as the driving rationale behind pay determination.

Definition

As explained in Chapter 1, never before in post-war Britain have private sector employers enjoyed so much unilateral freedom to determine the basis of employee pay, and in the interests of achieving purely managerial ends. Accordingly, pay is not purely a cost of hiring the necessary labour as before; nor is it determined in most parts of the private sector by collective bargaining. Instead, pay is a means of aligning a company's unique and inimitable asset – their employees – to the strategic direction of the organisation.

As Lawler (one of the greatest proponents of strategic pay) has said: 'The starting point for any pay system design process needs to be the strategic agenda of the organisation' (Lawler, 1990, p. 15). Once aligned with this agenda, pay becomes a powerful means through which firms may attract and retain desired talent, and elicit desired behaviour outcomes in the form of employee motivation, commitment and loyalty, all of which are conducive to positive organisational performance. With a particular focus on performance, strategic pay incorporates considerable scope for 'at risk' pay, with employees' pay potentially being contingent upon one, or a combination of, company performance, team/division performance, and individual performance (Armstrong and Murlis, 2004; see also Chapters 4 and 6).

The primacy of managerial choice as the determinant of pay practice is characteristic of strategic pay. Strategic pay differs substantially, therefore – conceptually and practically – in a number of important ways from traditional pay. The emergence to the fore of strategic pay has redefined the role and perceived contribution of pay organisationally and economically. Pay is no longer merely a 'cost of doing business', when used strategically it is a source of economic value added and, along with other human capital measures, the means by which firms can secure sustained competitive advantage (Pfeffer, 1994).

Existing research illustrates that organisations are embracing strategic pay widely. The Chartered Institute of Personnel and Development (CIPD) reviews pay arrangements in the United Kingdom (UK) annually. Their Annual Survey Report 2007, reports that 35 per cent of respondents have a formal pay strategy, with a further 40 per cent planning to introduce one. Large organisations are far more likely than smaller ones to have adopted a formal pay strategy, with 49 per cent of organisations, employing between 1,000–4,999 employees, having had one for the past four years or more, and 57 per cent of organisations, employing over 5,000 employees, having had one for the past four years or more (CIPD, 2007).

Respondents said that by far the most common goal for strategic pay is that of supporting the achievement of business goals (84 per cent), closely followed by paying high performers through performance differentiation (77 per cent), and the recruitment and retention of talent (68 per cent).

These developments are not confined to the UK alone, however. Proprietary consultancy data gathered from a sample of over one hundred Fortune 500 firms, all operating globally, reveal that all of them have had a global pay strategy in place for four or more years (Mercer Human Resource Consulting, 2004). The main reasons given by respondents for introducing global pay strategies include supporting global expansion (29 per cent), improved governance structures (17 per cent), cost management (15 per cent), compliance and reporting (12 per cent), and mergers and acquisitions (5 per cent). On a domestic, regional, and global level, the survey data indicate that firms are embracing strategic pay for the achievement of competitive advantage (ibid.).

Strategic pay: the theory

Rationalism

As noted, espoused theories of strategic pay are all predicated on the notion of strategic choice. Choice in the strategic sense involves decision makers selecting those pay strategies and systems that are judged optimal through rational deliberation. Weber, in his classic treatise on bureaucracy and authority, distinguished between two forms of rationality necessary as preconditions of 'ideal type' bureaucracies (Weber, 1924). *Formal* rationality was achieved when the best means to a given ends, whatever that may be, were chosen. Referring to the ends themselves, *substantive* rationality was achieved when the purpose itself was rational (ibid.). In the language of contemporary organisational behaviour, and work organisations in particular, we might equate formal rationality with organisational *processes* and substantive rationality with strategic *purpose*. The notion of the ideal type bureaucracy and optimal strategic pay investments shares a lot. Both emphasise management exercising rational choice over the ends, and the means through which those ends are achieved, as the route to economic maximisation in any given situation. In the context of strategic pay, rationality might therefore be thought of as (1) the selection of strategic pay practices which best achieve stated goals (the what) and (2) the selection of processes in support of the achievement of those goals (the how).

The influence of managerial choice on the shape and formation of pay practice is firmly rooted in the voluntarist tradition of free will and choice free from limitation. Rational actors, or 'classicists', view leadership as the primary moderator of organisational behaviour (Whittington, 1997). Managers choose pay strategies and dictate a path of action, whilst removed from the process of implementation. The parallel often drawn is that of a general directing the course of battle from atop a hill, but not personally taking up arms in combat. The presumption is that managerial decree equals corporate action. The organisation is in mission, design, and performance, because it has been chosen to be so by management (Gerhart and Milkovich, 1990).

Key to the rationalist argument is the assumption that causal conditions preceding choice (for example, deterministic pressures emanating from the environment) are not, of themselves, sufficient to produce that outcome (de Rond and Thietart, 2004). There exists an array of potential choices within any given situation, each with merits and disadvantages and which are, therefore, more or less attractive as a result. In the language of the rationalist, the process of differentiating between options is one of preference ordering, and it is the ability to discern that which is most preferable, or optimal, and exercise the best choice accordingly, that renders the decision maker as rational. In the context of pay determination, selecting the optimal means of supporting the achievement of corporate goals is using pay strategically (Lawler, 1990). The presumption of managerial ability to choose pay strategies and practices that result in predicted positive outcomes is a core belief of the prescriptive literature on strategic pay. Simplistically, the manager, as decision maker, reigns supreme.

In a related vein, de Rond and Thietart (2007) note that the libertarian viewpoint on choice and free will is relevant for contemporary strategic management, because it provides a justification for the belief that we have choices available and that we are free to deliberate rationally over our choices. Similarly, the rationalist viewpoint promotes individuals' responsibilities, and accountability for choices made and actions pursued, precisely because of the ability and freedom to choose. This is consistent with the current emphasis placed upon the contribution of leadership and their accountability for corporate performance (Reid, 1987).

Criticisms

Rationalism as the underpinning basis for pay strategy is, however, not without criticism, both theoretical and practical. First at a theoretical level, rationalism assumes that decision makers have no information problem, but in practice, they have only imperfect knowledge. 'We know only a fraction of the things we need to know' (Simon, 1957, p. 167). This lack of information about the environment prohibits a decision maker from achieving objectives through optimal means. Second, decision makers, due to limited calculative ability, are incapable of anticipating and considering all options to solve a problem. Standard theory, however, assumes that all actors have unlimited cognitive ability to capture, coordinate and process information. Third, decision makers are limited in the amount of attention that they are able to marshal for the capturing and processing of information. If one were to assume that decision makers had the computational ability to acquire and process all relevant data, they would be limited to considering the data piecemeal, and not holistically (Forest and Mehier, 2001). If the action determined is beyond the control of the individual, to what degree can individuals be truly held accountable for the resultant success or failure, and vice versa?

In the face of such limits, decision makers necessarily adopt a 'satisficing' path that permits attainment of needs at some satisfactory (reflexively specified by self) level (Simon, 1957). The fundamental characteristics of the satisficing 'organism', as defined by Simon, include first, a limitation on the ability to plan long behaviour sequences. The limitation is imposed by the bounded cognitive ability of the organism as well as the complexity of the environment in which it operates; second, the tendency to set aspiration levels for each of the multiple goals that the organism faces; third, a tendency to operate on goals sequentially rather than simultaneously because of the 'bottleneck of short term memory'; and lastly, satisficing rather than optimising search behaviour (ibid.). Maximising strategies, like Weber's ideal type bureaucratic scenarios, are inherently problematic to achieve, given cognitive limits.

Another criticism of rationalism centres on the way that decisions are made. Are they made at the start, on a once-and-for-all basis or by evolution? Evolutionists, fundamentally, contest the ability of managers to negotiate the range of competitive pressures through what is called detached calculation. Survival through competitiveness is a constant struggle, in which there will always be winners and losers for reasons other than the 'mere' formulation of sound strategy. Even when the organisation is in a privileged position of advantage over the competition, the process of natural selection still serves to condition the shape, formation, and intent of the organisation. It is markets and not managers that choose the prevailing strategies within a particular environment (Whittington, 1997), such as in global markets. Whilst theory has focused mainly on product market competitive pressure, market fit applies equally to all areas of capital, including innovation, technical capital, and, not least, labour. By definition, to survive is to be successful. Competitive pressures within markets naturally weed out weak performers and de-select them as part of the ongoing struggle for survival of the fittest (ibid.). This clearly has a bearing on pay strategy shape and formation.

Processualist theorists also have little confidence in the ability of managers to plan rationally to secure profit maximisation (Whittington, 1997). For processualists, recognition of the complexity of the internal states of organisations is crucial. They reject both rational actor and evolutionary (market forces) accounts as efficiency optimisers, and embrace two radical departures from the received wisdom: the cognitive limitations of rational action, already discussed, and the 'micro-politics' of organisations (Cyert and March, 1963). The micro-political view of the company rejects unitarist notions of companies constituting a single entity, with perfect unity of interest, but views the company and the management structure instead as comprising groups and individuals each with their own interests. As a result, no strategy is ever developed fully in accordance with the aspirations of everyone within the company, but reflects instead a set of joint goals more or less acceptable to all the decision makers (Whittington, 1997).

From a more practical perspective, and criticisms more closely related to pay, there is a question of how a decision maker is to know whether his/her decision is optimal. There are currently no generally accepted accounting procedures for measuring human resources (Armstrong, 1995), so there is no yardstick for gauging the success or otherwise of strategic pay. For instance, Ferguson and Berger (1985, p. 29) say:

> As tempting as it is to try to establish a balance sheet value for a firm's human assets, such attempts are probably doomed; at this point it is not possible to calculate a figure that is both objective and meaningful.

Similarly Scarpello and Theeke (1989, p. 275) say:

> At the theoretical level, human resource accounting is an interesting concept. If human resource value could be measured, the knowledge of that value could be used for internal management and external investors' decision making. However, until human resource accounting advocates demonstrate a valid and generalisable means for measuring human resource value in monetary terms, we are compelled to recommend that researchers abandon further consideration of possible benefits from [human resource accounting].

Even if one could measure human resource value, there remain a number of problems with asserting a linkage between human capital and human resource initiatives and organisational performance (Becker and Huselid, 1998; Guest, 1997; Legge, 2001). One problem is the problem of reverse causality. Are companies successful because of the way they manage their people (that is, the deployment of human capital/human resource management (HRM) practices), or is it simply the case that successful firms deploy those human resource (HR) practices perceived to be of value?

Furthermore, given that strategic pay is designed to enhance the organisation's competitive strategy, there are problems with classifications of competitive strategy, as such classifications are not mutually exclusive. Rather, it is apparent that those organisations, primarily competing on the basis of low cost, are also able to compete on the basis of quality: in effect minimising cost whilst maximising quality (Legge, 2001). This reflects, perhaps, some of the conceptual 'fuzziness' of dominant strategic management theories to which, prescriptive literature suggests, HRM strategies, systems, processes and practices, should be aligned (Legge, 1995).

Contingency and isomorphism

Having looked at rationalism and its critiques, we now turn to contingency theory. Contingency theory does not discount rationality and choice, nor is strategy formation viewed as an entirely determined outcome (Donaldson, 2001). The contextual characteristics of the organisation are treated as independent variables upon which the organisation's structure is dependent so contingency theory rejects the purist notion of universality, and redefines rationality as the choice of those strategies that best fit the organisation and its context. In one sense, this is the essence of strategic alignment.

The labour employed by the firm has been identified as a 'first order' variable upon which pay system choices are contingent (Gerhart and Milkovich, 1990). Other 'variables' such as firm size (Donaldson, 2001), organisational life cycle, and company performance also influence the pay system.

Relatively little work has explored the influence of institutional pressures upon the outcomes of pay determination (for a notable exception, see Kessler, 2001). Yet, research on the institutionalisation of organisational forms would suggest that they might have an important impact upon the nature and outcomes of pay determination (Gerhart and Rynes, 2003). In their seminal paper DiMaggio and Powell (1991, p. 189) ask, 'why is there such startling homogeneity of organisational forms and practice?' Their answer according to neo-institutionalist theory is isomorphism or conformity. DiMaggio and Powell identify three pressures leading to isomorphism: norms, mimetic behaviour (the desire to emulate the legitimate practice of 'influential others' due to uncertainty), and regulation.

Norms, which also embrace rules, rituals, and beliefs, influence organisations and their actors at multiple levels: at the individual level, in terms of informing the values of decision makers; at the firm level, the culture and politics of the organisation; and industry-wide norms at the inter-organisational level (Kessler 2001; Oliver 1997). Whilst an underdeveloped area, extant research not only highlights the highly influential nature of these determinants, but also reveals that they are often discreet in nature (DiMaggio and Powell, 1991). Measuring the impact and effect of such norms are, for this very reason, problematic (Donaldson, 2001).

As to mimetic processes, pay specialists reference the experiences and practices of others frequently, often emulating what is considered successful elsewhere, to inform choice and mediate risk in the form of failed change. Senior management (non-pay function) within multinational firms also have a significant input into pay determination. In terms of external expertise, management consultants and professional bodies stand out in terms of influence. Operating internationally, management consultancy firms offer advice and solutions to domestic and multinational firms on a range of pay and compensation issues. Despite marketing a tailored approach, much consultancy advice, methodologies, and technical solutions are seemingly, necessarily, standardised. This is perhaps inevitable because the bespoke development of solutions is time and labour intensive and ultimately less profitable in the face of strong competition and mounting cost pressures.

A number of factors contribute to the isomorphic outcomes of professionalisation. First, formal education encourages the development of organisational norms and shared rules amongst professionals which in turn are disseminated throughout the organisations in which they are employed. Second, developed professional networks typically span organisations and provide a mechanism through which new models, rules, and norms are diffused on an inter-organisational basis. The net result of professionalisation is

> a pool of almost interchangeable individuals who occupy similar positions across a range of organisations and possess a similarity of orientation and disposition that may override variations in tradition and control that might otherwise shape organisational behaviour. (DiMaggio and Powell, 1991, p. 175)

The largest professional association for personnel and human resources specialists in the UK with over one hundred and thirty thousand members is the CIPD. The CIPD provides codes of best practice relating to all aspects of employment management, including remuneration, guidance for practitioners on effective human resources practice in the form of conferences, seminars and workshops and, perhaps most significantly, an extensive range of taught courses and qualifications. The CIPD is not alone in doing so. There are a plethora of other institutions that provide similar services, including consultancies and business schools.

The transparency of financial markets also highlights winners and losers. Winners are regularly illustrated as best practice organisations, losers the opposite. Winners therefore become objects for other aspiring organisations to emulate, and institutions such as the CIPD facilitate such a process.

Standard theories of strategic pay do not recognise the importance of the role of institutions, nor the degree to which choices are informed by institutional forces, both consciously and in ways that are taken for granted by pay decision makers. Moreover, the greater the condition of uncertainty under which decisions are made, the greater is the likelihood that decision makers are likely to reference practice externally and become by degree, therefore, prone to the isomorphic institutional pressures pervasive within their organisational field. The implication is that pay system choices are not driven by purely economic interests nor formulated through purely rational means. Institutional pressures are primarily social and political and not economic, with *legitimacy* being the most valuable form of currency available, which places the reality of pay determination at odds with that assumed by standard theory. Pay systems are *selected* for reasons other than for purely economic maximisation.

Strategic pay: the practice

How well does strategic pay theory stand up to scrutiny empirically? What are leading organisations doing and most importantly – how well are they doing it? In response to these issues, and using both quantitative and qualitative methods, primary case-study based research conducted by the author reveals a portrait of strategic pay practice in stark contrast with prescribed theory and practice, with important implications for performance, organisations, and the people they employ (Trevor, 2007).

The research

A multi-level analysis

Existing research investigating strategic pay and related HRM practice does so according to assumptions about the causal linkages between practice and performance. The approach adopted here is not to view pay practice in such 'one-dimensional' terms. Consistent with other multi-level approaches (see Kochan et al., 1986, for example), a multi-level framework was created for the exploration of companies' attempts to manage managerial, professional, and technical pay strategically. The first level of analysis, the pay *approach*, reflects the implicit or espoused values, principles, and aspirations that underpin pay practice. The second level, the pay *design*, reflects the technical content of the intended pay policy. The third and final level, the pay *operation*, reflects what is achieved operationally as pay practice.

These three levels of pay practice are not mutually exclusive. Nevertheless, it is possible to differentiate between the three levels: between the principles underpinning pay, expressed in the form of pay strategies; between the technical designs of pay practice, expressed in the form of policy; and between achieved pay practices in operation. In being able to differentiate between the three states of the same pay practice, or system, it is therefore possible to assess any potential disconnection. What is desired (approach), and what is intended (design), may not be reflected in what is achieved in practice (operation). Such a nuance in the management of pay practice, as an example, is neglected by standard theories of strategic pay that assume linearity and discount the potential for disconnect between strategic conception and execution (Pfeffer and Sutton, 2000).

A tale of three case studies

The three case studies illustrated here are part of a wider study. They are called Alpha, Bravo, and Charlie. All three firms operate in the consumer goods market: food and beverage principally. All three are very large, the smallest employing some 56,000 employees and the largest employing at the time of research slightly fewer than 100,000 employees. All are multinational in scope, marketing and selling products in over one hundred countries in all cases, and with manufacturing and distribution facilities in multiple locations throughout the world. In addition to their sustained high performance, the organisations are also highly reputable, and referenced frequently as examples of best practice and as 'excellent', brand leading firms within the consumer goods sector and more broadly.

The research was conducted at multiple levels, including industry, organisation, division, and team. Primarily the fieldwork in these three organisations, which was conducted in 2005–2006, took the form of 50 interviews in nine countries and over twelve business divisions with senior managers, human resources directors, remuneration specialists, line managers and employees (see Trevor, 2007).

The findings

Given their similarity in terms of organisational form and circumstance, as described above, one might expect to see conformity of pay practice, if contingency theory has purchase. As market leading companies, standard theory would also presume that they are using pay strategically in support of their superior performance. We do indeed see three very similar profiles of pay practice. All three organisations subscribe to strategic pay. Emphasising the role of pay as being the attraction, retention, and motivation of valued talent and as the means by which desirable employee behaviours might be induced. Moreover, they all deploy very similar pay practices. For instance, all three firms deploy multiple forms of incentive systems on a broad basis (multiple occupations and at multiple levels throughout the organisations), using one or more schemes at any one time depending upon the role and level of the employee. Incentives are determined primarily by individual performance, but moderated in all cases by overall company performance depending on employee role and level.

Equity ownership at a discounted rate is also a key element in the form of all employee share ownership programmes, options (on a restricted basis), and stock purchase plans (SPP). All three also offer a comprehensive range of flexible benefits, or 'cafeteria benefits', emphasising flexibility and personal choice in individuals' benefits. Yearly referencing of internal pay structures against roles' external relativity – the external labour market – is the primary determinant of pay levels, and all three firms have dedicated pay professions that reside in all cases within headquarters operations. Interestingly, all three organisations make extensive use of specialist management and pay consultants when formulating pay strategies, even going so far as to use the same firm of consultants and even the same individual advisors.

Using the multi-level framework described above reveals a more nuanced and complex portrait of pay determination, however. At the level of approach, the portrait of pay practice of the three case companies is strikingly similar. In terms of the principles, values, and the philosophy that underpin their approach to pay, Alpha, Bravo, and Charlie are united. All three aspire to have pay systems that align employees to the mission and values of the firm. The aspiration, in all three cases, is expressed in terms of achieving a high performance work culture and the approach is, again, universally articulated in the form of a total rewards model.

The 'total reward' models in all cases emphasise the value to employees of both the financial and non-financial elements of their pay and all three organisations are self-professed employers of choice. Thus, in addition to financial base pay and bonus opportunities, pay and rewards also encompass career succession, development opportunities, stimulating work, lateral progression, flexible working, and a range of addition 'non-financial' measures.

In terms of the form of the pay approach and the related impact, as it is perceived within the broader organisation, we do see some variance between the three organisations, however. Bravo and Charlie adopt a guiding framework to define their pay *approach*. In organisational parlance, this guiding framework is often referred to as a corporate strategic statement. Irrespective, it defines for the organisation what is valued by senior management in terms of goals and corporate principles, and typically establishes a direct linkage with pay. In doing so, it fulfils a symbolic communicative role and is an important tool through which expectations (of both employer and employees) are made explicit.

Alpha, however, enjoys no such utility from its pay approach or the benefits because the approach is not communicated widely and remains, as a result, implicit and ambiguous. Indeed, whilst sharing many of the same strategic aspirations and corporate values of the other two cases, these are not communicated and remain a source of uncertainty organisationally. These differences are summarised in Table 2.1.

Where we have seen widespread conformity at the level of approach, we detect some notable differences between the three firms at the level of design. Unlike Bravo and Charlie, pay within Alpha is aligned almost exclusively to financial goals with profound implications for the determination of performance-based pay. Conformity to the prescribed design within Alpha is the intention driving the pay determination process at the level of design. Disseminated throughout the organisation as formal policy, the design is enforced through precise planning, rules, and checks. As such, the design in Alpha reflects a mandate to which the organisations (line management in business units and

Table 2.1 Strategic pay practice at the level of APPROACH

	Alpha	Bravo	Charlie
Aligned to	Mission & values	Mission & values	Mission & values
Aspiration	High performance work culture	High performance work culture	High performance work culture
Content	Total rewards model	Total rewards model	Total rewards model
Form	Implicit	Guiding Framework	Guiding Framework
Perceived impact	Ambiguous	Symbolic	Symbolic

divisions) are obliged to comply, and which is perceived to constrain the means by which line management in local markets might otherwise choose to remunerate their people.

Bravo and Charlie are qualitatively different from Alpha in their approach to pay practice design, being much less prescriptive. They too are different, however, in terms of what pay is aligned to and the form that the design (policy) should take. In Bravo, the pay design is aligned to business targets overall, that is, group level targets and metrics, with the intention of promoting the alignment of employees to group level performance and promoting corporate fit.

Charlie differs by placing the emphasis of the pay design on the local organisation – business unit/country/divisional targets and performance and not the corporation overall, as in the case of Bravo. What is intended is fit, or alignment, of employee interests and behaviours to the strategic goals of their immediate employing organisation. The design, as policy, constitutes guidance on good practice, upon which local line management might draw when determining pay within the context of their local organisation and labour market conditions. The form of the design is, then, one of minimum standards to which all are expected to comply, being non-negotiable. Pay determination of the design is largely decentralised and devolved, with central intervention being intended to be, and being perceived as, guiding local discretion and autonomy and not superseding it.

In terms of pay practice at the level of design, we might view each as placed on a continuum between centralised and decentralised pay design determination. Alpha represents a case of extreme centralisation (and standardisation), whereas Charlie is at the opposite end of the spectrum, with pay overall being characterised as a loose confederation of individual and stand-alone systems almost on a business unit/divisional basis. We might think of Bravo as having, intentionally at least, one overall system that applies to the entire organisation globally but with some expectation of adaptation locally, see Table 2.2 for a summary.

Table 2.2 Strategic pay practice at the level of DESIGN

	Alpha	Bravo	Charlie
Aligned to	Financial goals	Business overall	Local organisation
Intended	Conformity	Corporate fit	Local fit
Content	Precise planning, rules & checks	Practice prescription	Guidance on good practice
Form	Mandate	Policy	Minimum standards
Perceived impact	Constraining	Informing	Guiding

How well are the three shared approaches, and three distinct modes of design, operationalised? In Alpha, our most extreme example of centralised pay determination, what is experienced operationally are pay systems, across all sub-organisations of the business overall, that are aligned to centrally determined targets and enforced by headquarters. These systems do indeed direct effort and behaviours towards these centrally determined targets. In the context of the local organisation and unique market and organisational conditions, however, these behaviours are not complementary to performance and are viewed as misleading by local management; that is, employee behaviours and effort are misdirected.

By contrast, operationally, pay systems within Bravo emphasise corporate targets (with concession made necessarily to local targets), with the expectation that local management will not only adapt the prescribed design to the conditions of the local organisation, but also foster a sense of employee ownership of corporate success and promote consistency throughout the organisation. Conventionally, Bravo conforms most to what one might perceive in general terms as 'best practice'.

Charlie, on the other hand, emphasises local targets, as per the design illustrated above, with local autonomy and discretion constituting the primary determinants of employee pay. Local management, having such discretion, chooses in the vast majority of the divisions investigated to use performance-based pay as a means of rewarding effort, commitment, and loyalty on a post-hoc basis. This is perhaps in recognition of the difficulty of defining appropriate performance targets and measures *a priori* as one might expect with expectancy theory (see, for example, Vroom, 1964). Instead, local management within Charlie uses pay (superficially the same pay interventions that are used in both Alpha and Bravo) to reinforce desirable behaviours and levels of effort, and to bind the local organisation to that of the group overall, within the umbrella of the values espoused at the level of approach. See Table 2.3 for a summary of strategic pay practice at the level of operation.

Alpha is a good example of the potential risk of attempting to use pay strategically. In a best-case scenario, it is unclear what the impact, perceived or actual, is organisationally.

Table 2.3 Strategic pay practice at the level of OPERATION

	Alpha	Bravo	Charlie
Aligned to	Centrally determined targets	Corporate and local targets	Local targets
Achieved	Enforced scheme	Adaptation	Autonomy
Content	Directional	(some) line of sight	Post hoc reward
Form	Misleading	Leading	Reinforcing
Perceived impact	Best – unclear Worst – risk	Corporate consistency	Culturally binding & context specific

At worst, however, the pay systems deployed pose a significant business risk and result in a number of unintended consequences, many of which are damaging.

In terms of pay outcomes overall, we can summarise that Alpha is characterised by a highly centralised and instrumental approach to pay and by the degree to which it is standardised. There is little or no concession made to local business or cultural conditions within divisions and sub-organisations of the overall group business and this results in business *risk*. Pay, in this instance, directs wrong behaviours, diminishes motivation and pay systems themselves are often subverted or rejected by local (line) management without the knowledge of the central human resources function or senior management.

In Bravo, by contrast, pay is viewed as an important managerial tool that influences behaviours; symbolically communicates those principles and values considered important by senior management; and, to a degree, promotes alignment of employees worldwide to the overall strategic direction and goals of the global organisation. Pay only does so when endorsed and managed locally, and may prove ineffective otherwise.

Pay in Charlie is both substantively and formatively different from both Alpha and Bravo. Pay is deemed as important in motivational terms, but only from the perspective of 'hygiene' (Herzberg, 1975). In effect, pay only becomes of high strategic importance when *wrong* by producing dysfunctionality such as conflict, inefficiency, and counterproductive behaviours. This reflects in Charlie a perspective on what pay can and cannot achieve organisationally. Pay is merely a function of *hygiene* and, when not wrong, is just one element of the glue that binds the organisation overall. This is especially important in the case of Charlie where growth in the past has been through acquisition and not traditionally organic growth strategies. Performance-based elements of the pay package, such as performance related pay and bonuses in particular, are post-hoc pay reinforcing recognition over incentivisation.

Observations and implications of the findings

What can we observe from analysis and comparison of the three case studies? First, all three organisations, which are very similar when assessed using criteria such as industry, size, age, and lifecycle, share at first sight very similar profiles of pay practice, but deeper analysis highlights profound differences. The role of pay in Alpha might be characterised as corporate control. In Bravo this is less so, and might be instead characterised as an attempt to *lead* the overall organisation corporately in a defined strategic direction. The emphasis in Charlie is fostering and sustaining a commitment-based culture orientated around the local organisation, but operating under the umbrella values of the group organisation overall.

Second, and perhaps most significantly, what is intended is not what is always achieved in practice. A simple observation conceptually but of grave significance practically, is the existence of a disconnection – or *gap* – between the three levels of the pay determination process. At the heart of strategic conceptions of pay (and HRM generally) is the value chain illustrated in a previous section. All classical conceptions of strategic management assume that intent translates directly into action (Whittington 1997; Wright and Nishii 2004). The findings illustrate clearly, however, the pervasiveness of a gap between pay strategy, policy, and execution in each of the case study companies – albeit to a greater or lesser degree per case. The implication is that, irrespective of strategic desire or the saliency of the design, ineffectual execution results in ineffectual pay practice which then impacts negatively upon the pay outcomes experienced as a result. Whilst mainstream studies continue to investigate the nature of the linear relationship between practice and performance, such studies are questionable if 'realised' pay practice differs from the 'espoused" (Mintzberg, 1978). The neglect of the gap between strategy and execution is therefore a critical weakness of strategic theories of pay.

This distinction between intended and actual practice is largely omitted from strategic management literature. Very little of the research underpinning standard theories of strategic pay recognise that 'not all intended HR practices are actually implemented and, those that are, may often be implemented in ways that differ from the initial intention' (Wright and Nishii, 2004), and the findings clearly lend support to this. Despite rational planning at the design stage, selected pay systems are rarely perfectly applied or enacted by those charged with implementation – typically line management – for a variety of reasons. In the language of Gerhart and Rynes (2003), functional pay strategies are neither successfully implemented nor executed. In light of this observation, many of the rationalist assumptions that form the bedrock upon which strategic theories of pay are founded – substantive and formal – seem narrow and misplaced.

The implications of the gap between pay strategy and execution are all too real. Contrary to espoused pay theory and the prescriptions of strategic pay proponents, the experience of strategic pay in practice, when observed through the lens of multiple dimensions, reveals a highly complex process of pay determination where the outcomes are far from certain *a priori*. Indeed, in the case of Alpha, and in the cases of Bravo and Charlie albeit to a much lesser extent, a great many unintended consequences are encountered as a result of the strategic pay systems deployed in the hope (and expectation) of positive performance outcomes. As a result of these unintended consequences, these three similar firms using the same pay practices do very different things operationally and experience very different outcomes.

Third, pay may not fulfil the stated strategic objectives of motivating managerial, professional, and technical employees to work harder. Alpha represents a cautionary tale for those attempting to use strategic pay systems. The desired outcomes of a high performance work culture, an organisation aligned to mission and goals and desirable behaviours and productivity are, if they are present in Alpha, not the result of the strategic pay. Rather the organisation, which is of course market leading, is successful in spite of pay, not because of it. Arguably, more than merely ineffectual, the pay systems used are positively damaging and are quite the opposite of what was desired (approach) or intended (design). Indeed, there are numerous examples in Alpha of conflict arising from poorly managed strategic pay practices – not only conflict that is overt and manifest, and therefore apparent to management, but also conflict that is discreet and therefore much more difficult to remedy. Such discreet conflict takes the form of employee demotivation, disengagement, and disenfranchisement, resulting in poor performance, employee attrition, and behaviours that consume or destroy value.

Moreover, the centralised and standardised ethnocentric nature of the enforced pay design – which in many divisions is a poor fit for the local organisation – creates a great deal of work for local line management who are necessarily required to adapt (or subvert in extreme cases) the imposed system to avoid the inevitable conflict. Implementing such poorly aligned systems is not only problematic but also extremely time consuming, and therefore a burden, and distracts from the strategic goals in hand.

Fourth, analysis of the case studies provides renewed support for contingency. At organisational level, contingency predictions are borne out by empirical observations of the pay practices of the case organisations. However, the same contingency effect at sub-levels of the three organisations encourages divergence which is observed particularly at the level of operation. In short, the influence of contingency is a key factor shaping pay practice at all levels of the organisation and at each stage of the pay determination process.

Finally, in addition to the importance of contingency, this research provides strong support for the salience of isomorphism. Isomorphism or conformity as a result of social and political pressures is observed especially at the level of approach. The three competing organisations draw on the same pool of managerial employees, who frequently move interchangeably from one employer to another and, as noted above, all three use the same advisors, and thus inevitably according to neo-institutionalist theory, adopt essentially the same pay practices.

In summary, the findings suggest that attempting to use strategic pay systems, such as incentive pay, results often in unintended consequences and negative outcomes that destroy value and do not create it. The research study findings overall are littered with examples of strategic pay systems producing outcomes precisely the opposite of what was desired strategically, including employee de-motivation and disengagement, misdirected behaviours and conflict. In process terms, strategic pay systems place significant demands on managerial time and effort operationally, particularly when managers have to reconcile the negative tensions that arise as a by-product. Strategic pay can, therefore, represent a significant organisational risk if managed improperly and a far cry from the value-added means of securing competitive advantage envisaged by strategic pay proponents.

Conclusions

The main implication of the findings from this research is that theory is out of step with reality and may represent a largely unattainable ideal in practice. It would be overly pessimistic and wrong, however, to conclude that pay cannot be strategic in any sense because of the managerial limitations identified. Choice may be limited, but managers are still able to exercise a *degree* of choice. Thus, it is argued here that a revision and not an abandonment of strategic pay is required.

Clearly, attempting to use pay strategically is not as straightforward as prescriptive commentary, or advocates of strategic pay, suggest. Despite the difficulties encountered by all, some case study companies clearly experience better outcomes than others – in large part because of their approach to the use and management of strategic pay systems. In the light of the findings, firms should approach the prescriptions of strategic pay advocates with caution and adopt more modest expectations of the desired pay outcomes.

A key implication of the research is that standard theory has established an ideal with little practical grounding that is, as a result, inherently challenging to achieve operationally. Moreover, practitioners not only cannot avoid achieving only limited success, but also run the risk of incurring negative outcomes as an unintended consequence of attempting to use pay strategically. Thus, the findings of this study challenge many key aspects of standard theory and provide the basis for a grounded reorientation of standard theory to reflect more clearly the reality of strategic pay in practice.

A revision to theory would necessarily have to incorporate sensitivity to the managerial aspects of pay practice and the importance of effective management of pay systems to pay system effectiveness, an issue overlooked by existing commentary. The current focus on the practice and performance linkage to the neglect of the gap between strategy and execution is one such area requiring revision. If sensitive to such issues, a revised approach to strategic pay would necessarily be less ambitious in terms of promised outcomes.

Whilst challenging a compelling and enduring corpus of literature, this view is consistent with some of the most recent commentary on strategic pay. Armstrong and Brown (2006), formerly two of the most vocal advocates of strategic pay having produced over nine practitioner orientated books between them alone, reflect on developments to strategic pay and call for a 'new realism'. They say:

> When mostly North American concepts of strategic HRM and pay first entered into management thinking and practice in the UK we were some of their most fervent advocates, writing and advising individual employers on the benefits of aligning their pay systems so as to drive business performance. We helped articulate strategic plans and visions, and to design the pay and pay changes that would secure better alignment and performance .... Some 20 years later, we are a little older and a little wiser as a result of these experiences. We remain passionate proponents of a strategic approach to pay management .... but in conducting this work *we have seen some of the risks* and opportunities .... at times *there has been an over-ambition and optimism in terms of what could and couldn't be achieved by changing pay and pay arrangements'*. (Armstrong and Brown, 2006, p. 1 – emphasis added)

In principle, strategic pay remains a laudable ambition. Companies continue to aspire to use pay strategically and, despite the challenges encountered, show little sign of deviating from their current trajectories nor adopting alternative approaches – indeed, alternative approaches are not obvious, such is the pervasiveness of the strategic approach. Can firms move beyond the orthodoxy of strategic pay? Any change to the prevailing status quo would necessarily have to be incremental, given the inertia of company practice, the taken-for-granted associations developed in the minds of decision makers and the norming effects of a labour market where the so-called strategic pay interventions are not simply commonplace, but benchmarks to which both firms and employees attach great value. Nevertheless, the findings presented in this chapter prompt a call for a fresh perspective that better reflects the reality of strategic pay.

A fresh perspective

What might a fresh perspective look like? Whilst having concluded that even leading companies struggle to manage strategic pay effectively with the result that pay is often non-strategic operationally, the research does not in any way contest the continued importance of pay. The findings suggest that an alternative approach to the use of pay systems *in support* of strategy is required: one that acknowledges the relative limits on the ability of companies to manage pay strategically by the terms of standard theory and incorporates provision for a redefined contribution that would better serve the aim of securing competitive advantage.

The use of pay was not always thought of, or practised, in strategic terms. As discussed previously, pay within post-war Britain was determined primarily as a result of collective bargaining conducted at multiple levels – occupational, industry, and multi-employer. Such centralised pay determination served to take wages out of competition between employers. Management was neither free, in principle, nor empowered, in practice, to determine pay unilaterally for the achievement of purely managerial ends. Pay represented a 'cost of doing business' or, more particularly, the cost of hiring the labour necessary to do business.

The philosophy underpinning the employment relationship differed too, emphasising the pluralism of interest between employer and employee. Bargaining arrangements were focused predominately on the avoidance of conflict through negotiation. The risks of not reaching a mutually acceptable settlement included strikes and other forms of well-publicised industrial action. Whilst not expressed in such terms, industrial action, in its various forms, represented a significant business risk. Pay was not, itself, used to secure competitive advantage, but was considered a critical risk that required careful management to avoid the crippling effects of industrial conflict. The value-added outcomes of pay are hard to define and equally difficult to measure, but the negative consequences of 'getting pay wrong' are all too obvious.

In trying to move beyond the dominant logic of strategic pay, do we perhaps need to reflect on what pay was – old pay? The research illustrates that many of the features of old pay continue in practice to pervade the operational management of pay, strategic or otherwise. Despite the underlying ideology of strategic pay being one of unitarism, the management of pay operationally continues to be characterised by pluralist relations between employer and employee, and by pluralism within the management structure itself. Given these, and other challenges involved, our definition of what constitutes strategic pay might be re-scaled to reflect more clearly the reality of pay in practice. The strategic contribution of pay should not be to maximise value, given the constraints on the ability of companies to do so, but to minimise the inherent risks associated with pay, whether used strategically or not. Indeed, what is maximisation in pay determination? In practice, pay professionals are not 'strategic partners', but risk managers, and continue to fulfil a great number of the tasks and activities characteristic of old pay, such as conflict resolution. Effective pay management, in practice, is effective risk management and attempts to manage it on any other basis are inherently, and inevitably, problematic. Future research on pay might profit greatly by developing further the risk thesis proposed above.

It is recognised that such a revision will not prove popular with large sections of the pay profession, remuneration and management consultants, academics, and others with a vested interest in the success of strategic pay conceptually and prescriptively. They will find it overly negative – pessimistic perhaps – and may challenge the conclusions drawn from the findings by citing numerous counter examples and stories of success. The methods used here, necessary to gain the insights presented as findings, may also be criticised on those same grounds that relegate qualitative studies of pay to a secondary position in terms of importance to dominant positivist studies – namely reflexivity, lack of the ability to generalise, and other such acknowledged limitations. The research upon which this chapter is based, however, was not conducted with the aim of reforming the opinion of the faithful, but to put forward an alternative perspective garnered as a result of grounded experience. It is hoped that, ultimately, the findings and conclusions presented here will resonate most with those for whom attempts to use strategic pay systems prove the most problematic – a frustrated and often much maligned pay function and long-suffering line management.

References

Armstrong, M. (1995) 'Personnel and Accounting' in Storey, J. (ed.) *Human Resource Management: A Critical Text*, London: Thompson.

Armstrong, M. and Brown, D. (2006) *Strategic Pay: Making It Happen*, London: Kogan Page.

Armstrong, M. and Murlis, H. (2004) *Pay Management*, 5th ed., London: Kogan Page.

Becker, B. and Huselid, M. A. (1998) 'High Performance Work Systems and Firm Performance: A Synthesis of Research and Managerial Implications', *Research in Personnel and Human Resources Management*, 16, 53–101.

Chartered Institute of Personnel and Development (CIPD) (2007) *Pay Management Survey 2007*, London: Chartered Institute of Personnel and Development.

Cyert, R. and March, J. (1963) *A Behavioral Theory of the Firm*, Englewood Cliffs: Prentice Hall.

de Rond, M. and Thietart, R. A. (2004) *Chance, Choice and Determinism in Strategy*, Judge Institute of Management Studies, working paper series.

de Rond, M. and Thietart, R. A. (2007) 'Choice, Chance and Inevitability in Strategy', *Strategic Management Journal*, 28, 5, 535–551.

DiMaggio, P. and Powell, W. (1991) 'The Iron Cage Revisited: Institutional Isomorphism and Collective Rationality' in Powell, W. and DiMaggio, P. (eds) *The New Institutionalism in Organizational Analysis*, Chicago: University of Chicago Press.

Donaldson, L. (2001) *The Contingency Theory of Organizations*, Auckland, NZ: Sage.

Ferguson, D. H. and Berger, F. (1985) 'Employees as Assets: A Fresh Approach to Human Resource Accounting', *The Cornell HRA Quarterly*, 25, 4, 24–29.

Forest, J. and Mehier, C. (2001) 'John R. Commons and Herbert A. Simon on the Concept of Rationality', *Journal of Economic Issues*, 3, 35, September.

Gerhart, B. and Milkovich, G. T. (1990) 'Organizational Differences in Managerial Compensation and Firm Performance', *Academy of Management Journal*, 33, 663–691.

Gerhart, B. and Rynes, S. (2003) *Compensation: Theory, Evidence and Strategic Implications*, New York: Sage.

Guest, D. E. (1997) 'Human Resource Management and Performance: A Review and Research Agenda', *International Journal of Human Resource Management*, 8, 265–276.

Herzberg, F. (1975) *One More Time, How Do You Motivate Employees?* Harvard Business School: Harvard Business School Press.

Kessler, I. (2001) 'Pay System Choices' in Storey, J. (ed.) *Human Resource Management*: A *Critical Text*, London: Thomson Learning.

Kochan, T. A., Katz, H. and McKensie, R. (1986) *The Transformation of American Industrial Relations*, New York: Basic Books.

Lawler, E. (1990) *Strategic Pay: Aligning Organizational Strategies and Pay Systems*, San Francisco: Jossey-Bass.

Legge, K. (1995) 'HRM: Rhetoric, Reality and Hidden Agendas' in Storey, J. (ed.) *Human Resource Management: A Critical Text*, London: Routledge.

Legge, K. (2001) 'Silver Bullet or Spent Round? Assessing the Meaning of the High Commitment Management / Performance Relationship' in Storey, J. (ed.) *Human Resource Management: A Critical Text*, London: Thomson Learning.

Mercer Human Resource Consulting (2004) *Global Compensation Survey* (proprietary consultancy data).

Mintzberg, H. (1978) *The Structuring of Organizations: A Synthesis of Research*, New York: Prentice Hall.

Oliver, C. (1997) 'Sustaining Competitive Advantage: Combining Institutional and Resource Based Views', *Strategic Management Journal*, 18, 9, 697–713.

Pfeffer, J. (1994) *Competitive Advantage through People*, Boston: HBS Press.

Pfeffer, J. and Sutton, R. I. (2000) *The Knowing-Doing Gap: How Smart Companies Turn Knowledge into Action*, Boston: HBS Press.

Reid, G. (1987) *Theories of Industrial Organization*, London: Blackwell.

Scarpello, V. and Theeke, H. A. (1989) 'Human Resource Accounting: A Measured Critique', *Journal of Accounting Literature*, 8, 265–280.

Simon, H. (1957) *Models of Man*, New York: Wiley.

Trevor, J. (2007) Can Pay Be Strategic? A Critical Exploration of Strategic Pay in Practice (Unpublished PhD thesis), Judge Business School, University of Cambridge.

Vroom, V. H. (1964) *Work and Motivation*, Jossey Bass: San Francisco.

Weber, M. (1924) 'Legitimate Authority and Bureaucracy' in Pugh, D. S. (ed.) *Organization Theory* (1997), 4th ed., Penguin, London.

Whittington, R. (1997) *What Is Strategy and Does It Matter?* London: Thomson Business Press.

Wright, P. M. and Nishii, L. H. (2004) *Strategic HRM and Organizational Behavior: Integrating Multiple Levels of Analysis*, Erasmus University Conference 'HRM: What's Next', 2004.

3

Employee voice in pay determination

Esmond Lindop

'I sometimes wonder, Mr Deakin, who governs this country – the government or the Transport and General Workers Union.' This comment by a post-war Home Secretary to the then TGWU General Secretary (cited in Barnes and Reid, 1980, p. xiii) sounds almost incredible to anyone only familiar with employee relations in Britain in the early years of the twenty-first century. The sheer significance of trade unions on the political stage as well as within the British workplace from the 1940s to the 1980s is hard to overstate.

It is therefore unsurprising that when thinking about employee voice in pay determination, the customary starting point is the role played by trade unions. Collective bargaining was the dominant means of employment regulation in Britain for most of the twentieth century, covering some four-fifths of all employees at its height. As recently as the 1980s, the emerging concept of employee voice was seen as virtually synonymous with trade unionism. Only in the past few years has it started to be seen as something broader, which can be expressed – and which can influence pay decisions – through other mechanisms.

This chapter seeks to analyse the new and diverse forms that employee voice is taking in relation to pay. Trade unions remain important, though playing a diminished role, in pay setting through the long-established institutions of collective bargaining. A new and major institutional force in pay setting, particularly one affecting employees in the private sector, is the Low Pay Commission. Both it and the expanded Pay Review Bodies (PRBs) in the public sector have generated new forms of employee voice as input to their pay decisions. Moving away from pay-setting institutions, I will also examine the greatly expanded role of direct communication systems such as employee attitude surveys in shaping pay decisions within individual organisations. There are also early signs of new forms of collective voice emerging to influence pay, most notably demonstrated in the United Kingdom (UK) by the London living wage campaign, using mechanisms different from traditional collective bargaining. It is argued that it is misleading to see these new forms of voice as inherently inferior to collective bargaining by trade unions. We must start, however, with an outline of the concept of employee voice itself, and a look at the remarkable changes that have taken place in the involvement of trade unions in the UK in the process of pay determination.

The emergence of employee voice

> It would generally be recognised that employed persons can justly claim the right to have their interests taken into account. In order to be assured that these interests are taken into account, the needs and experience of workpeople must be known to the employer. ... Trade unions are the unique means whereby men and women in employment can themselves decide how their interests can best be furthered. (TUC, 1966, p. 29)

The view put forward by the Trades Union Congress (TUC) in its evidence to the Donovan Commission in the 1960s is in many respects a classic statement of trade unions as the 'unique means' of employee voice being expressed. That was a view shared by Freeman and Medoff (1984) when they adapted ideas about consumer behaviour in the face of problems to apply them in an employment context, coining the concept of employee voice in the process. In essence, they identified the strategies available to employees as 'exit', in other words leaving less desirable jobs for better ones, or 'voice', defined as 'direct communication to bring actual and desired conditions closer together' (ibid., p. 8). In their view, for employee voice to be effective in influencing employer behaviour, it must be trade union voice (Bryson, 2004). Only the collective mechanism of a trade union offered a realistic prospect of success and individuals, in the absence of an independent collective mechanism, would be unlikely to press for changes affecting the well-being of other employees.

Subsequent commentators have been rather less impressed by the assumption that, for all practical purposes, there could be no employee voice other than trade union voice. As expressed recently by Bryson et al. (2007):

> Our conception of employee voice is not, as was Freeman and Medoff's (1984), based solely on unionism. Rather, it is closer to Hirschman's (1971) conception, embracing any form of employee voice as Hirschman embraced any form of consumer voice: it is the institutionalisation of two-way communication between employers and employees designed to reduce transaction and exit costs for both parties. It is thus a contractual governance mechanism with mutual benefits. (pp. 3–4)

As we shall see below, other work by Bryson suggests that there are good reasons to believe that trade unions do not play a uniquely effective role in enunciating employee voice. I will also argue that, in the context of pay setting, the effectiveness of employee voice on occasion relies on its vocalisation to bodies other than the contractual employer, depending on the locus of decision-making. First it is appropriate to review the declining, but still important, role of British trade unions in the process of pay determination through conventional collective bargaining from the early 1980s onwards.

The changing pattern of trade unions and pay bargaining[1]

The growth in trade union membership and the rapid spread of collective bargaining as the prime means of regulating pay and conditions in the UK during the twentieth century are a familiar tale. By the mid-1960s, the TUC claimed some 80 per cent of employees (18 out of 23 million) had their wages and salaries determined by some type of joint negotiating machinery (TUC, 1966, p. 86). While these figures may be viewed with some scepticism, the expansion of trade union membership and collective bargaining is not in doubt, as evidenced by less partial sources. By 1979, some 55 per cent of all employees were trade union members, and in 1984, some 70 per cent of all employees were covered by collective bargaining over pay (Millward et al., 2000).

The Workplace Employment Relations Surveys (WERS) and their predecessors, the Workplace Industrial Relations Surveys (WIRS), stretch back to 1980 and provide a rich vein of information about the nature of work in Britain. Successive surveys have grown in depth and complexity, and the composition of questions has changed to reflect the transformation in British workplaces over the period. One area covered by the surveys that has experienced particularly radical change is collective bargaining, that is, the joint regulation of the terms and conditions of employment.

In an analysis of the first four WERS surveys, Millward et al. (2000) were able to produce comparable measures of collective bargaining coverage for the period 1984–1998. These data are reproduced in Table 3.1. The figures refer to the percentage of workplaces where certain pay determination methods were in use.

The most striking feature to emerge from the data is that collective bargaining coverage shrank from setting pay in three-fifths of all workplaces in 1984 to less than one-third just 14 years later – a fall of 50 per cent. Thus, in less than a generation, the principal traditional means by which rank and file workers could influence the terms and conditions of their employment, including their remuneration, had become a minority activity.

The other notable feature of the data presented in Table 3.1 concerns the level of decision-making about pay. In 1984, multi-employer collective bargaining was the single most important method of pay determination in the economy, accounting for two-thirds of all bargaining. From the early 1980s onwards, individual employers increasingly opted out of multi-employer bargaining arrangements across much of the private sector. The result was the demise of national bargaining machinery across a swathe of industries, from engineering, food retailing, and banking to docks, food manufacture, textiles, and road transport (Brown, 1991). By 1998, multi-employer bargaining was used to determine pay in only 13 per cent of workplaces, which represented less than half of the collective bargaining that was taking place in Britain.

Table 3.1 Pay determination methods 1984–1998

	Column percentages		
	1984	1990	1998
Collective bargaining	60	42	29
Most distant level of negotiation:			
Multi-employer bargaining	41	23	13
Multi-site, single employer bargaining	12	14	12
Workplace bargaining	5	4	3
Don't know	1	1	–
Not collective bargaining	40	58	71
Most distant level of decision-making:			
External to organisation	7	9	14
Management at a higher level in organisation	11	16	25
Management at workplace level	21	30	30
Don't know	1	3	2

Source: Millward et al., 2000, p. 186.

Where collective bargaining remained intact, it was most commonly taking place at the level of single employers – a striking feature of the results is the stability of multi-site, single employer bargaining arrangements in terms of reported frequency.

If collective bargaining was in retreat, what was replacing it as the means of pay determination? Table 3.1 appears to provide the answer. Joint regulation of the terms of employment was apparently being replaced by simple management authority. The data show that whereas in 1984 management were reported as having sole control of pay setting in a third of workplaces, this figure had risen to 55 per cent by 1998. At its starkest interpretation, it seems that while in 1984 the single most prevalent form of pay determination was national or industry-level bargaining, by 1998 this had been replaced by management diktat at the level of the individual workplace. Thus, there is prima facie evidence from the WERS data that employee voice in the area of pay determination was significantly eroded during a relatively short period from the mid-1980s to the late 1990s.

As so often in analysis of social and economic issues, the glass of collective bargaining can be perceived as half-full or half-empty, depending on the viewpoint of the observer. Despite the sharp decline in collective bargaining coverage, it remains an important means of pay determination in Britain. Before turning to other forms of employee voice, it is therefore appropriate to analyse the current contours of collective bargaining, drawing on the most recent iteration of the WERS series (Kersley et al., 2006).

A comparison of the 1998 and 2004 WERS data is also enlightening as the period corresponds almost exactly to that covered by the incoming New Labour government. Tony Blair's electoral landslide in 1997 might have been expected to herald an upturn in fortunes for the labour movement and collective bargaining. As Brown and Nash (2008) state 'after the long, lean years of Conservative hostility and often depressed economic conditions, the six-year period following the 1998 WERS, with its sympathetic government, supportive legislation, low unemployment, and uninterrupted economic growth, might have been expected to witness a collective bargaining renaissance'. Analysis of WERS 2004 allows us to examine the extent to which these expectations were met.

According to WERS 2004, there has been no upturn in collective bargaining coverage since 1998. In fact, the decline that was observed prior to 1998 has continued, albeit more slowly, with the proportion of workplaces covered by bargaining falling from 29 per cent in 1998 to 27 per cent six years later.

As might be predicted, there was a stark division between the public and private sectors in terms of bargaining coverage. In the public sector, the proportion of workplaces that were covered by collective bargaining was 83 per cent, which corresponds to 82 per cent of employees. In the private sector, however, only 14 per cent of workplaces used collective bargaining to determine pay. The fact that this corresponds to 26 per cent of employees indicates that bargaining is concentrated in large organisations. This interpretation is reinforced by the disaggregated data on workplace size shown in Table 3.2. The data show a very strong positive correlation between workplace size and bargaining coverage. In workplaces of 10–24 employees only 17 per cent of employees were covered by bargaining. This proportion increases to over two-thirds of the workforce for workplaces of over 500 employees. Kersley et al. also find that workplace ownership is an important determinant of bargaining coverage. Their analysis shows that joint regulation is lower where an individual or family holds a controlling interest in the workplace. The same is also true of stand-alone workplaces as compared to those that are part of a larger organisation (ibid., p. 181). Thus, the majority of workers who had their pay set by collective bargaining in 2004 were either in the public sector or in large organisations with multiple establishments.

Table 3.2 also illustrates bargaining coverage according to industrial sector. The patterns here are broadly predictable and follow the contours of union strength. Sectors such as public administration, health and social work, education and other community services are predominantly in the public sector, which is far more heavily unionised than the private sector (though this picture of stability in the public sector is not the full story, as we shall see below). Other sectors where bargaining coverage has remained high such as electricity, gas and water, and transport and communication, although now in the private sector, have a legacy of high unionisation from the pre-privatisation era. In sectors where unionisation is traditionally weaker, such as wholesale and retail, hotels and restaurants, and other business services, then collective bargaining coverage is correspondingly less widespread.

It might have been expected that collective bargaining coverage would have recovered under the more benign political climate of the Labour government. Using time-consistent measures Kersley et al. find that bargaining has continued to contract.

Table 3.2 Incidence and coverage of collective bargaining as depicted by WERS 2004

	Workplaces with any collective bargaining	Employees covered by collective bargaining
	% workplaces	% employees
All workplaces	27	40
Workplace size:		
10–24 employees	19	17
25–49 employees	33	26
50–99 employees	31	27
100–199 employees	48	42
200–499 employees	57	52
500 or more employees	65	68
Sector of ownership:		
Private sector	14	26
Public sector	83	82
Industry:		
Manufacturing	20	39
Electricity, gas and water	96	87
Construction	17	26
Wholesale and retail	9	17
Hotels and restaurants	2	5
Transport and communication	43	63
Financial services	63	49
Other business services	10	12
Public administration	93	90
Education	67	58
Health and social work	36	60
Other community services	32	46

Source: Kersley et al., 2006, p. 180.

They calculate that aggregate collective bargaining coverage declined at an average annual rate of 0.7 per cent between 1998 and 2004. This compares to an annual rate of 3.3 per cent for the period 1990–1998 and 2.9 per cent over the 1984–1990 period (ibid., p. 188). Thus, the extent of collective bargaining has continued to fall under New Labour, albeit more slowly. These aggregate data, however, mask distinct variations within the private sector. In private services, the rate of decline in bargaining slowed from an average of 4.7 per cent between 1990 and 1998 to 1.1 per cent per year from 1998 to 2004. This is in marked contrast to private manufacturing where the rate of decline in bargaining coverage has doubled from 1.3 per cent per year to 2.6 per cent over the two periods. Given that bargaining coverage has always been lower in private services, this difference may simply be because there was further to fall in the manufacturing sector.

The locus of private sector pay fixing has continued its shift downwards, irrespective of whether firms bargain with unions. Kersley et al. report that the most significant change in pay determination 'has been the growth in the percentage of workplaces where all pay was set by management at workplace level: this was the sole method of pay determination in over two-fifths (43 per cent) of private sector workplaces in 2004, compared with one-third (32 per cent) in 1998' (op. cit. p. 184). Brown and Nash claim that the underlying cause of this decentralisation of pay setting has been the diminishing pressures of comparability. They state that 'for decades employers with multi-plant organisations had centralised control over pay. They have done this as a precaution against their employees' perceiving anomalous pay comparisons that might provoke discontent or be used as bargaining levers' (ibid.). As trade union influence diminished, employers have felt freer to set pay in relation to local labour market conditions and to develop performance-related pay schemes, which were traditionally opposed by unions (Heywood et al., 1997). Evidence from the WERS Panel Survey suggests that the proportion of continuing workplaces which had performance-related pay rose from 20 per cent in 1998 to 32 per cent in 2004 (Kersley et al., p. 191). This trend of decentralisation is evident even where unions are still involved, even if more weakly. Brown and Nash find that in every sector except transport and communications there has been a substantial decentralisation of pay fixing to the level of the workplace (ibid.). It seems that employers no longer feel the need to set pay at industry or sector level and have been emboldened to respond to local labour markets and to design their own incentive pay schemes.

Employee voice: new outlets and influences

With the rapid decline in trade union power and subsequent diminution of collective bargaining coverage, attention has shifted to the means by which employees' views and interests are incorporated into the process of wage determination. What, if anything, has filled the void left by the retreat of collective bargaining? Before we look at some of those mechanisms, we should conclude discussion of the decline of collective bargaining with a brief assessment of the impact of trade unions, which may help in understanding the patterns shown by the WERS data.

One of the features of discussion of the decline in trade union membership and collective bargaining is the implicit assumption that somehow alternative mechanisms are second rate. However, as Dundon et al. (2005) comment, 'the decline in unionisation does raise questions as to the efficacy of union-based systems for employee voice'. In considering pay matters, the issue of whether and how far those represented by trade unions gain a wage premium over other employees because of collective bargaining has long preoccupied observers. As one recent analysis puts it, 'the empirical literature on the union wage premium is one of the largest in labour economics' (Blanchflower and Bryson, 2007, p. 2). This is not the place to explore this literature in detail but, in recent years, most of those investigating the field have concluded that the union premium has been in decline. Blanchflower and Bryson's most recent analysis of the impact of trade union coverage in the UK concludes that 'with workplace fixed effects there appears to be no statistically significant union membership wage premium among covered workers in the private sector' (ibid., p. 12), though the study did identify a union wage premium in the public sector after controlling for workplace fixed effects, workers' occupations, their job characteristics, qualifications, and worker demographics. This finding seems logically consistent with the pattern of falling union density and a decline in the significance of collective bargaining in the private sector and broad stability in the public sector. It should be noted, however, that there is some evidence that unions remain effective in providing a fringe benefit premium and have the effect of compressing differentials (Kersley et al., 2006).

Further work by Bryson (2004) used WERS data to probe the effectiveness of different employee voice mechanisms within the workplace, based on employee perceptions of managerial responsiveness. Contrary to common expectations, the results showed 'employees perceive managers to be more responsive in the presence of non-union voice than they do where union voice is present' (ibid., p. 228). Indeed, even on issues such as grievance resolution and the promotion of fair treatment, often seen as areas where unions have more to offer than other mechanisms, Bryson concludes that union voice is often less effective than some non-union voice mechanisms.

At this point, as the basis for further exploration, it may be useful to introduce a classification scheme for the channels of employee voice. In their assessment of the changing patterns of employee voice in the UK and the Irish Republic, Wilkinson et al. (2004) developed a framework for employee voice differentiated along two dimensions. One dimension reflected the direct (based on employees themselves) to indirect (based on a union or collective grouping) nature of voice, while the other axis reflected the extent to which there were shared or contested agendas. Instead of this two dimensional figure, however, this Chapter proposes what I consider is a more useful device in relation to employee voice on pay decisions: a figure with four quadrants, distinguishing the individual/collective dimension and the institutional/non-institutional dimension. If we think in this way, then figure 3.1 is a graphical representation of how employee voice can be exercised in relation to pay determination.

The top left quadrant of Figure 3.1 could be termed the 'traditional' form of worker voice, populated as it is primarily by collective bargaining or, occasionally, other formal, collective arrangements such as company councils. The historical importance of collective bargaining is clear, and as we have already seen in this chapter, its

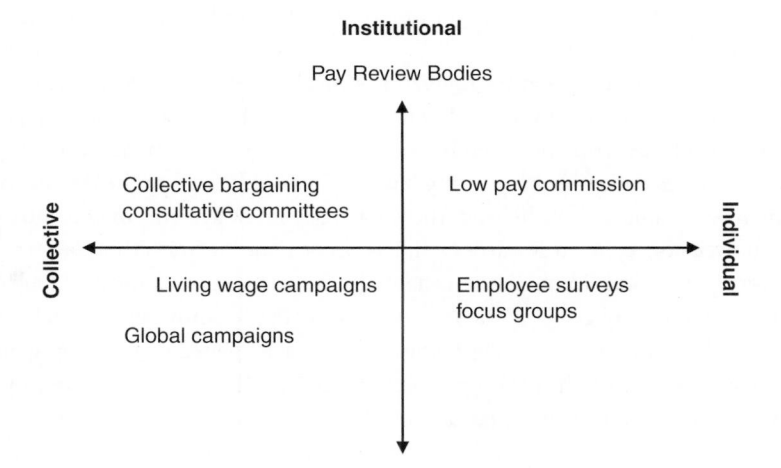

Institutional

Pay Review Bodies

Collective bargaining consultative committees   Low pay commission

Collective ← → Individual

Living wage campaigns   Employee surveys focus groups

Global campaigns

Non-institutional

Figure 3.1   A topography of employee voice mechanisms

continuing significance should not be underestimated in the public sector and in a shrinking but still large part of the private sector.

As to company councils or equivalent mechanisms, they exist both as a complement to collective bargaining, discussing non-pay matters, and as a substitute for collective bargaining (Marchington, 1994). The Workplace Employment Relations Survey 2004 (Kersley et al., 2006) found that there was a decline from 1998 to 2004 in the number of workplaces that had a joint consultative committee (JCC) both at the workplace and at a higher level than the workplace (region, division, or head office), with the decline most marked in non-union workplaces, as well as a decline from 1998 to 2004 in the number of consultative committees. Where there were workplace JCCs, however, 66 per cent discussed pay issues, a rise from 47 per cent in 1998. In short, the number of JCCs had declined, but those that remained were more likely than before to discuss pay issues.

There is yet little evidence of a widespread upsurge in new collective institutional mechanisms in response to the Information and Consultation of Employees (ICE) Regulations 2004 (Hall, 2006). Where such bodies exist, however, the evidence suggests that they are involved in discussing reward issues. This applies in situations where trade unions hold collective bargaining rights as well as where the company council is the only formal representative body. Recent research on implementation of the new regulations in 13 case-study organisations, for example, found that 'if pensions issues are included, then all of the organisations have consulted their I&C bodies on reward issues' (Hall et al., 2007, p. 58). It may therefore be that, in the future, as these bodies become more widespread, they may emerge as a significant influence on pay and benefit decisions. Given the overlap in many cases with organisations where collective bargaining exists, this could further erode the traditional role of trade unions.

The remainder of this chapter reviews the mechanisms of employee voice in the other quadrants in turn and the different ways in which they influence the pay-setting process. The central argument is that these alternative mechanisms have grown in importance as collective bargaining has diminished. Far from the decline of bargaining leaving a black hole behind, there have been new systems of voice to articulate employee concerns on reward as well as other issues in ways that have required employers to respond. In particular, the major new institutions for pay determination, notably the public sector PRBs and the Low Pay Commission, which are not often considered in discussion of employee voice, have opened up new opportunities for employee voice to be heard on pay matters in ways that have been overlooked in the literature. We look at this quadrant of Figure 3.1 next.

The rise of the new pay determination institutions

The above analysis of WERS data over the period 1980–2004 may seem to have carried the implication that rather little had changed in pay determination in the public sector in that time. In reality, the results of the 1990 WERS highlighted major changes in parts of the public sector, with coverage of collective bargaining dropping from 95 per cent of the workforce in 1984 to 78 per cent of public sector employees in 1990: 'much of this fall in the public sector must reflect two large groups of workers losing their negotiating rights – the teachers and the nurses' (Millward et al., 1992, p. 94). This observation is one of the relatively rare instances of commentators recognising the scale of change that has occurred since the 1980s in the institutional mechanisms for pay determination across important parts of the public services, with consequent changes in the employee voice.

Table 3.3 provides some data on the timing and scale of the changes. Creation of the first three PRBs was announced in 1970 with the role of making recommendations on pay for the armed forces, doctors and dentists, and senior public servants such as the judiciary and senior civil servants. The rationale was summed up by the then Secretary of State for Employment as meeting 'a clear need for co-ordinated machinery for advising Government on the remuneration of certain groups for whom no negotiating machinery is, for one reason or another, appropriate' (The Times, 1970, p. 9). In other words, PRBs were first created as institutions to advise on pay for relatively small, specialist groups some of whom had never been covered by conventional pay bargaining arrangements and which successive governments had found hard to deal with satisfactorily. A key feature of the first three groups was the inherent limitations on their bargaining power, with either statutory (Armed Forces) or ethical (doctors and dentists, senior civil servants etc.) barriers to industrial action.

The 1980s saw more, larger groups drawn into this 'too difficult to deal with category'. By this time, however, they were large groups with long traditions of conventional collective bargaining and experience of taking industrial action. As Table 3.3 indicates, by 2007 the six PRBs covered more than two million employees, accounting for more than a third of the public sector workforce. The most recent expansion occurred in July 2007, when the Review Body covering nurses, midwives, and related professions in England, Wales, and Scotland had its remit extended, first to cover the National Health Service (NHS) staff not previously within its remit but who were nevertheless paid under the Agenda for Change pay system; and second to include staff working in Northern Ireland. The Review Body was renamed the NHS Pay Review Body (NHSPRB) to reflect these changes. This change added a huge number and variety of staff – ancillary and maintenance staff such as cleaners, porters, catering, domestics, electricians, plumbers, builders; administrative and clerical staff, administrative managers, and many more.

What is significant about this development in the context of the current discussion are the implications for employee voice mechanisms in relation to decisions on pay. Across swathes of the public sector, conventional collective bargaining involving employee voice being vocalised to the employer side at the bargaining table by trade unions and professional associations has either been replaced or augmented by new arrangements.

The methods of working used by the PRBs have rarely received attention. Made up of independent members drawn from varied backgrounds, their role is to respond to remits from the relevant government ministers by making recommendations on pay and, in some areas, conditions for the employee groups concerned. In doing so, the review bodies receive written and oral evidence from the major representative bodies, such as the teaching trade unions in the case of the School Teachers' Review Body (as well as from the employer side and other bodies). But this is not the only

Table 3.3 The growth of the Pay Review Bodies

	Yr set up	Number (approx)	Coverage in 2007
The Senior Salaries Review Body (formerly The Top Salaries Review Body)	1971	5,000	UK
The Armed Forces' Pay Review Body	1971	210,000	UK
The Review Body on Doctors' and Dentists' Remuneration	1971	160,000	UK
The NHS Pay Review Body (formerly The Nursing and Other Health Professions Review Body but extended 2007)	1984	1,300,000	UK
The School Teachers' Review Body	1991	500,000	E&W
The Prison Service Pay Review Body	2001	34,000	E,W,NI
Total		2,209,000	

Source: Corby, 2003; Office of Manpower Economics, 2008.

way in which employee voice is vocalised to the PRBs. During the course of the year, members of the review bodies make visits to relevant workplaces, talking to groups and individual employees on the ground, and the results from these informal discussions feed into the decision-making process. For example, the 2007 report of the Armed Forces' Pay Review Body comments, 'our visits included some 320 formal and informal discussion groups enabling us to hear, first hand, the views of around 4,000 service personnel and spouses' (2007, p. 1). So, while the methods of working therefore include what may be viewed as elements of mediation or arbitration, they go wider in terms of gathering views and information from employees affected by the decisions, using direct communication methods.

As noted above, these PRBs often replace collective bargaining, but they do not always do so. The consultants' contract and the new pay system for non-medical staff in the National Health Service (Agenda for Change) were negotiated by conventional collective bargaining outside the relevant PRBs. That is why, in Figure 3.1, the PRBs are positioned straddling the collective/individual intersection.

The Low Pay Commission, the institution set up by the New Labour Government in 1998 to make recommendations on the national minimum wage, has made a point of gathering views and evidence from varied sources, in a similar way to PRBs. As the Commission put it in its first report:

> We invited and analysed written and oral evidence from major organisations and interested parties. But we wanted to go beyond such traditional consultation ... we were determined to have direct contact with a wide range of employers, workers and the unemployed to understand the realities of their circumstances. We were particularly keen to reach small firms, rural businesses, businesses operating on the fringes of the formal economy and, above all, low-paid workers and the unemployed. We travelled throughout Britain to meet a wide range of people. (Low Pay Commission, 1998, p. 21)

In terms of their significance for pay determination, the six PRBs and the Low Pay Commission in their different ways have had an important impact. Taking the review bodies first, a study by Elliott and Duffus of how 25 public sector employee groups fared in relative pay terms over the 22 years to 1992 found 19 of them losing ground relative to the private sector while six improved their position (Elliott and Duffus, 1996). The results suggested that the form of pay machinery seemed to be the key determinant of relative performance, with those groups covered by PRBs or other special mechanisms tending to do somewhat better than those covered by collective bargaining.

A more recent study covering the decade to 2003 came to similar conclusions, indicating that groups covered by the independent PRBs have tended to fare better than those public sector employees having their pay set by collective bargaining (Makepeace and Marcenaro-Gutierrez, 2005). In short, the ending of conventional collective bargaining for these groups has not silenced employee voice and worsened employees' pay situation; rather the PRB mechanism has opened up enlarged systems of employee voice and seen relative pay levels maintained or improved.

Turning to the Low Pay Commission with its much wider remit, the national minimum wage has become the foundation of pay structures across much of the private sector. Indeed, in some sectors there are substantial proportions of the workforce paid at the level of the minimum wage itself – according to the Commission's 2007 report, some 12 per cent of all employees in the retail sector were paid at the minimum, while in cleaning, hospitality and hairdressing, over 20 per cent of employees were in minimum wage jobs in April 2006 (Low Pay Commission, 2007, pp. 35–36). Pay structures for higher graded employees in these and many other sectors are built on the national minimum rate, so both the minimum wage and the processes – including employee voice processes – used by the Commission in formulating it have become of major importance in pay determination in Britain. In brief, the setting of the national minimum wage is now the single most important pay decision in Britain in terms of the numbers directly and indirectly affected.

Moving clockwise around Figure 3.1, we now look at individual, non-institutional voice mechanisms (the lower right quadrant).

Individual, non-institutional mechanisms of voice

'We work for a multibillion dollar company and still cannot pay for rent, utilities and food. With overtime, I cannot support my family of three. Shame on you!' (Sirota et al., 2005, p. 84). Frank comment of this kind about reward, both positive and negative, has become an established feature of life across major corporate employers as a result of employee attitude surveys. From modest beginnings in the 1960s in global corporations such as IBM, surveys of this sort, offering a non-institutional, individualised form of employee voice, have come to be viewed as key management indicators and communication mechanisms on pay as on other facets of working life.

The provision of employee survey services is now a major area of business in its own right (Incomes Data Services (IDS), 2004). Many survey providers offer normative data so employers can benchmark their results against others, as well as assisting with the interpretation of an organisation's own results and supplementing them, for example by running focus groups. The consequence has been the development of increasingly sophisticated measurement of employee views as the basis for management action. Companies such as the Royal Bank of Scotland use employee survey results – with views in the case of the bank contributed by some 87 per cent of employees – to shape their 'employee proposition', including all elements of reward (Incomes Data Services, 2007). This type of annual, or more frequent, gathering of views from employees and the weight attached to it in modifying practice in major employers is a form of employee voice that is too often overlooked. It is for example almost unexplored in the WERS research, apart from noting that such surveys were conducted in 42 per cent of all workplaces in the 2004 survey (Kersley et al., 2006 p. 137), far higher than the proportion of workplaces where trade unions were recognised. As Dundon et al. comment, 'employees now expect to have a voice, and both middle and senior managers are more used to and empathetic with such expectations' (Dundon et al., 2005, p. 318). At first glance, the expression of employee voice through a survey mechanism may seem to lack the punch provided by traditional union approaches. But this is to miss the importance now attached by senior managers within most large employers to securing high levels of employee engagement. The concern with employee engagement or commitment as a key factor in competitiveness means that employee views are accorded a greater significance than in earlier decades when trade unions were more influential.

The new collectivist voice

> The trade union movement has failed to come to terms with the character and geography of contemporary work... The contracting out of what were core functions of business activity – such as manufacturing, distribution, cleaning, catering, information technology and business administration – has quietly become paradigmatic. Subcontracting is now a feature of employment in all sectors and spaces of the global economy. (Wills, 2006, p. 5)

Our last quadrant of Figure 3.1 covers those new forms of campaigning that have emerged in response to these trends, a collective expression of employee voice that does not rely on traditional trade union processes of collective bargaining to bring actual and desired conditions closer together.

One of the best-known examples of this type of campaign in a UK context is the living wage campaign launched by the East London Communities Organisation (TELCO). Briefly, the London living wage campaign was launched in 2001 by a broad-based coalition including faith groups, trade union branches, schools, and community groups. The successes claimed for it include securing 'living wage' contracts for domestic workers at a number of NHS Trusts and for contract cleaners at several corporate banks at Canary Wharf and in the City of London, as well as living wage clauses in the Olympic 2012 procurement process and establishing a living wage unit at the Greater London Authority (GLA) (Wills, 2006).

The significance for our purposes is that the TELCO and similar campaigns are focused on voicing employee demands for improved pay and conditions in new ways. First, they have targeted the organisations perceived as the end user, those which can be viewed as 'the "real employer" at the top of any contracting chain' (Evans et al., 2007, p. 87), rather than the direct contractual employer of the employees, an approach that has been seen as of prime importance in view of the increasingly subcontracted nature of work. Second, their broad-based community character has enabled them to adopt different approaches to those open to conventional trade union-based collective bargaining. As Wills puts it in her account of the London living wage campaign for cleaning staff at the Homerton Hospital, 'whereas trade union organisation – where it exists – remains focused on each workplace as a separate entity or bargaining unit, the living wage campaign has found a means of connecting separate contracts together' (Wills, 2006, p. 12). It has also generated a mechanism for voicing their demands to those in a position to influence pay decisions: 'while the Trust could refuse to negotiate with the workers who were no longer their employees, they could not refuse to negotiate with representatives of their local community' (Wills, 2006, p. 21).

It would, of course, be wrong to exaggerate the scale of these types of activities currently in the UK. The numbers of employees affected by this variety of voice are tiny yet by comparison with conventional trade union membership. But in the USA, where private sector trade union membership has fallen even lower than in the UK, so-called 'community unions' have grown rapidly. They have been described as:

> organisations of low wage workers that focus on issues of work and wages in their communities... mediating institutions that are based in specific ethnic and geographic communities (as opposed to specific workplaces). (Fine, 2005, p. 154)

Their activity has focused on raising wages and improving working conditions primarily via public policy avenues rather than through traditional collective bargaining. As Fine puts it,

> neither tarred with the same 'special interest' label nor burdened by the same institutional imperatives as traditional unions, community unions have been able to speak and act with moral authority'. (Fine, 2005, p. 155)

Moral authority has also been the key form of pressure brought to bear on an international basis in recent years by activists trying to mobilise consumer power and embarrass leading corporations to improve conditions of those working in their production networks. For example, the non-governmental organisation Women Working Worldwide (WWW) has pioneered this approach, linking women workers in the export processing zones of the developing world, particularly in the garments, electronics, and horticultural industries, with consumers and activists in the developed countries (Wills, 2006). The growth of codes of conduct, social auditing and bodies such as the Ethical Trading Initiative (the organisation created to ensure that the working conditions of workers producing for the UK market meet or exceed international labour standards) bear testament to the impact of this activity, a form of employee voice that rarely features in the literature.

Conclusion

In their discussion of WERS findings over the period 1980–1998, Millward et al. posed the question of whether employees have lost their voice. They concluded at that stage that 'the answer must be "no" – but with important qualifications' (Millward et al., 2000, p. 135). While the great majority of workplaces had some form of communication channel between employees and managers, the period had seen a major shift from channels involving representatives – usually trade union representatives – to direct modes of communication, largely on occasions and terms set by management themselves.

Turning from communication overall to the determination of pay and conditions, we have seen that collective bargaining has been of decreasing significance as a means of regulating reward in Britain. It currently applies to under a third of the workforce, less than half the coverage of 30 years ago. Collective bargaining continues to play an important, if reduced, part in the determination of pay in the public sector. The largest change has been in the private sector where coverage was down to one in five workers by 2004 and continuing to decline. In the private sector, therefore, traditional collective bargaining offers a diminished and patchy voice for a still substantial but shrinking minority of workers. There are yet no signs that this period of collapse is drawing to a close.

The conclusion that many observers have drawn is that pay determination is increasingly being left to the discretion of local managers within individual workplaces. Employee voice is felt to be fading – and by implication losing its power. The core argument presented here is that employee voice is changing its form rather than fading away. As far as the issue of power in pay setting is concerned, other contributors have pointed to the growing importance of market influences and the impact of globalisation. Certainly these have served to blunt the effectiveness of traditional collective bargaining strategies in pursuit of pay ends, but they have also arguably increased the weight attached to employee voice expressed through more individualised avenues by employers seeking to foster employee engagement and to manage the increasing cost/value of skilled employees (Gosling et al., 1994). In the end, power must be judged by the outcomes achieved.

The key diminution of collective bargaining in the public sector has been the result of the more widespread adoption of PRB mechanisms, which have receptiveness of employee voice as an integral element of their work. Across the wider economy, the growing importance of the national minimum wage has given rise to different forms of voice influencing the work of the Low Pay Commission. Within individual organisations, direct employee voice through processes such as employee attitude surveys has an impact on decisions that, I would argue, has been underestimated in the debate. Lastly, while still in their infancy, we are seeing signs of the emergence of new forms of collectivist employee voice distinct from traditional trade union approaches. As Dundon et al. counsel, 'our intellectual lens needs to be open rather than skewed by shunting such processes off into a pre-packaged box marked "non-union and inadequate" in contrast to a box marked "union and effective"' (2005, p. 317).

Note

1. The analysis of WERS data in this section was contributed by David Nash, Lecturer in Human Resource Management at Cardiff Business School.

References

Armed Forces' Pay Review Body (2007) *Thirty-Sixth Report*, Cmnd 7019, Norwich: HMSO.

Barnes, D. and Reid, E. (1980) *Governments and Trade Unions: The British Experience*, London: Heinemann.

Blanchflower, D. and Bryson, A. (2007) *The Wage Impact of Trade Unions in the UK Public and Private Sectors*, IZA Discussion Papers 3055, Bonn: Institute for the Study of Labor [IZA].

Brown, W. and Nash, D. (2008) 'What Has Been Happening to Collective Bargaining Under New Labour? Interpreting WERS 2004', *Industrial Relations Journal*, 39 (2), 91–103.

Brown, W. and Walsh, J. (1991) 'Pay Determination in Britain in the 1980s. The Anatomy of Decentralization', *Oxford Review of Economic Policy*, 7, 44–59.

Bryson, A. (2004) 'Managerial Responsiveness to Union and Non-Union Worker Voice in Britain', *Industrial Relations*, 43, 213–241.

Bryson, A., Willman, P., Gomez, R., and Kretschmer, T. (2007) *Employee Voice and Human Resource Management: An Empirical Analysis using British Data*, London: Policy Studies Institute.

Corby, S. (2003) 'Public Sector Disputes and Third Party Intervention' *ACAS Research Paper* 02/03, London: Advisory, Conciliation and Arbitration Service.

Dundon, T., Wilkinson, A., Marchington, M., and Ackers, P. (2005) 'The Management of Voice in Non-Union Organisations', *Employee Relations*, 27, 307–319.

Elliott, R. and Duffus, K. (1996) 'What Has Been Happening to Pay in the Public-Service Sector of the British Economy? Developments over the Period 1970–1992', *British Journal of Industrial Relations*, 34, 51–85.

Evans, Y., Wills, J., Datta, K., Herbert, J., McIlwaine, C., and May, J. (2007) '"Subcontracting by Stealth" in London's Hotels: Impacts and Implications for Labour Organising', *Just Labour: A Canadian Journal of Work and Society*, 10, 85–97.

Fine, J. (2005) 'Community Unions and the Revival of the American Labor Movement', *Politics and Society*, 33, 153–199.

Freeman, R. and Medoff, J. (1984) *What Do Unions Do?* New York: Basic Books.

Gosling, A., Machin, S., and Meghir, C. (1994) 'What Has Happened to Men's Wages since the Mid-1960s?', *Fiscal Studies*, 15, 6387.

Hall, A. (2006) 'A Cool Response to the ICE Regulations?', *Industrial Relations Journal*, 37, 456–472.

Hall, M., Hutchinson, S., Parker, J., Purcell, J., and Terry, M. (2007) *Implementing Information and Consultation: Early Experience under the ICE Regulations*, Employment Relations Research Series No. 88, London: Department for Business, Enterprise and Regulatory Reform.

Heywood, J.S., Siebert, W.S., and Wei, X. (1997) 'Payment by Results Systems: British Evidence', *British Journal of Industrial Relations*, 35, 1, 1–22.

IDS (2004) Employee Attitude Surveys, IDS HR Study 777, London: Incomes Data Services.

IDS (2007) 'The RBS Links Employee Engagement to Improved Business Performance', *IDS HR Study 846*, London: Incomes Data Services.

Kersley, B., Alpin, C., Forth, J., Bryson, A., Bewley, H., Dix, G., and Oxenbridge, S. (2006) *Inside the Workplace*, London: Routledge.

Low Pay Commission (1998) *The National Minimum Wage*, Cmnd 3976, Norwich: HMSO.

Low Pay Commission (2007) *The National Minimum Wage*, Cmnd 7056, Norwich: HMSO.

Makepeace, G. and Marcenaro-Gutierrez, O. (2005) *The Earnings of Workers Covered by Pay Review Bodies: Evidence from the Labour Force Survey*, London: Office of Manpower Economics.

Marchington, M. (1994) 'The Dynamics of Joint Consultation' in Sisson, K. (ed.) *Personnel Management*, Oxford: Blackwell.

Millward, N., Bryson, A., and Forth, J. (2000) *All Change at Work?* London: Routledge.

Millward, N., Stevens, M., Smart, D., and Hawes, W. (1992) *Workplace Industrial Relations in Transition,* Aldershot: Dartmouth.

Office of Manpower Economics (OME) (2008) http://www.ome.uk.com/review.cfm?body=6 (accessed 7 January 2008).

Sirota, D., Mischkind, L., and Meltzer, M. (2005) *The Enthusiastic Employee,* New Jersey: Wharton School Publishing.

The Times (1970) 'Three Review Bodies to Scrutinize Public Sector Salaries', The Times, London, 3 November, p. 9.

Trades Union Congress (1966) *Trade Unionism,* London: Trades Union Congress.

Wilkinson, A., Dundon, T., Marchington, M., and Ackers, P. (2004) 'Changing Patterns of Employee Voice: Case Studies from the UK and Republic of Ireland', *Industrial Relations Journal*, 46, 298–322.

Wills, J. (2006) *Subcontracting, Labour and Trade Union Organisation: Lessons from Homerton Hospital and the London Living Wage Campaign*, Working Paper Two, London: Queen Mary College, University of London.

Part II
Pay issues

4

Paying for progression – ever onwards and upwards?

Steve Palmer

Why might someone choose to enter one occupation as opposed to another, or work for one employer rather than another? A literature review carried out recently by *Frontier Economics* identified a long list of potential factors ranging through pay, job security and work environment, the labour market for the individual's skills, family background, status of the career/profession, and other personal characteristics (age, gender, ethnicity etcetera). *Frontier Economics* boiled down the list to four main determinants: relative wage, work environment, family background, and the prospects for pay advancement (*Frontier Economics*, 2006).

This last determinant is the subject of this chapter. But strangely, given its important role in career choice – and hence recruitment and retention – the literature on how employees progress within pay structures is remarkably limited. It tends to fall into two categories. General textbooks sometimes deal with the principles of progression but not in great depth. Other publications tend to cover progression in the context of specific pay approaches. For example, Armstrong and Murlis consider progression in the context of contribution-based pay, that is, progression based on a mix of performance and competence (Armstrong and Murlis, 2004). Armstrong and Brown examine the issue in the context of 'new pay' approaches such as broadbanding and job families, and set out the progression arrangements they consider best suited to these structures (Armstrong and Brown, 2001). Other authors note it is often difficult to disentangle discussion on progression from wider considerations around, for example, scale revalorisation and performance-related pay (Wright, 2004).

The emphasis seems to be more on how progression should operate, and less on what processes employers actually use, despite the fact that survey evidence shows a wide range of practices are in operation and, outside the public sector, few are simple one-factor approaches (CIPD, 2006; e-reward, 2004). It was to address this lacuna and get a better understanding of how progression actually operated in the wider economy that the Office of Manpower Economics (OME) and Chartered Institute of Personnel and Development (CIPD), supported by Incomes Data Services (IDS), jointly agreed in 2005 to research the area. The research took three forms: a literature review, case studies in a range of organisations, and a quantitative survey of practice. This chapter examines the results of that and other research.[1]

The chapter is in three main sections. It starts with a review of pay and progression arrangements since the 1970s: a movement away from quasi-automatic incremental based progression to progression based on performance and from narrow grades to broad bands. The second section looks at the present position and, particularly, the difference between the public and private sectors in terms of pay and progression arrangements, the extent of line manager discretion, and pay drift. The final section summarises the evidence and ends by considering the challenges facing those concerned with pay and progression.

Readers should note that what are reviewed here are the systems by which employees may progress their pay *within* pay ranges. Promotion, the movement *between* pay ranges, is another form of progression, but it is largely self-explanatory and is not covered in detail.

Pay progression – changing times, changing attitudes

Progression and service

It is worth bearing in mind that pay progression was always largely a white collar/non-manual worker concept (Thompson, 2000). Largely it still is, particularly in the private sector. Manual workers usually received either a spot time rate or were paid in relation to their output through payment by results and/or productivity schemes, and had little scope for structured progression. On this score at least, little has really changed, although in its 2006–2007 review of pay in engineering, IDS notes that of the 54 companies surveyed, 39 said that manual employees could earn higher rates through pay progression, mostly through the acquisition of additional skills (27 companies), with some also using individual performance, competency, service, or a combination of factors. However, over a quarter of the companies had no progression arrangements at all for manual employees, and even where it existed progression was most often to do with promotion to higher-paid roles, rather than the traditional movement within a pay band (IDS, 2006a). Consequently, the remainder of this chapter focuses largely on arrangements for non-manual employees.[2]

Thompson argues that the origins of white-collar pay progression systems lie with the concept of 'salaried' employment and connotations of a long-term relationship between employer and employee, which itself provided the opportunity for career development beneficial to both parties. This tended to translate into reward for service as a proxy for experience and increased employee value (Thompson, 2000). (Interestingly, in the recent *Cadman* case the European Court of Justice reaffirmed its earlier view that employers did not have to objectively justify pay differences resulting from incremental payment schemes designed to reward experience (Industrial Relations Law Reports, 2006); see Chapter 8 for a fuller discussion.)

The process for progressing white-collar staff was incremental progression through narrow pay bands. In larger companies pay bands typically started at 80 per cent of a market-related mid-point,[3] were usually determined by job evaluation, and contained a number of pay steps or increments. Increments of around 4 per cent of the mid-point would ensure that a new starter in a grade would, with satisfactory performance, progress to the midpoint in five years. In theory, at least, exceptional performers could progress quicker, through the award of double increments, and could continue to progress beyond the midpoint, whereas poorer performers could have increments withheld (IDS, 1977). Generally speaking though, the vast majority of employees covered by such schemes advanced by one increment per annum.

In crude terms, the attraction to employees of such schemes is obvious, especially since the structures themselves were annually revalorised to maintain their real and/or relative value, and employees below the maximum therefore benefited in pay terms from both uprating and progression. The attraction to employers lay in the fact that in 'mature' structures attrition (the replacement of higher-paid employees with lower-paid employees as staff leave or are promoted), reduced the paybill effects of progression to zero or thereabouts. Indeed, pay rises resulting from incremental progression were usually excluded from the dictates of 1970s statutory incomes policy on the basis that they did not involve an increase in the paybill (IDS, 1978). The progression 'certainties' inherent in incremental pay structures were also powerful recruitment and retention tools.

More subtly, incremental progression also reflected and supported the concept of internal labour markets, where staff are developed within organisations and provide the labour pool for recruitment to fill posts, other than 'entry' posts. A number of benefits accrue. For employees there is the scope for progression and promotion once within the organisation; for employers, there are reduced transaction costs and lower staff turnover, increased employee commitment, creation of a 'high trust' environment, and the benefits of a transparent and easy to manage pay structure (Thompson, 2000).

In the private sector, at least, the 1980s marked the end of this 'relationship' model, and a move to a more 'transactional' model. One casualty was incremental payment systems with service as the prime determinant of pay progression. Some of the reasons have been set out in Chapter 1 – political pressures towards decentralisation and individualisation, economic pressures through monetary policy to control inflation, and organisational pressures occasioned by open markets and fierce competition. The effect has been to fragment internal markets, with less emphasis on hierarchy and more on cross-functional teams and a concomitant reduction of career structures and promotion opportunities (Thompson, 2000). Much of this, of course, underpins the attraction of broad banded pay structures for employers.

Progression and performance

In terms of the pay structure there was a growing management sense that incremental payment systems were failing to motivate employees (Cannell and Wood, 1992). This coincided with greater interest in pay systems which emphasised linking reward to individual performance (IDS/IPM, 1985). Looking back over the previous decade Thompson noted that 'the dominant shift has been away from progression scales based on seniority or age to a consensus that some form of performance measurement should be the main determinant' (Thompson, 2000, p. 147).

A survey of 274 private sector organisations in 1991 found that over a quarter of them had introduced individual performance-related pay for all employees, a figure that rose to 40 per cent with schemes covering some or all non-manual employees, and 57 per cent looking solely at service sector organisations. The incidence of performance-related pay varied by broad employee group with well over half of directors, managers, and clerical staff covered (Cannell and Wood, 1992).

The trend towards the greater use and incidence of performance-related pay continued through the 1990s and into new decade (Kersley et al., 2006).

The early days of performance-related pay effectively resulted in progression based on service being replaced with progression based on an appraisal against agreed objectives. Employees might still have been employed on incremental scales, but their movement through ranges – their access to incremental points – was determined through a performance management process and the allocation of a performance 'mark'. Individuals could, therefore, progress more quickly or slowly than the average or 'satisfactory' performer on the basis of their performance assessment. The more common approach, however, was to have no specified steps within pay ranges, and staff progressed solely on the basis of the percentage award deemed appropriate to their level of performance (IDS/IPM, 1985).

Great debate ensued about the design of performance pay schemes, for example, the avoidance of bias in appraisals, whether or not to force distributions on performance marks to avoid all employees being marked as 'satisfactory', how to ensure stretching personal objectives, and how to ensure that pay was not used to manage poor performance (ibid.). Some of these concerns are still with us (see, for example, Houldsworth and Jirasinghe, 2006). A few employers even questioned the need to link pay to performance in the first place, and some argued that a robust and well-implemented performance management system could achieve the same results in terms of employee motivation without the emotional link to pay outcomes (IDS/IPM, 1985).

Criticisms emerged about how motivating performance-related pay actually was, especially in the public sector. For example, an analysis of the views of Inland

Revenue staff of their own motivational responses to performance pay showed that substantial majorities did not consider it had any impact in areas such as quantity of work, quality of work, working beyond job requirements, or ensuring sustained high performance, views endorsed by their line managers when responding to questions about the impact of performance pay on their staff (Marsden and Richardson, 1991). Another difficulty emerged once inflation fell to very low levels, as lower inflation meant smaller merit budgets. It became much harder in the 1990s to provide meaningful performance payments and differentiation out of budgets of 3 per cent than it had been in the 1980s when inflationary pressures meant budgets were much larger. The fact that 'real pay' outcomes were the same under both regimes made little impression on employees used to large percentage 'nominal' pay increases. Employers also had concerns that the consolidation of performance awards into base pay were adding to fixed costs with no guarantee that previous performance would be maintained. However, perhaps the biggest failing of 'traditional' performance-related pay schemes was that the sole focus for progression was employee outputs, whereas a greater emphasis on customer satisfaction in competitive marketplaces called for rewards related also to *how* people performed their work and not just what they did.

At this point, some parallel developments in pay and grading systems that have had a bearing on approaches to progression in recent years should be considered.

In the 1970s, we have noted that structures were generally based around quite narrow pay ranges of 20 per cent. It would not be unusual to have different, and occasionally overlapping, structures for different staff groupings, for example clerical and administrative staff, craft workers, professional and technical staff, and various level of management. So another feature of narrow banded structures would be a comparatively large number of pay grades. (In the public sector, the grading structure often linked across to a pay spine of equal incremental points covering all staff. However, these systems also involved overlapping grades within and between occupational groups.)

By 2007, the CIPD annual Reward Survey showed that things had become much 'looser'. Looking at arrangements in 466 organisations drawn from across the economy, CIPD reported 44 per cent using individual rates, ranges or spot salaries, 40 per cent with broad bands, and 31 per cent using job families or career grades. Only 22 per cent now used narrow bands, and 16 per cent had pay spines, in both cases, these were much more prevalent in the public sector (CIPD, 2007). We look at individual rates, broad bands, and job families, and their implications for pay progression, in more detail below.

Broad bands and pay progression

Reporting on the results of a survey carried out in 1999/2000, Armstrong and Brown commented that the research confirmed 'there is no generally accepted definition of what a broad banded system is, except that it comprises fewer and wider bands than a traditional graded structure' (Armstrong and Brown, 2001, p. 36). A slightly unpromising conclusion, but the authors fleshed out the bones by noting that over half of respondents had five or fewer grades for their senior executives, managerial/professional staff and other employees, and that in nearly half of pay structures band width exceeded 50 per cent (and in nearly a fifth, 80 per cent).

They outline several reasons why organisations might choose a broad banded route: to achieve greater pay flexibility, to reflect a reduced job hierarchy in a delayered organisation, to break down 'silo' mentalities and encourage cross-team working and lateral movement between jobs, and to reduce the importance of job status. The concept places much more emphasis on employee development via lateral moves within bands, and much less emphasis on promotion (ibid.).

Bergel suggested that three pay delivery mechanisms worked particularly well in broad banded structures: pay related to career development, skill-based pay, and merit pay (Bergel, 1994). These themes are picked up by Armstrong and Brown who argue that important features of broadbanding are its emphasis on lateral and in-job progression rather then vertical career growth (Armstrong and Brown, 2001), and who also quote Gilbert and Abosch's view that broadbanding helped employees understand that their pay growth was only limited by their ability to have an impact on the organisation (Gilbert and Abosch, 1996). It was therefore an initial tenet of broad banding that employees should be able to progress to the top of their band on the basis of their individual merit.

In contrast to traditional pay structures, with their fairly prescriptive approaches to pay progression, progression in broad banded structures is much more flexible, and likely to be based on judgements around performance, competence, contribution (both performance and wider competences), and individual development (Armstrong and Brown, 2001). Couple this with much greater scope for individuals to influence job content and in these circumstances 'progression is people-orientated rather than job orientated' (ibid., p. 98). Certainly, incremental progression is rarely used in broad banded structures (IDS, 2005).

Where progression is unstructured – there is no limit to progression within a broad band – the important factors determining pay are the market worth of the individual, their competence level relative to others, and their contribution. In these systems, line managers have a high degree of freedom and discretion, but with it go a clear need for robust and defensible market data, well-trained and capable managers, and financial flexibility to operate unstructured progression systems.

That is the theory, but several things have combined to make broad banding slightly less than it seems. First, budgetary constraints are bound to impose some limit on progression rates. Second, the system turned out harder to manage than expected, movement between bands could be more difficult to justify than movement between grades, and there were equal pay concerns arising from the unstructured nature of pay progression and the heavy reliance on market data (Armstrong, 2004).

Third, employers found that broad bands created progression expectations that could not be met (ibid.). Employees appeared uneasy about the lack of structure to their progression within broad bands, and, as economic theory predicts, wanted more certainty about how their pay would develop over time, the level they were likely to reach in the structure, and when (IDS, 2004).

The result is that structure crept back in the shape of *reference points* and *anchor points* related to the market, *zones* which enabled progression up to and beyond reference points, and *segments* with defined pay ranges. How this approach differs from narrow banded structures is not always obvious, but the main differences are the flexibilities provided by zones (they could, for instance, be built around individuals or small groups of workers), the scope they allow for movement, and the fact that they do not appear as 'hierarchical' as traditional structures.

Progression in the newly defined broad banded structures is what Armstrong and Brown call 'semi-structured'. It can arise either in relation to competence or performance or both, or because the individual's role has expanded, but not enough to justify movement to another segment or zone, or because they have increased their responsibilities. Progression can be through the whole range, or up to a market-related reference point with variable unconsolidated payments beyond that (Armstrong and Brown, 2001).

Considering how broad banding would develop in future, Armstrong suggested there was likely to be more zoning, greater use of broad *grades* – narrower than broad bands but wider than narrow grades, more use of job evaluation to support the pay structure, and more use of career grades (Armstrong, 2004). We look at this latter development below, considering first the job family structure to which it is related.

Job families, career families, and pay progression

Incomes Data Services (2006b, p. 3) defines job families as

> clusters of jobs or roles that share similar characteristics. While the exact level of responsibility, skill or competence required of roles within a job family may vary, the essential nature of the activities carried out and the skills used tend to be similar.

Armstrong and Brown point out that this approach is likely to figure where management considers different occupations require different reward and/or career development practices. Job families are therefore usually arranged by functional groups, for example finance, information technology (IT) or personnel, or by work categories such as administration or customer services, or by occupation, for example scientists, IT specialists. Each family is split into 'levels' (or grades) to reflect the knowledge or competency required of different roles. Levels can vary across families depending on their complexity. Job families often entail fewer and wider grades than traditional structures, and therefore can be accommodated within broad banded structures (Armstrong and Brown, 2001).

Pay rates are determined by market data and for this reason, pay ranges for levels across different families do not necessarily align. Job families anyway often entail fewer grades than traditional structures, and many therefore tend to share some of the characteristics of broad banded structures (so-called 'hybrid' systems), including the pay progression approaches based on a mix of competence and performance. The same progression approach may not be used across all families, with more use, for example, of unconsolidated bonus payments in areas such as sales.

Career families are a recent refinement on job families. Whilst the former look at career progression primarily *within* a job family, career grades offer progression *across* job families. Career family grades are also based on levels relating to competency, knowledge, and skills, but define career paths between families. Unlike job family structures, career families have a common grade and pay structure; therefore, jobs at the same level are considered to be the same size, and share pay ranges. 'In effect, a career structure is a single shared graded structure in which each grade has been divided into families'; the grade definitions are the same, even if the definitions of levels differ across families (Armstrong, 2005, p. 21). Whilst different in principle, pay progression in career families also relies on the familiar mix of performance and competency, looking at both outputs and inputs.

Individual rates, ranges, and pay progression

Structures can be based on individual employees, having a separate pay range for each role, generally governed by market data. This system is much more common for senior employees than other staff. The approach is also generally associated with broad banded structures, with zones or segments reflecting individual job ranges. Progression through ranges is usually linked to performance and/or some other measure, and can be limited by the use of market data (for example, an employee can progress to the market median on the basis of performance, with only those showing sustained exceptional performance progressing to the upper quartile market rate). Some organisations do not have scale minima or maxima. Staff are appointed as the market dictates, and progression is related to not only performance but also to their position in relation to some 'control' point, usually the market median. This enables higher earners to continue to progress, albeit typically more slowly than those below the control point (IDS, 2005).

Other progression systems

The CIPD has identified eight different progression systems (CIPD, 2005). In later work to inform joint OME/CIPD research, IDS narrowed the field to seven (Incomes Data Services, 2005). Three of these are service, performance, and market-related progression, which we have considered above, and another is promotion. The other three are competency and skills-based progression, and hybrid schemes, which we review here.

Competency-based progression

Competency-based progression arose out of the growing use of competency assessments for purposes of recruitment, retention, and employee development.[4]

Competencies were not necessarily intended to determine reward, but the emphasis in some employment areas – especially customer-facing roles – on behaviours rather than outputs, and the view that performance could be enhanced by doing so, has led some employers to use competency frameworks to replace, or at least modify, progression based simply on performance. In these systems, competency assessments determine movement either through pay ranges, or solely above the range mid-point. 'Pure' competency-based progression schemes are complex and therefore quite rare, and are often leavened by reference to performance and/or more objective skills measurement.

Skills-based approaches

Skills-based approaches relate progression to the acquisition of new skills, typically to enable manual or craft employees to operate and maintain high-tech equipment. It is based around reward for specific skill modules, and is rare for white-collar workers.

Hybrid schemes

As early as 1973, the OME highlighted:

> the wide variety [of incremental pay] systems in operation and the difficulty of categorisation...In practice not only were most systems encountered of a hybrid character but often two or more systems coexisted within the same organisation for different categories of staff. (OME, 1973, p. 14)

Thirty years later e-reward reported that although 68 per cent of survey respondents reported basing progression solely on performance, contribution, or service, 32 per cent used hybrid systems, combining two or more approaches. Fifteen alternative approaches were identified, with seven combinations emerging around performance, service, competency, and contribution (e-reward, 2004). In its analysis of company practice IDS noted that whilst individual performance appraisal was the most popular approach to progression for white-collar staff, hybrid schemes were nearly as popular (IDS, 2005). More recently, in 2007 CIPD found that 79 per cent of survey respondents used a hybrid approach, although the incidence varied by occupation and sector (CIPD, 2007).

Incomes Data Services identified four main hybrid systems, and noted that they tended to be industry specific. These were: a combination of *service and performance*, the simplest and most common approach; *performance and skills/competency*, which aims to reward the use of skills, not just their acquisition; *performance and market*, which provides quicker performance-related pay progression to the market rate; and *market and competency*, where progression to market 'markers' is based on personal development in the role.

A fifth approach, the use of *contribution-based progression* is also attracting interest. These schemes typically combine performance with a quite wide definition of competency which might include personal development, use of new skills, innovation, adaptability, use of IT and so on. Progression looks at the 'how' inputs of performance as well as the output by measuring performance against objectives and performance. It is particularly useful at senior levels (IDS, 2005).

Pay progression reviewed

In summary, progression pay trends in the past thirty or so years, particularly in the private sector, show a move away from quasi-automatic incremental progression based on service, initially to systems based on assessments of individual performance, and more latterly to systems based on performance and competence, or some other combination. This has gone hand in hand with moves away from narrow grades to the use of broader bands or grades, possibly with internal zones or sectors, job families, or career grades. As these latter approaches place at least as much emphasis on career development as on pay progression, they have contributed to an alignment of reward strategies with wider HR objectives.

However, it would be unwise to assume that the changes to progression arrangements are universal, even in the private sector and certainly not in the public sector; or that they always follow the pristine principles set out in the text books. Things are often more complex. In the next section, we will examine the evidence on pay progression as it is practised in the twenty-first century.

Pay progression – the state of the art

OME/CIPD research

In 2005–2006 OME and CIPD jointly worked to use the Institute's annual Reward Survey of pay practitioners to examine the scope and operation of pay progression systems across the UK economy. The main criteria used are set out in Table 4.1.

Two things are immediately striking about the table. The first is that progression based solely on one measure is very much the minority. The highest proportion of responses relating to a single measure concern length of service, which is a largely public sector approach, and the second highest relates to individual performance. Second, and the other side of the coin, is the predominance of combination approaches. The main factors likely to appear in combination with another or others are individual performance, competency, market rates, and organisational performance. The CIPD re-examined progression again in its 2007 survey, this time focussing solely on combination approaches. The results are reproduced in Table 4.2.

Unfortunately, the data do not tell us anything about the actual combinations, as opposed to the potential components and their incidence. But they do suggest that combination schemes mostly comprise performance (whether individual, corporate

Table 4.1 Criteria used to manage pay progression, by occupation, 2006

	Percentage of respondents			
Progression based on	*Senior management*	*Middle/line management*	*Technical/ professional*	*Clerical/ manual*
Individual performance only	15	13	13	10
Competency only	4	4	6	5
Skills only	0	0	0	0
Service only	11	17	16	19
Market rates only	2	2	1	3
Organisational performance only	1	0	0	1
Team performance only	0	1	0	0
Individual performance combination	58	53	52	43
Competency combination	36	40	41	40
Skills combination	22	22	27	27
Service combination	8	11	16	15
Market combination	33	28	31	26
Organisational performance combination	31	20	18	15
Team performance combination	10	9	6	5

Source: CIPD 2006, table 11.

Table 4.2 Pay progression criteria used within a combination approach, by occupation, 2007

	Percentage of respondents			
Progression based on	*Senior management*	*Middle/line management*	*Technical/ professional*	*Clerical/ manual*
Individual performance	89	87	85	77
Competency	54	55	58	53
Skills	36	38	43	43
Length of service	17	18	17	19
Market rates	71	71	70	67
Organisational performance	62	50	45	41
Team performance	30	28	22	21

Source: CIPD 2007, table 12.

and/or team based), market rates, and/or competence. Skills may also be a component. Interestingly, other than organisational performance, which is more likely to be a factor for senior management, there is little variation in the use of factors across broad occupational groups.

We also need to consider the variation in progression arrangements across sectors. Analyses from IDS, CIPD, and the OME provide some interesting insights.

Private sector

The private sector is much more likely to use a combination of individual pay, broad bands, and job families than are either the voluntary or public sectors. This is particularly so of larger organisations. As a result, private sector organisations have fewer grades by broad occupational classification than the public sector, and market rates are easily the main determinant of pay rates, followed by ability to pay. In terms of progression, given the weight the private sector puts on performance and the market, the main progression emphasis is on a combination of performance, skills, and competences, and on individual performance.

Where there are pay ranges, about half of organisations expect 'satisfactory' employees to progress to some 'target rate', which is set at 40 per cent to 50 percent of the range in around 40 per cent of manufacturing organisations (and 51 per cent to 90 percent in a further 40 per cent of organisations). In the private service sector, just fewer than 70 per cent of organisations have a target rate set at 40 per cent to 50 per cent of the range. As the target rate falls *within* the pay range rather than at the range maximum, three-quarters or thereabouts of private sector organisations in both manufacturing and services have scope for progression above the target, and for recruitment above the target. Progression above target is most likely to be related to new skills/responsibilities, performance or career development (OME, 2006).

Practice on progression also varies within these broad private sector classifications, as in-depth reports on specific areas indicate. For example, pay ranges are used in three-fifths of call-centre organisations, with progression based, in order of importance, on individual performance, and/or competency, and/or service. Performance-only progression is used in just over a quarter of organisations, typically those linked to the finance sector, with about a sixth each using service or competence. Hybrid arrangements using combined measures (for example, performance and skills; performance and competence; or performance and competence or service) were comparatively unusual (IDS, 2006c). In engineering, a survey of 50 companies showed that they all allowed white-collar employees to earn more through pay progression, typically linked to performance, additional skills, or competency. Fewer than one in ten had service-related increments, and just over a quarter used two or more factors (commonly chosen from performance, additional skills, and competency; IDS, 2006a).[5]

The public sector

A fifth (20 per cent) of the UK workforce is employed in the public sector, and its total pay bill approaches some £130 billion. Unsurprisingly, governments, whatever their political persuasion, are interested in what they are getting for their investment. Pay progression is part of that interest. Thus in 1991, the then Conservative Government argued that pay systems in the public sector needed to make a regular and direct link between a person's contribution to the standards of the service provided and his or her reward (Citizens' Charter, 1991).

The theme was picked up by the Labour government in 1999. In *Modernising Government*, Ministers identified a number of changes they wished to make to public sector pay arrangements. The first was to challenge 'outdated assumptions about public sector pay, for example the idea that "fair pay" means everyone should get the same increase, or that pay and conditions must all be set nationally' (Cabinet Office, 1999, chapter 6, paragraph 20). Second, they argued that 'a person's pay should reflect their output, results, and performance. This means the best performers both individuals and teams and those who contribute most, should be best rewarded' (ibid.), and that pay systems and performance pay in particular must be used 'in creative ways to provide effective incentives to achieve high quality performance and to encourage innovation and team-working' (ibid., paragraph 21).

However, looking across the entire public sector, the divergence of 'typical' practice compared to the private sector is stark – it is equally stark if only comparing public sector practice with that of large employers in general. The CIPD/OME work shows that

- The public sector is more likely than the private sector to use pay spines, including incremental points.
- This is true for all occupational levels, including senior managers.
- The public sector is also more likely to have a comparatively large number of pay bands (six or more), especially for technical and professional and clerical & manual staff.
- There is an emphasis on 'formal' progression within pay ranges, usually based on service and over a long time. (Staff at all levels in the public sector are much more likely to take over four years to reach their range target rate.)
- These target rates are set high in the structure, typically over 80 per cent of the pay range.
- Consequently, there is little scope for employees to progress beyond their range target (other than by promotion), or for employers to recruit specialised staff from outside the public sector at above target rates (OME, 2006).

Another key difference with the private sector is that public sector employees are more likely to receive progression *in addition* to annual 'cost of living' adjustments, both when compared to employees in manufacturing and, in particular, when compared to employees in private sector services.

The overall picture does, however, obscure the progress that has been made in some public sector areas towards changing public sector pay structures and establishing a clearly discernable link between performance and progression. Pay arrangements for senior civil servants, for example, include broad bands with progression totally determined by performance, supported by non-consolidated bonuses (albeit these latter are low compared to private sector practice, and there are other differences, see Towers Perrin, 2006).

For the rest of the civil service grades the traditional approach of service-related increments loosely based on individual performance was strongly criticised in the review by Makinson (2000). He argued that performance should be rewarded separately from progression via non-consolidated merit payments, and that the levels of current basic awards were too low to allow adequate progression. He recommended that civil service pay should be based on the market and that the market rate should be reached within three to four years. Recent trends have indeed been towards making pay more performance related, whilst shortening pay scales and speeding progression to the market rate. Departments have been keen to ensure that staff are aware of future salary levels, and how long it will take them to progress there given satisfactory performance. However, one result, according to IDS is that 'effectively, this has meant a severing of the link between basic salary and individual performance, which was the touchstone of civil service pay systems through the latter half of the 1990s' (IDS, 2007a, p. 50).

The National Health Service (NHS) has pay bands containing varying numbers of incremental points with the assumption that non-medical staff will normally progress by one increment per annum. There are two 'gateways' where further progression relies on an assessment of the application of the necessary knowledge and skills (Department of Health, 2004).

The parties covering university staff agreed a new model spine for all employees. Individual universities are free to negotiate their own grade arrangements locally, including the number and size of increments. Whilst staff have a normal expectation of annual progression, the national framework allows for the introduction of a contribution threshold near the top of each band. Progression beyond that point is discretionary, and may be designed, for example, to reward sustained individual contribution in terms of high levels of outcomes and competences exceeding those expected of the role (JNCHES, 2003).

The local government employers have noted a number of weaknesses with traditional service-based progression systems, not least that Councils found it difficult in practice to withhold increments, and the fixed costs of progression increases without performance gains. Their 2003 survey found that whilst the vast majority of respondents still used progression based on service, others were using competence, performance, or contribution-based progression (Employers' Organisation for Local Government, 2004). They quoted the Local Government Pay Commission:

> Rather than seeing the issue of progression as service or contribution we suggest consideration should be given to a combination of a limited number of service related increments followed by some form of contribution based pay progression. This could include progression based on the acquisition of skills, competences, qualifications etc. as appropriate. (Local Government Pay Commission, chapter 6, paragraph 50)

It seems, though, that whilst some progress has been made towards adopting private sector practice, implementation of new pay and progression structures in the public sector remains patchy. The general impression is still one of narrow pay bands where the maximum equates to the market rate, incremental progression is fundamentally service related but with some performance element, and an emphasis on control rather than flexibility. The OME identified four key factors accounting for this pattern of public sector practice (OME, 2006):

First, affordability: survey evidence suggests that financial constraints are the main determinants of public sector pay policy, reinforced more recently by the Government's 'policy for pay', crudely interpreted as a 2 per cent limit on base pay rises. Finance is probably also an issue in the private sector, but discussion there is more likely to consist of an outline of corporate objectives, followed by an assessment of the HR (and other) strategies needed to deliver them, including reward structures and processes, rather than a simple 'what's left for pay'.

As to bargaining structures, public sector respondents to the CIPD's 2006 survey saw collective bargaining as a key influence on pay, while private sector employers hardly gave it a mention. Doubtless, this reflects the much higher union density in the public sector, and the greater use of pay negotiations, but it also represents a limitation on managerial discretion and flexibility.

Trust: we have noted in Chapter 1, evidence that line managers are not 'trusted' to operate reward systems either effectively or objectively. Given the financial constraints on the public sector and other concerns around equal pay (see below), narrow pay structures with prescriptive appointment and progression rules may be a means for employers themselves to control managerial discretion. For example, the local government employers' body notes:

> In any large organisation the arbiters of pay levels and progression are likely to be line managers. There is always the risk that they will not apply progression criteria consistently over time.... The narrower the grades/bands the less this is likely to happen because there isn't so far for an individual to move. (Employers' Organisation for Local Government, 2004, p. 17)

Finally, equal pay concerns are very real in the public sector and mistakes are very expensive. This may explain the rigidity of pay progression arrangements. Expanding on its observation that line managers may not apply progression criteria consistently, the local government employers note the risk that 'over time, unfair or, at worst, discriminatory practices will emerge across the organisation' (ibid.).

Paying for progression

In *principle* progression costs should tend to zero because of attrition effects, as noted above (although newer pay structures can face substantial on-costs from, first, the assimilation of staff to the newer grades, and second from the fact that new structures often open up the scope for progression to staff previously at the top of their grades). In *practice*, however, progression usually costs money so, for employers, there is always a tension between meeting employee expectations on pay advancement and the need to control costs. Work by IDS suggested that there were two approaches: tight control via a line manager budget for progression, and separating progression from any general pay rise and funding it separately, but actual evidence on the costs of progression is difficult to find (IDS, 2005).

The issue has recently taken on an added dimension in the public sector where the Treasury already seeks data from central government departments on paybill growth in support of their pay proposals. The six pay review bodies have also been asked to consider the effects of their recommendations on the paybill. Specifically, the measures to be considered are paybill growth, which reflects the total employer cost of awards, and paybill per head growth, which gives an indication of resulting changes in average earnings. This latter includes the effects of pay progression, and has raised the entire 'pay drift' issue with the implication that its costs should be taken into account in determining base pay awards.

Pay drift

It is easy to observe that earnings usually grow faster in percentage terms than base pay increases, although the actual level of difference is volatile and somewhat cyclical. When the OME looked at pay drift in 1973, the main causes were secondary bargaining and the poor management of output related schemes for manual workers in the private sector (OME, 1973). More recent research commissioned by the OME suggests a much more complicated picture, with large contributions from elements of pay 'drive', that is, pay increases resulting from deliberate employer strategies, with only a residual pay 'drift' element (IDS, 2006d). Pay drive includes pay progression, market adjustments, performance pay, actions to address equal pay concerns etcetera, and it is arguable the degree to which, if at all, these should be offset against base pay adjustments. Pay drift includes the effects of strategies to 'fiddle' pay structures, for instance to retain key employees by re-grading jobs or by giving higher than justified performance awards. Whilst such strategies usually indicate that pay structures have slipped behind the market, progression systems can anyway contribute to drift – and therefore costs – if not carefully managed, and, where they are used, tight grade, performance, and competency definitions are essential.

Staff at the maximum: the end of the road?

Eventually staff will progress to their salary maximum for their grade. A common problem is how to keep these staff motivated when their only pay rise is likely to be some periodic revalorisation of the pay structure. Besides some disillusionment on the part of employees, one risk is re-evaluation of posts to justify their movement to a higher grade (grade drift).

This is a particular problem in the public sector where staff tend to progress quasi-automatically to a high point in the pay range, but it can also cause problems with private sector grading structures owing to a commonly adopted approach which slows down performance progression beyond the market rate (usually the scale mid-point). Some institutions, particularly in the private sector, 'gear' performance awards so that they are determined in relation to performance and distance from the market rate combined, so that the highest awards go to high performers below their designated market rate. Leaving aside whether telling higher-paid employees that they are being paid the market rate and that they shouldn't complain is much consolation, Armstrong and Murlis note that it can be difficult to explain to people why they are getting smaller percentage increases than others lower down the scale even though they are performing satisfactorily (Armstrong and Murlis, 2004).

Some approaches for dealing with this problem are introducing a higher performance range, with tight limits on entry and progression, or rewarding performance with variable and non-consolidated bonuses based on performance, or guaranteeing at least a 'cost of living' adjustment provided performance levels are maintained (IDS, 2005).

Summary and some challenges

Armstrong has argued:

> In the good old days of salary administration the only types of grade and pay structures were multi-graded or pay spines. But it could not last … and the light dawned with the concept of reward management as the inadequacies of narrow grade and … pay spines became apparent. But … reward management does not stand still. Reward structures have probably seen more startling changes than the rest of HRM policies and practices put together. (Armstrong, 2005, p. 21)

What this has meant for pay progression was summarised by Thompson as the shift away from progression based on seniority or age to performance measurement as the main determinant (Thompson, 2000).

Changes to progression arrangements have gone hand in hand with changes to pay structures, and processes are clearly more complex – and, some would argue, less transparent – than 30 years ago. They are clearly also now more rounded, often taking account of a multitude of factors, and focussed on employees as individuals. These changes have not been without their challenges, as we have noted, and others lie in wait for progression systems. We conclude by looking at what some of these might be.

Equal pay and age discrimination

Chapter 8 reviews recent developments in discrimination law. These raise interesting issues around pay inequalities that may arise from the operation of long incremental payment systems in respect of gender (women may lose out because of the nature of their career patterns) and age (younger workers have less time in a grade and may not have progressed as far as older workers). Some employers in the public sector are already looking to speed up progression to the market rate to avoid potential traps from the legislation. There are other concerns about the transparency of some of the 'new pay' systems, especially where progression is based on assessments of performance or competence. Wright observes that these structures 'are quite simply not going to have anything like the easily recognisable or transparent pay rate or narrow range for the job evident in a traditional graded structure' (Wright, 2004, p. 82).

Employee expectations

A criticism of broad banded pay approaches is that they disrupt employee expectations. Armstrong noted that broad bands created employee expectations that they would progress to the top of bands, and these could not be met. Employees therefore lacked the progression certainty they had previously enjoyed (Armstrong, 2005). Thompson has also raised the implications of newer pay approaches for the psychological contract (Thompson, 2000)

Variable pay

The inclusion of elements of variable pay[6] in remuneration packages is now widespread, see Chapter 6, and especially at management levels in the private sector, and they can amount to substantial percentages of base pay. Variable pay is one option for continuing to reward excellent performers who are at the market rate in base pay terms, and can therefore be a replacement for (an element at least) of pay progression. This concept might go further.

Chapter 1 highlights the tendency of American remuneration practice to migrate to the United Kingdom, and in this context, it is interesting to note Cotton's review of the *World at Work* conference[7] held in the United States (US) in May 2007:

One response to an increasingly global market is that many US employers are shifting from merit-based salary increases to a system of market-based rates coupled with performance-based spot bonuses. American firms are beginning to suspect that merit-based pay increases may be nothing more than the traditional pay award in drag. To get away from the upward movement in the payroll, salaries are being decoupled from performance and being linked to the market. Instead, contribution is being rewarded through non-consolidated performance-related bonuses (Cotton, 2007, p. 2).

In this context, analysis of earnings indices for the financial intermediary sector, carried out by Incomes Data Services based on ONS data, is revealing. It shows hardly any movement in base pay over time, with all the year-in-year movement in earnings accounted for by non-consolidated bonuses (IDS, 2007b). Perhaps the future for progression systems elsewhere will be similar: a mix of limited quasi-automatic movement to a market rate, coupled with unconsolidated variable payments to reward performance.

Acknowledgements

Much of the analysis contained in this chapter derives from the joint research project carried out by OME, CIPD and IDS to examine progression practice in the UK economy. The author is particularly grateful to Duncan Brown and Charles Cotton (CIPD) and Alastair Hatchett, Nicola Alison and colleagues (IDS) for their input to this earlier work, and to the staff of the CIPD Library for their patience and assistance. The views expressed here are nevertheless those of the author.

Notes

1. Most of the research carried out by the Office of Manpower Economics and referred to in this chapter is available on its website www.ome.uk.com. The research carried out by Incomes Data Services in 2005 was entitled 'Organisational practice on pay progression'. Owing to agreements of confidentiality with organisations taking part it has not been possible to publish the report. However, IDS has published a short extract of the findings in IDS Report 945. Some of the case studies have also been separately published, for example Airbus and Suffolk County Council (IDS Report 929).
2. Public sector manual staff are sometimes covered by formal progression systems, for example, the NHS and Universities, but pay ranges are narrow with few incremental steps. Progression arrangements are as for non-manual staff.
3. Some schemes operated on the basis of a range of 80 per cent to 120 per cent of a market-related mid-point with quasi-automatic incremental progression to the mid-point. The area above the mid-point allowed flexibility to reward exceptional performers, or to aid retention of staff with particular skills.
4. For a review of the role of competencies in staff recruitment and retention, see PA Consulting Group (2007). Practices in assessing Employee 'Quality'. London, OME.
5. For a further example of progression arrangements by sector see Incomes Data Services (2006). Pay in electricity, gas, and water industries. London, IDS.
6. Variable pay in this context is taken to mean elements of earnings that are performance related and not consolidated into base pay. Bonus payments schemes are a typical and increasingly frequently used example.
7. 'World at Work' incorporates the American Compensation Association.

References

Agenda for Change Project Team (2004) *Agenda for Change – Final Agreement*, Leeds: Department of Health.

Armstrong, M. (2005) 'Career Family Structures', *Executive Compensation Review*, *290*, London: IDS.

Armstrong, M. and Brown, D. (2001) *New Dimensions in Pay Management*, London: CIPD.

Armstrong, M. and Murlis, H. (2004) *Reward Management*, 5th ed., London: Kogan Page.

Bergel, G. (1994) 'Choosing the Right Pay Delivery System to Fit Banding', *Compensation and Benefits Review*, 26, 4, July–August 1994, 34–38.

Cabinet Office (1999) *Modernising Government*, London: Stationery Office.

Cannell, M. and Wood, S. (1992) *Incentive Pay: Impact and Evolution*, London: Institute of Personnel Management.

Chartered Institute of Personnel and Development (CIPD) (2005) *Reward Management. Annual Survey Report*, London: CIPD.

Chartered Institute of Personnel and Development (CIPD) (2006) *Reward Management. Annual Survey Report*, London: CIPD.

Chartered Institute of Personnel and Development (CIPD) (2007) *Reward Management. Annual Survey Report*, London: CIPD.

Citizens' Charter (1991) Cmnd 1599, London: HMSO.

Cotton, C. (2007) 'Reflections on the World at Work Conference', *Reward Review*, Autumn, London: CIPD.

e-reward (2004) 'What is Happening to Grade and Pay Structures Today', *Survey Report 26*, Stockport, Cheshire.

Employers' Organisation for Local Government (2004) *Reviewing and Modernising Pay Frameworks*, London: Employers' Organisation.

Frontier Economics (2006) *Wages and Public Sector Hiring*, London: OME.

Gilbert, D. and Abosch, K. (1996) *Improving Organizational Effectiveness through Broadbanding*, Scottsdale, AZ: American Compensation Association.

Houldsworth, E. and Jirasinghe, D. (2006) *Managing and Measuring Employee Performance*, London: Kogan Page.

Incomes Data Services (IDS) (1977) 'Salary Increments', *Study*, 145, London: IDS.

Incomes Data Services (IDS) (1978) 'Pay Policy and Stage Four Rules', *Study*, 184, London: IDS.

Incomes Data Services (IDS) (2004) 'Broadbanding', *IDS Report 906*, London: IDS.

Incomes Data Services (IDS) (2005) Organisational Practice on Pay Progression, London: OME, unpublished.

Incomes Data Services (IDS) (2006a) *Pay and Conditions in Engineering 2006/07*, London: IDS.

Incomes Data Services (IDS) (2006b) 'Job Families', *IDS HR Studies*, 814, London: IDS.

Incomes Data Services (IDS) (2006c) *Pay and Conditions in Call Centres 2006/07*, London: IDS.

Incomes Data Services (IDS) (2006d) *An Assessment of the Causes of Pay Drift in UK Organisations*, London: OME.

Incomes Data Services (IDS) (2007a) *Pay in the Public Services 2007*, London: IDS.

Incomes Data Services (IDS) (2007b) 'Highest Ever Bonus Season in Finance Boosts Earnings Growth', *IDS Report 978*, London: IDS.

Incomes Data Services (IDS) and Institute of Personnel Management (IPM) (1985) *The Merit Factor: Rewarding Individual Performance*, London: IDS.

Industrial Relations Law Reports (2006) *Cadman v Health v Safety Executive*, 969.

Joint Negotiating Committee for Higher Education Staff (JNCHES) (2003) *Framework Agreement for the Modernising of Pay Structures*, London: JNCHES.

Kersley, B., Alpin, C., Forth, J., Bryson, A., Bewley, H., Dix, G., and Oxenbridge, S. (2006) *Inside the Workplace: Findings from the 2004 Workplace Employment Relations Survey*, London: Routledge.

Makinson, J. (2000) *Incentives for Change: Rewarding Performance in National Government Networks*, London: HM Treasury.

Marsden, D. and Richardson, R. (1991) *Does Performance Pay Motivate? A Study of Inland Revenue Staff*, London: Inland Revenue Staff Federation.

Office of Manpower Economics (OME) (1973) *Incremental Payment Systems*, London: HMSO.

Office of Manpower Economics (OME) (2006) *Public/Private Approaches to Pay Progression*, London: OME.

Thompson, M. (2000) 'Salary Progression' in White, G. and Druker, J. (eds) *Reward Management: A Critical Text*, London: Routledge.

Towers Perrin (2006) *Bonus Scheme Design and Effectiveness,* London: OME.

Wright, A. (2004) *Reward Management in Context*, London: CIPD.

5

Local pay

Bob Elliott

Over the past twenty-five years, the impact of trade unions on pay setting in the United Kingdom has diminished. Less than one in five private sector employees (19.6 per cent) were covered by a collective agreement in 2006. The equivalent figure for public sector employees was 69 per cent. Fewer than one in six employees in the private sector were members of a trade union (Grainger and Crowther, 2007). Trade unions now play a modest role in private sector pay setting though they retain influence in the public sector. Pay in the private sector is now more likely than at any time in the past 60 years to reflect underlying conditions in the markets in which labour is hired. In the private sector, rates of pay for the same type of job now differ between regions and localities: in many jobs pay has become localised. In the public sector, pay is less localised and less responsive to underlying labour market conditions. This difference between how pay is set in the public and private sectors affects the ability of the public sector to attract and retain the labour it requires. The Treasury has advocated a move away from national pay structures in the public sector and the introduction of 'measures to ensure that public service pay systems are more responsive to regional labour market conditions'.[1]

This chapter explores the arguments for and the limits to local pay. It not only reports evidence to support a move to greater localisation for some public sector workers, but also shows that it is not appropriate for all. It details the degree of local pay variation in the private sector and explores the consequences of this for public sector pay setting. It details the mechanisms through which pay is localised and discusses some of the practical issues that arise when seeking to localise pay.[2] The first section of this chapter explores the technical issues involved when estimating the pattern of local pay, and therefore involves a very simple discussion of the econometric method that is used. The rest of the chapter explores public/private sector differences in respect of local pay determination and explores industrial relations considerations.

Regional or local pay variation?

Data on average pay by region typically show very little variation outside London and the South East. Incomes Data Services (IDS), reporting data for April 2006, record that the median pay levels (earnings) in eight of the 12 regions in Great Britain (GB) are clustered between £399 and £422 and comment that it seems 'remarkable that with such a wide variety of types of jobs the medians are so similar' (Incomes Data Services 2006a, p. 14). Or is it remarkable? Are such statistics very meaningful?

The type of jobs, the industrial structure, the training, and skills of the workforce all differ between regions and all of these factors affect earnings. It may at first glance seem surprising that given all these drivers of pay there is not more variation, but these are highly aggregated statistics and they tell us little that is of any real interest. We learn little from comparisons of average pay levels. We are not comparing like-with-like. To make meaningful comparisons we must compare like-with-like and that means standardising the pay data.

Differences between private sector labour markets in the balance of supply and demand for labour will result in spatial variations in pay. Regions are not labour markets and therefore data at the regional level mask important differences between localities within regions. Aggregate regional data also mask differences between the patterns of pay in the private and public sectors. The pay setting systems are different in the two sectors. In the private sector, where most pay setting is unilaterally by management, not jointly with unions, pay is more likely to reflect underlying labour market conditions.

One way to ensure we are making like-for-like comparisons between different localities is to calculate Standardised Spatial Wage Differentials (SSWDs). This is done by taking observations on individual employees' personal characteristics, such as their age and gender, and job characteristics such as the occupation and industry in which they work. The data can then be interrogated using the standard regression technique of Ordinary Least Squares. This method allows the researcher to control for all the measured differences that are known to affect pay and to distinguish those differences in pay that do not relate to personal and job characteristics but to the locality in which the employee works.

The equation for generating the SSWDs can be written as:

$$\ln(w_{ij}) = x'\beta + v_j + \varepsilon_{ij} \tag{1}$$

where w_{ij} is the hourly earnings of individual i who works in locality j, the vector x contains the 'controls', the measured differences between the jobs and productive attributes of workers in the different localities, v_j captures the area-specific effects and ε_{ij} constitutes the individual-specific error terms.[3]

The 'controls' used will be determined by the data set available to the researchers. In a widely used data set, the Annual Survey of Hours and Earnings (ASHE), which is a 1 per cent sample of all employees in Great Britain, details are available on the age, gender, and employment status of those sampled, together with considerable details of the industry, occupation, and area in which they work. In the equation above age, gender, employment status, industry, and occupation make up the vector *x,* they are the controls. The area-specific effects, vj can then be estimated by assigning a unique identifier, a dummy variable, to all those employees working in the same area. In the ASHE data set, England can be divided into 353 Local Authority Districts (LADs) and so there are potentially 353 different identifiers. A different identifier is assigned to each area save for one which is called the omitted area and serves as the reference area against which the difference in pay in every other LAD can be measured. The coefficients on the dummy variables then provide estimates of SSWDs and by taking the exponent can be expressed as percentage differences in pay from the omitted area or the UK national average as in Table 5.1. below.

Table 5.1 reports SSWDs calculated for the private sector of the economy in England for the period 2003–2005 (See Elliott et al., 2007b). The Table illustrates the importance of controlling for differences between localities (here LADs) in individuals' personal and job characteristics. Standardised Spatial Wage Differentials have been estimated in stages, introducing progressively more controls. Where there are no controls and the data are simply clustered by area, by LAD, average pay in the lowest paying area is 61.5 per cent of the all areas mean and in the highest paying area, it is 250.4 per cent of the all areas mean (see the first column of Table 5.1). Note

Table 5.1 Distribution of private sector SSWDs with different control variables

Statistic	(1)	(2)	(3)	(4)	(5)
	LAD identifiers only	Model (1) with age and sex dummies added	Model (2) with occupational dummies added	Model (3) with industry dummies added	Model (4) with part-time dummy added
Mean	103.3	103.1	101.3	101.2	101.2
standard dev.	21.2	19.6	10.9	10.2	10.1
Minimum	61.5	72.6	80.8	82.1	82.5
10th percentile	84.4	85.7	91.2	91.8	91.6
50th percentile	98.1	97.9	98.6	98.5	98.4
90th percentile	128.6	126.4	114.4	114.9	114.7
Decile range	44.2	40.7	33.2	23.1	23.1
maximum	250.4	237.7	166.6	159.4	158.6
Adjusted R²	0.139	0.334	0.621	0.639	0.640

Note: For the calculation of these statistics, each LAD value assumes equal weight. The decile range is the difference between the 90th and 10th percentiles of the distribution.

Source: Elliott et al. (2007b).

that this single control, which identifies the LAD in which the employee works, explains only 13.9 per cent of the variance in individual pay.

Once controls are added, these controls identifying first the employees' gender and age, then the occupation and industry in which they work and finally whether they work full or part-time, we observe that the variation of pay between different areas falls. The standard deviation decreases, the decile range narrows and the difference between the highest and lowest LADs falls. Adding in these controls increases the proportion of the variance of individual pay that is explained: it rises from 0.139 to 0.64 (see the last column of Table 5.1). Clearly, when seeking to distinguish between pay in different localities it is important to standardise for measured differences between areas.

Even so, substantial differences in pay between different areas of England remain as the final column of Table 5.1 reveals. The pattern that emerges might be described as the 'underlying' pattern of local pay differentials, for it has emerged once all measurable differences between areas in the type of jobs that are done and the productive characteristics of the workers who do them have been included in the estimation.

It has been argued that SSWDs estimated as above overstate the underlying variation in pay between localities because the ASHE data set does not allow researchers to control for all the relevant differences in jobs. One difference between jobs that has been judged important and the subject of recent research is the level of responsibility (Morris et al., 2007). It has been argued that managerial jobs in London pay more because they carry more responsibility than managerial jobs in the rest of England and that the occupational controls available in ASHE do not allow researchers to measure and therefore control for this difference between jobs in different localities. Morris et al. (2007) have revealed that when measures of responsibility are taken from another data set and included alongside occupational controls then this changes the underlying pattern of pay. They find that including a measure of higher responsibility in the equation above results in an average reduction in the estimated SSWDs for localities in central London of around three percentage points. For some localities in central London, the City of London, and Westminster, the reduction was around five percentage points.

Does this underlying pattern truly reflect the differences in pay that employers must offer in different localities? Critics argue that economic analysis of variations in average earnings using large data sets recording data on individual employees' pay overstate the variations in pay that employers in different localities find necessary to offer to recruit and retain labour. They point to the smaller differences between localities in rates of pay that are found in the pay scales and pay schedules of large private sector companies. However, focus on pay rates misses the other mechanisms that employers use to adjust pay to local market conditions. Some locate new employees further up the pay scale and advance existing employees more quickly up the scale in high-cost low amenity areas, where labour would otherwise be difficult to attract. Others offer additional overtime payments or accelerated promotion in hard to recruit areas. These adjustments do not show up in basic salary scales and can only really be distinguished in data on average earnings. They make it extremely difficult, and from a practical perspective impossible, to map the pattern of regional and locality pay by taking basic pay data then adding to them all the pay additions that can be identified because some of the adjustments which employers use are just not evident in the data.[4] It is for this reason most analysts argue that earnings data, once appropriately adjusted are the only way of mapping the true patterns of regional and local differences in pay. Estimating the underlying pattern of pay presents some empirical challenges, but having standardised for individuals' personal and job characteristics, substantial variations in pay between different localities remain. Why?

Why regional pay variation?

Cost of living

One reason we expect to observe regional and local pay variations is that the cost of living differs between areas of the United Kingdom. The only data available on this comes from the Office for National Statistics who have recently begun to publish data on regional price levels and these are now available for 2000 and 2004. They are reported in Figure 5.1.

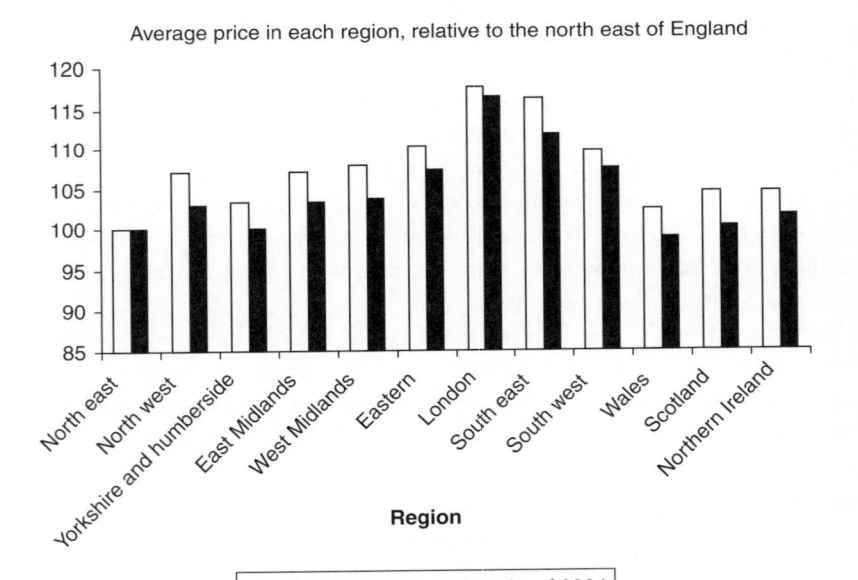

Figure 5.1   Regional price levels in 2000 and 2004

Source: Ball and Fenwick (2004) and Wingfield D., Fenwick D., and Smith K (2005).

Though regions do not give the level of detail we require, they do show that there are substantial differences in the cost of living between different parts of the country. They show that in 2000 the North East was the lowest price area and London the highest. London was again the highest in 2004 and the North East was the second lowest.

Nominal pay would be expected to reflect variations in the cost of living. Employees are concerned about real pay and, all else being equal, employees would tend to move from high-cost to low-cost areas. This migration would drive nominal pay up in the high-cost areas and down in the low-cost areas until nominal pay reflected cost of living differences.

However, all else is not equal and there are further important differences between localities that drive nominal pay. Localities differ in their attractiveness as places in which to work.

The amenity of different localities

A second major reason why pay will differ between localities is because localities differ in attractiveness, more generally amenity, as places in which to work. Some jobs will be located in localities judged unattractive, perhaps because the area is physically unappealing or suffers high crime. Where this happens employers will need to pay more to attract employees to work in these localities. Employees may seek to minimise exposure to some of the unattractive features of the area in which they work by living in a different area, but this then requires them to commute to work. Commuting is generally thought unattractive and employers will have to pay more to compensate employees for the disutility of commuting: again, pay will be higher in unattractive areas.

Theory of net advantages

Differences in the cost of living and amenities are drivers of regional and locality pay differences. Both are aspects of the net advantages of jobs in different areas of the country. In 1776, Adam Smith set out the theory of net advantages and explained how, as a result of the forces of competition, all the advantages and disadvantages of different jobs would tend to equality. This would not result in equality of nominal pay but rather pay would be higher where it was necessary to compensate employees for a higher cost of living or for area disamenities. Smith wrote:

> The whole of the advantages and disadvantages of different employments of labour – must in the same neighbourhood, be either perfectly equal or continually tending to equality. If in the same neighbourhood there was any employment either evidently more or less advantageous than the rest so many people would crowd into it in the one case, and so many desert it in the other, that its advantages would soon return to the level of other employments. (Smith, 1776 book 1 chapter 10)

Provided that employees have the same preferences for (or aversion toward) the amenities (disamenities) of different localities, and are informed of these differences and free to move, then competition in labour markets will ensure that the net advantages of different jobs will tend to equality.[5] Some areas of the country will be distinguished by higher pay to compensate for the higher cost of living, some by higher pay to compensate for a less pleasant working environment, and some by compensation for both these factors.

Empirical research has provided support for this theory of regional and local pay differences. Differences between geographical areas in the working environment, as proxied by the industrial mix, and in the attractiveness of the external environment in which they live and work have been found to be important in explaining the patterns of geographical pay differences in the United Kingdom (see Blackaby and Murphy, 1995; Reilly, 1992; Shah and Walker, 1983).

However, in labour markets the forces of competition are mediated by institutions. Local and regional patterns of pay reflect the ways in which companies and trade unions interpret and respond to the supply of labour and the demand for labour in local and regional labour markets.

Until recently trade unions played a major role in setting pay in the UK economy and the effect of union wage bargaining was to reduce pay dispersion. The idea of 'equal pay for equal work' was a powerful driver of union wage policy and was for the most part interpreted to mean equal *nominal* pay for equal work. This had the effect of narrowing differences in pay between localities. Additional payments to those working in London through the payment of allowances were the only acknowledged exception.

In the private sector trade union presence (membership and density) is now low and unions play only a modest role in setting pay (Brown et al., 2003; Cully et al., 1999; Grainger and Crowther, 2007). The weakening of trade unions has widened the distribution of earnings (Machin, 1997, 1999; Metcalf et al., 2001). In the private sector of the UK economy, the weakening of unions will have affected the distribution of pay between localities. The mechanisms that employers use to set pay now determine the patterns of local and regional pay. However, there are significant differences between the ways in which pay is set in the private and public sectors of the UK economy. They result in quite different geographical patterns of pay in the two sectors which we now discuss.

Private sector

The system of pay setting in the private sector differs between large and small employers. Small employers, with factories or workplaces in only one locality, will set pay to reflect conditions in the labour market for that locality. The UK Labour Force Survey reveals that 26 per cent of all employees in Great Britain in 2003 worked in organisations that had only one workplace. The patterns of regional and local pay among the employees of these small firms will reflect conditions in the local labour markets in which they operate.

Large employers with a network of offices or factories in different localities have long recognised that they must offer additional pay to offset the higher cost of living associated with working in London and have therefore paid London Allowances. Incomes Data Services (2006a, b) report that many companies in the finance sector now also pay both higher basic salaries to those who work in London, while continuing to pay London allowance.

Simply distinguishing between London and the rest of the country is unlikely to be sufficient for many large companies. The cost of living varies between the regions and localities of the United Kingdom and of course, the cost of living is not the only driver of the requirement to localise pay. Where large employers operate in a number of localities they will seek to set pay that is competitive in all these localities. But in doing this they must balance the advantages of a system that adjusts pay to conditions in all these localities against the costs of such a system.

One model for localising pay is decentralised pay setting which affords local managers complete autonomy to set pay. In practice, this model is seldom adopted for it is typically a high-cost system. The high costs arise from the duplication of time and effort that is associated with multiple centres of pay setting and decentralisation can result in higher wage bills or increased turnover where local managers do not have the skills and experience to set pay at the 'right' level for the local market.

To avoid these costs most large employers operate a framework which clearly identifies the conditions under which higher pay can be awarded in some localities. The framework will make specific provision for setting different rates of pay in different geographical areas. The different areas are increasingly described as 'pay zones' and different pay bands attach to each zone. Though some of these zones will cover London and the South East, the remaining bands cover other localities. Although such arrangements are not infrequently called 'regional salary bands' the geographical areas they detail do not correspond to regions and therefore this description is inappropriate.

Frameworks specify rules and procedures designed to adjust pay to the local market conditions and the rules are designed to remove discretion from local managers inexperienced in pay setting. These rules identify the conditions under which higher pay is offered. Typically, the rules require evidence of the rates paid by local competitors, of the local cost of living, and perhaps of local unemployment or turnover rates as evidence of market tightness (Incomes Data Services, 2002).

Incomes Data Services (2007b) report an example of such a scheme for clerical staff in retail banking employed by the Royal Bank of Scotland. The scheme introduced in 2007 distinguishes five local salary bands with Band 5, the highest, covering central London, and Band 4 covering the area of outer London. But Bands 2 through 5 are defined by town names and do not map to regions. Pay in Band 5 is over 30 per cent higher than pay in Band 1. The regional allowances previously paid have been incorporated into basic salary. Changes to the allocation of towns to any of the pay bands are determined centrally by reference to a number of factors evidencing recruitment and retention pressures: among them are data on turnover, time-to-fill vacancies, and competitors' pay. Data on travel to work distances are also collected – it is presumed – to map the spatial dimensions of the local market and of the pay band (Incomes Data Services, 2007b).

There are fewer institutional constraints on pay setting in the UK private sector than in the public sector and private sector employers are motivated to set competitive, market rates. We should therefore expect the patterns of local and regional pay in this sector to map closely the drivers of regional and local pay differences: differences in cost of living and amenities. Estimates of the local patterns of pay in the private sector in the United Kingdom have been produced by Blanchflower et al. (1996), by Elliott et al. (1996), by Wilson et al. (1996, 2002), by Davies and Owen (2004), and by Elliott et al. (2007b). They all reveal very substantial variation as reported in Table 5.1.

Public sector

Pay setting arrangements in the public sector are very different. In most parts of the public sector there are national agreements and national pay scales, and, with the exception of London and the South East, pay is usually the same regardless of the area of the country in which the employee works. Employees in London and the South East receive additional payments to cover acknowledged differences in the cost of living and in some agreements there is now provision for areas outside the South East to make additional payments if they experience recruitment and retention difficulties. But as a general rule there is little scope for adjusting pay to local or regional labour market conditions.

The pay of most public sector employees is set through an institutional, not a market process, and arguments different from those employed in the private sector motivate the setting of pay. Trade unions play an important role in pay setting, and pay therefore deviates from the rates that would otherwise be paid in the market. Trade unions are concerned about equity and fair pay, and seek to negotiate a national rate for the job (see Metcalf et al., 2001). They narrow the distribution of pay and the resulting spatial pay structure is flatter than would otherwise occur. The scope for local pay in each of the major pay agreements that cover the public sector is detailed below.

Local government

The pay and conditions of Administrative Professional Technical and Clerical (APT&C) staff and manual workers in local government in England and Wales are covered by a Single Status Agreement. Introduced in April 1997 this has integrated and

harmonised pay and conditions following local job evaluation. Progress towards implementation has been slow (see Incomes Data Services, 2007a). Market supplements can
be paid for hard to recruit or retain posts. It is difficult at this stage of partial implementation to say whether these arrangements will result in more or less geographically
differentiated rates of pay for APT&C and manual staff than existed before 1997. No
robust analysis of the spatial impact of the new arrangements has yet been conducted.

Police service

The UK-wide salary scales cover each of the Federated ranks: Constables, Sergeants,
and Inspectors. The payment of additional allowances – rent allowance, housing
allowance, and London and South East allowance – result in geographical differentiation of total financial reward.

Education

Different institutional arrangements set the pay of teachers in England and Wales
and Scotland. Main grade teachers in England and Wales and classroom teachers in
Scotland are paid on national pay scales. Progression through the main scales is by
years of completed service while access to an upper scale is conditional on evidence
of performance, in England and Wales, and competence in Scotland. In England
and Wales, there is scope for local pay through initial placement and progression up
the scale. In England, separate pay scales offer higher pay to those working in inner
and outer London and fringe areas. In England and Wales, further discretionary
payments are available to address recruitment and retention problems. Payment is at
the discretion of schools but these latter are neither substantial nor widespread. The
School Teachers' Review Body (STRB) argues that 'there is scope for significant local
discretion over pay policy and practice' (see STRB, 2005, para. 5.55) and almost two
years earlier had advocated a local pay mechanism for schools based on pay zones
but this has yet to be implemented (STRB, 2004, part 2, chapter 4). Scotland has only
the Islands allowance.

National Health Service (NHS)

Since 2004 all non-medical staff have been covered by a new pay structure called
'Agenda for Change' (AfC) which was introduced progressively from the middle of
that year. The AfC provides for additional payments in 'high cost areas' (high-cost
area supplements) and the payment of local and national recruitment and retention
premia. High-cost area supplements are paid in inner and outer London and fringe
areas but national recruitment and retention premia have only been implemented for
maintenance staff. Doctors and dentists are paid London Weighting. This was frozen
at 2005/06 levels for both 2006/07 and 2007/08 because the Review Body on Doctors'

and Dentists' Remuneration (2005) argued that there was no evidence of recruitment and retention problems among these staff groups in London. We shall visit the evidence for this later in this chapter. Scotland again pays Islands allowance.

Central government

Pay and grading decisions in central government have been devolved to ministries and agencies. Since April 1996, each department and agency has been able to establish its own pay and grading structure. Many are located only in London and therefore have no need to devise a pay structure for geographically differentiating pay. However the three largest have employees throughout the United Kingdom and thus need to address this issue. They are the Department of Work and Pensions (DWP), Ministry of Defence, and Her Majesty's Revenue and Customs. Together they employ around 300,000 of nearly 500,000 civil servants in the United Kingdom. Decentralisation has given rise to a diversity of pay and grading practices in the UK civil service. Some departments have separate London pay scales and some pay London allowances. Department of Work and Pensions have identified four 'location pay zones': national; inner London; outer London and; Specified Location Pay Zones (SLPZ) where this latter covers a number of the remaining South East and east of England towns.

Overview of recent developments

A general feature of public sector pay arrangements in the past few years has been the drive to shorten the length of pay scales. Shorter pay scales offer fewer opportunities to use accelerated incremental progression to respond to tight labour markets. The new pay scales have been underpinned by the increased use of job evaluation. Both these developments have reduced the scope for geographical differentiation of pay within the main pay scales. Special area payments, London and contiguous area payments remain the main vehicle for differentiating pay geographically. Where there is provision for more local pay this has generally not been used, with the possible exception of local government. Once we get beyond London and the south east of England pay in the rest of the United Kingdom is, with few exceptions, the same for any job in the public sector.

The consequences of public – private differences

Figure 5.2 presents a stylised graphical representation of the spatial patterns of pay in the private and public sectors. The slopes of the lines reflect the increments to pay that are associated with working in different areas of the country. They map the spatial patterns of pay in the two sectors that are distinguished by estimating SSWDs. The slopes are described by the exponents of the coefficients on the area-specific effects, vj, estimated in equation (1). The difference in slopes reflects the much smaller geographical variation in pay in the public sector than in the private sector.

Where the slope of the line, the increment to pay, in the public sector is less than the increment to pay in the private sector the pay premium for working in a particular locality is lower in the public sector than it is in the private sector. It follows that the public sector would be expected to find it more difficult to attract and retain employees and vacancy and turnover rates will be higher in the public sector in these areas. Where the premium is higher in the public sector than in the private, the reverse will be expected. The public sector will have low vacancy rates, vacancy rates which are below the natural or equilibrium vacancy rate, and turnover will be low. In these localities, the public sector will be paying above what it needs to attract and retain labour. It is not difficult to understand why if this is indeed the case the Chancellor of the Exchequer proposed in April 2003 to introduce 'measures to ensure that public service pay systems are more responsive to regional labour market conditions'. The higher vacancy rates in localities in which the public sector is paying less than required will have an adverse effect on the volume and quality of public services delivered in those areas and will give rise to higher indirect costs, in the form of higher turnover and bills for agency and temporary staff to plug the gap. Realigning the pay structure to ensure it is more closely aligned to local market conditions would produce greater equality of vacancy rates. Indeed realignment is complete when vacancy rates in all localities are at their natural or equilibrium rates. Realigning rates means distributing resource away from those areas which are paying more than is required, to those paying less than required. Though it will offer efficiency gains, it will be controversial.

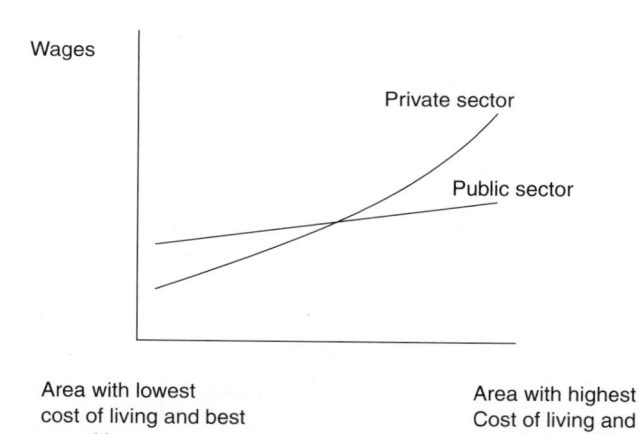

Figure 5.2 Spatial patterns of pay in the public and private sectors

The argument above proposes an association between the size of the gap between the two lines and the ability of the public sector to attract and retain the labour it requires. The greater the difference between the premium in the private and the public sectors the more difficult it will be for the public sector to attract and retain labour. Is there empirical support for this hypothesis? In a direct test of this hypothesis Ma et al. (2007) took vacancy rates as a measure of the ability of the public sector to recruit and retain labour and regressed these on the size of the gap between SSWDs estimated for the private and public sectors. The research focused on two homogeneous groups of public employees: NHS doctors and nurses. It built on earlier work by some of these researchers which had shown an association between the gap and the vacancy rate for qualified nurses (Elliott et al., 2007a).

Ma et al. (2007) mapped the patterns of pay in both the private sector and for NHS nurses and NHS doctors across 354 Local Authority Districts in England. The SSWDs for the private sector were mapped using data on all employees in the private sector and for specific groups of occupations that were judged comparators for nurses and doctors. The comparators in both cases were clusters of occupations at equivalent levels of skill, and in the case of nurses, those in which we find qualified nurses working when they are not working as nurses in the NHS. For doctors the comparators were occupations of similar professional standing including those used by the Review Body on Doctors' and Dentists' Remuneration (2002, p. 17, para. 1.81). The argument proposed was that these professions likely had similar preferences to doctors about the amenities of different areas. In fact, it made no difference to the results whether all private sector employees, or a more narrowly defined occupational group, were chosen. The researchers found the expected positive association between vacancy rates for nurses in England and the size of the gap – the larger the gap between what the private sector paid and what nurses were paid, the higher the vacancy rate for qualified nurses. No such relationship was found for doctors.

Should pay be localised?

In the private sector, the appropriate degree of spatial disaggregation will emerge from the operation of market forces. The discussion here will therefore focus on the public sector. The empirical results of the study by Ma et al. (2007) are revealing in this respect. The association between nursing vacancy rates and the gap between what nurses were paid and what the private sector paid at a local level arose because the labour markets in which nurses are recruited are localised. Nurses have transferable skills and are recruited in localised labour markets. What other employers pay in the local labour market matters to nurses and what other employers paid varied between localities. The same will be true for many of the other jobs done in the public sector; those done by clerks and administrators, cleaners, drivers, porters, gardeners, security staff, teaching assistants, and community police support officers, all are recruited in highly localised labour markets and pay differences between localities matter. It might also be true for social workers, police officers, teachers, and other non-medical health professionals, but this has yet to be evidenced.

All else being equal there will also be a need to differentiate pay between localities where employees are recruited in national or even international labour markets. But these employees may have a wider choice of localities in which to work, and other characteristics of these localities may assume importance. Doctors, in common with senior managers, senior judges, civil servants, the most senior police officers, and university lecturing staff operate in national and even international labour markets. Ma et al. (2007) found that some other characteristics of localities mattered more than just cost-of-living and amenities to doctors. Identifying what these other characteristics are, why they matter to the professional group being studied, and how they differ between employers in different localities is key to understanding the appropriate spatial variation in pay for these occupations.

Defining the labour markets in which staff are recruited is therefore a first step for determining the importance of localising pay. We have some information on the boundaries of labour markets, collected from data on travel to work patterns. These patterns define Travel To Work Areas (TTWAs) which constitute largely self-contained labour markets. They are areas of the country in which the majority of people (at least 75 per cent) who live in the area also work in the area and vice versa. They are distinguished by analysing the commuting patterns of the population reported in the periodic censuses. Those available from the Office for National Statistics (see http://www.statistics.gov.uk/geography/ttwa.asp) at the time of writing were defined in 1998 using information from the 1991 Census on home and work addresses.[6] At the time of writing there were 308 TTWAs covering the United Kingdom, of which 207 cover England.

The problem with TTWAs is that they are defined across all occupations and we know that commuting patterns (Coombes et al., 1990) and the geographical boundaries of labour markets differ between occupations. Each TTWA therefore effectively constitutes a weighted average of several different labour markets defined for the occupations in that area. Employing goodness-of-fit statistics and the most stringent out-of-sample prediction tests Elliott et al. (2007b) found that Local Authority Districts better described the labour markets in which the NHS operates than did TTWAs.

The research by Ma et al. (2007) revealed interesting results for medical staff: when the gap was larger doctor vacancies were lower, which was not what the simple theory would predict. Doctors' vacancies were lower in the high-cost (less attractive?) areas; doctors were attracted to work in these areas. Evidently the gains from working in high-cost areas exceeded the higher cost of living that was encountered in such places. The reasons why doctors were attracted to work in high-cost areas were explored. It was hypothesised that doctors might be attracted to work in high-cost areas because this is where more teaching hospitals are located. Teaching hospitals may offer more opportunities to undertake research, and this research activity may enhance promotion prospects. It was also hypothesised that there might be more opportunities to earn income from private work in posts in high-cost areas such as London and the South East. Finally, it was recognised that the specialty composition of the medical workforce would vary between hospitals and, because vacancies differ by specialty, variations in vacancy rates between hospitals could reflect more than local labour market conditions.

An extended model was therefore estimated including indicators of hospital types, and a measure of the share of private sector income in total income. The empirical results revealed that the type of hospital made a difference; it was easier to recruit to teaching and Acute Specialist hospitals than to other hospital types. Private sector income proved insignificant but this might have been because it was distinguished only by region, as a finer geographical breakdown was not made available. However, the central result remained; when the gap was larger doctor vacancies were lower, doctors appeared to be attracted to high-cost areas.

The economic rationale for the payment of London allowance is that this payment is required to address recruitment and retention issues in London. The results of the studies by Elliott et al. (2007b) and Ma et al. (2007) undermine the case for paying a London allowance to doctors. The Review Body on Doctors' and Dentists' Remuneration (2007 p. ix) concluded:

> We continue to view London weighting as a labour market issue and as we have not received any evidence of problems of recruitment and retention in London, we see no reason to revise last year's recommendation to freeze London weighting.

In its 2006 report (para 2.26), the Review Body had concluded:

> There is no basis, on labour market grounds, for increasing the current level of payment and indeed, there is an argument for removing it completely. We recognise however that its immediate removal could create considerable problems in morale and motivation terms.

These results for doctors illustrate that there may be no need to set different rates of pay for different geographical areas. In the case of doctors, there were evidently features of the high cost, poor amenity areas which offset these disadvantages. But this may not always be the case. Where the net advantages differ between different areas and pay does not reflect these differences in advantages there will then be differences between areas in their ability to recruit and retain labour. This will be the case even where employees work in a national labour market. The areas between which pay is differentiated may not be finely described localities and they may not be labour markets. In the case of some occupations, a more meaningful distinction may be between urban areas and rural and remote areas. Scotland has long found it necessary to offer General Practitioners and nursing staff a Distant Island Allowance to attract them to practice in the remote islands.

When deciding how to, or indeed whether to, localise pay or to distinguish pay along some other geographical dimension a sound initial hypothesis is that the highest pay should be offered in the highest cost least attractive areas, but this is just the initial hypothesis. It is driven by a prior view of the disadvantages of some areas and further enquiry, as in the case of the doctors above, may reveal other compensating advantages. The appropriate geographical differentiation of pay for any occupation is therefore an empirical question. In the private sector, it will emerge from the operation of market forces, but in the public sector, it must be distinguished by administrators informed by robust empirical evidence.

The starting point for the empirical enquiry is evidence of difficulties in some areas of the country in their ability to recruit and retain labour. Where these difficulties are confined to just some areas of the country, it is a signal that the geographical distribution of pay needs rebalancing. When the difficulties are experienced in all areas, it is a signal that the general level of pay needs adjusting upwards. Contingent on confirmation that some greater geographical differentiation is required, the benefit of greater differentiation must be balanced against the costs of setting up and administering the system. Evidently, multi-site private sector employers judge that this can best be achieved within some broader framework agreement.

Refining the analysis

Finally, it is important to consider further the robustness of the empirical analysis reported above. The line of enquiry above assumes that the pattern of local pay differentials in the private sector (which is in effect used to benchmark public sector pay) reflects underlying differences in the cost of living and amenities of different localities. But if the net advantages of jobs in different areas are to be equalised, labour must be mobile and pay structures flexible. These appear strong assumptions and where they are not met, net advantages may remain unequal.

One indicator that these conditions may not be satisfied is differences in geographical unemployment rates, though these differences alone do not provide sufficient evidence of labour market disequilibrium. Natural rates of unemployment may differ between localities and where they do recorded unemployment rates will differ. Another possible distortion to the private labour market could be the dominance of the local market by the public sector. Reporting results from the 2005 Labour Force Survey Ma et al. (2007) reveal that the public sector accounted for 22.8 per cent of all employment in the average LAD but that this ranged from 7.0 per cent to 42.6 per cent. At the upper end, it is conceivable that such presence by the public sector might distort the private sector rates of pay in that locality.

Testing for the impact of both these effects on their earlier results Ma et al. (2007) reported that this did not change the central results for either doctors or nurses, though there was a small change in the size of the coefficients and a small reduction in significance.

Remaining issues

One further puzzle has emerged from discussion of the empirical evidence on SSWDs. If SSWDs accurately measure wage differences between otherwise identical employees working in different areas of the country, why are employers in parts of London prepared to pay a premium of nearly 60 per cent over employers in other parts of the United Kingdom? Why do employers congregate in these high-cost areas? Are they paying more for different, non-identical, higher quality labour and again are the SSWDs we have estimated comparing like with like?

Where services must be delivered locally, as are the services of bars, restaurants, hotels, retailers, transport, and some public services, the answer is clear. This is where the customers are located. But where the enterprise is providing services to a national and even international customer base it becomes less clear. Why do not enterprises move their business to lower costs areas? This question has recently been addressed by spatial economic theory. Recent advances in urban economics, and the development known as the new economic geography, point to the advantages of agglomeration and to the higher profit opportunities that arise in areas of high density of economic activity. Whether these arise from a combination of greater access to markets (both their own and neighbouring markets), the size of markets, and the degree of competition within markets or through increasing returns from the enhanced supply of non-traded producer services in denser areas is the focus of current research. Empirical evidence reveals that high-cost areas offer private sector firms enhanced profit opportunities and these result from the benefits of agglomeration not from employing non-identical employees. It is for this reason that many enterprises chose to locate in high-cost areas.[7]

Conclusions

In the private sector of the UK economy, the appropriate degree of spatial disaggregation will emerge from the operation of competitive labour market. Private sector firms are motivated to pay what is required to attract and retain the employees they require and a pattern will emerge from the profit-maximizing decisions of the myriad of firms that comprise the private sector. In the public sector, the pattern of pay is determined by the institutions of wage setting and for most groups it is different from that in the private sector. The starting point for determining whether there is a need to adjust the spatial pattern of pay in the public sector, whether to localise or move to some other spatial disaggregation of pay, is evidence of differences between areas of the country in their ability to recruit and retain labour. Where the net advantages of jobs in different areas of the country are not equalised there will be differences between areas in recruitment and retention. Distinguishing differences in the net advantages of jobs in different areas of the country and relating these to measures of recruitment and retention is the key to distinguishing the appropriate spatial disaggregation of pay. The appropriate geographical differentiation of pay for any occupation in the public sector is, therefore, an empirical question.

Notes

1. HM Treasury, Budget Statement, April 2003.
2. For a much earlier but more comprehensive review of theories of pay setting and of the empirical evidence on the determinants of pay setting in local markets from an era in which trade unions exerted a more powerful influence over private sector wage setting see Molho 1992.
3. There is some discussion as to the appropriate set of controls. The data set we use here, ASHE, contains no data on employees educational attainment which is known to be an important determinant of an employees' pay. The ASHE contains detailed information on the employees' occupation and this is used by researchers instead of educational controls. Blanchflower et al. (2005, 2.3.1) have argued that occupation dummies should not be used because they are close to being percentiles of the pay distribution so including them as controls can be like regressing a variable on itself. They have argued that when calculating SSWDs for the United Kingdom an alternative data set, the Labour Force Survey, should be employed. Other researchers have argued that education controls are a very blunt instrument for controlling for variations in employees' skills and occupational controls should be included as standardising variables (see Hirsch in Blanchflower and Bryson, 2007).

    Occupational dummies also control for many other important characteristics of jobs which determine pay. Factors such as the risk of an accident or injury at work and the nature of the working environment are not measured by any other variables included in either data set. Thus there are strong arguments for including occupational controls.
4. Periodically researchers have sought to map the underlying patterns of regional and local pay by identifying and adding up all the elements of pay that can differ between areas. This method is called the Specific Cost Approach and is reported in Elliott et al. (1996) and most recently in Crystal Blue (2007).
5. For a review of this theory and a survey of empirical work see Rosen (1986).
6. New Travel To Work Areas are intended to be available in the autumn of 2007. See '1991-based Travel-to-Work-Areas', Office for National Statistics and M. G. Coombes, London, Office for National Statistics, 1998.
7. See Fingleton (2003) and (2006) for a useful discussion of these issues.

References

Ball, A. and Fenwick, D. (2004) 'Relative Regional Consumer Price Levels in 2003', *Economic Trends*, 603, 44–53.

Blackaby, D. H. and Manning, D. N. (1999) 'Industry Characteristics and Inter-Area Pay Differences', *Scottish Journal of Political Economy*, 38, 2, 142–161.

Blackaby, D. H. and Murphy, P. D. (1995) 'Earnings, Unemployment and Britain's North-South Divide: Real or Imaginary?', *Oxford Bulletin of Economics and Statistics*, 57, 487–512.

Blanchflower, D. G. and Bryson, A. (2007) 'The Wage Impact of Trade Unions in the UK Public and Private Sectors', mimeo, www.dartmouth.edu/~blnchflr.

Blanchflower, D. G., Hern, R., and Oswald, A. (2005) *Area Cost Adjustment: A Review*, London: NERA.

Blanchflower, D. G., Oswald, A., Baker, B., and Sandbach, J. (1996) 'The Area Labour Cost Adjustment: Empirical Analysis and Evidence of a New Approach', Project C, Report to the Department of the Environment, *National Economic Research Associates*, London.

Brown, W., Marginson, P., and Walsh, J. (2003) 'The Management of Pay as the Influence of Collective Bargaining Diminishes' in Edwards, P. (ed.) *Industrial Relations*, 2nd ed., 189–213, Oxford: Blackwell.

Coombes, M. G., Green, A. E., and Owen, D. W. (1990) 'Substantive Issues in the Definition of "Localities": Evidence From Sub-Group Local Labour Market Areas in the West Midlands', *Regional Studies*, 22, 4, 303–318.

Crystal Blue Consulting (2007) *Review: Staff Market Forces Factor – Specific Cost Approach*, Report to Department of Health, London.

Cully, M., Woodland, S., O'Reilly, R., and Dix, G. (1999) *Britain at Work: As Depicted by the 1998 Workplace Employee Relations Survey*, London: Routledge.

Davies, R. and Owen, D. (2004) 'Options for the 2004 MFF: Final Report', *Warwick Institute for Employment Research*, October.

Elliott, R. F., Bell, D. N. F., Scott, A., Ma, A., and Roberts, E. (2007a) 'Geographically Differentiated Pay in the Labour Market for Nurses', *Journal of Health Economics*, 26, 190–212.

Elliott, R. F., Sutton, M., Ma, A., Skåtun, D., McConnachie, A., Morris, S., and Rice, N. (2007b) 'Distributing Public Funding: Taking Account of Differences in Local Labour Market Conditions', *Health Economics Research Unit*, Aberdeen: University of Aberdeen.

Elliott, R. F., McDonald, D., and MacIver, R. (1996) *Local Government Finance: Review of the Area Cost Adjustment*, Aberdeen, University of Aberdeen on behalf of the Department of the Environment.

Fingleton, B. (2003) 'Increasing Returns: Evidence from Local Wage Rates in Great Britain', *Oxford Economic Papers*, 55, 716–739.

Fingleton, B. (2006) 'The New Economic Geography Versus Urban Economics: An Evaluation Using Local Wage Rates in Great Britain', *Oxford Economic Papers*, 58, 501–530.

Grainger, H. and Crowther, M. (2007) *Trade Union Membership 2006*, London: Department of Trade and Industry.

Incomes Data Services (2002) 'Pay Differentiation Practice in UK Organisations'. *A Research Report for the Office of Manpower Economics*, London: Incomes Data Services.

Incomes Data Services (2006a) *Pay Report 965*, November.

Incomes Data Services (2006b) *Pay Report 962*, October.

Incomes Data Services (2007a) *Pay in the Public Services*, London: Incomes Data Services.

Incomes Data Services (2007b) *Pay Report 975*, April.

London Assembly (2002) *Report of the London Weighting Advisory Panel*, London: London Assembly, June.

Ma, A., Elliott, R., Sutton, M., Skåtun, D., McConnachie, A., Morris, S., and Rice, N. (2007) 'Spatial Wage Variation in the Public and Private Sectors and Its Impact on Public Sector Recruitment and Retention: The Case of the UK National Health Service', *Health Economics Research Unit*, Aberdeen: University of Aberdeen.

Ma, A., Roberts, E., Elliott, R. F., Bell, D. N. F., and Scott, A. (2006) 'Comparing the New Earnings Survey (NES) and the Labour Force Survey (LFS): An Analysis of the Differences between the Data Sets and their Implications for the Pattern of Geographical Pay in the UK', *Regional Studies*, 40, 6, 645–665.

Machin, S. (1997) 'The Decline of Labour Market Institutions and the Rise of Labour Market Inequality in Britain', *European Economic Review*, 41, 4, 647–657.

Machin, S. (1999) 'Pay Inequality in the 1970s, 1980s and 1990s' in Gregg, P., and Wadsworth, J. (eds) *The State of Working Britain*, Manchester: Manchester University Press.

Metcalf, D., Charlwood, A., and Hansen, S. (2001) 'Unions and the Sword of Justice', *National Institute Economic Review*, 176, April, 61–76.

Molho, I. (1992) 'Local Pay Determination', *Journal of Economic Surveys*, 6, 2, 155–194.

Morris, S., Elliott, R. F., Sutton, M., Ma, A., Skåtun, D., McConnachie, A., and Rice, N. (2007) 'Using the Labour Force Survey to Adjust for Higher Responsibility and Seasonal and Temporary Employment in the Review of the Market Forces Factor', Oxbridge, Brunel University, Mimeo.

Reilly, B. (1992) 'An Analysis of Local Labour Market Pay Differentials', *Regional Studies*, 26, 3, 257–264.

Review Body on Doctors' and Dentists' Remuneration (2002) *Thirty Fourth Report*, Cm 5340, London: The Stationery Office.

Review Body on Doctors' and Dentists' Remuneration (2005) *Thirty Fourth Report*, Cm 6463, London: The Stationery Office.

Review Body on Doctors' and Dentists' Remuneration (2006) *Thirty Fifth Report*, Cm 6733, London: The Stationery Office.

Review Body on Doctors' and Dentists' Remuneration (2007) *Thirty Sixth Report*, Cm 7025, London: The Stationery Office.

Rosen, S. (1986) 'The Theory of Equalising Differences' in Ashenfelter, O. and Layard, R. (eds) *Handbook of Labor Economics*, Vol. 1, Amsterdam: Elsevier, 641–692.

School Teachers' Review Body (2004) *Thirteenth Report, Part 2*, London: The Stationery Office.

School Teachers' Review Body (2005) *Fifteenth Report*, London: The Stationery Office.

Shah, A. and Walker, M. (1983) 'The Distribution of Regional Earnings in the UK', *Applied Economics*, 15, 507–519.

Smith, A. (1776) *An Inquiry into the Nature and Causes of the Wealth of Nations*, London: Methuen and Co. Ltd., Edwin Cannan (ed.) 1904. 5th ed. First published: 1776.

Wilson, R., Assefa, A., Briscoe, G., Elias, P., Green, A. E., McKnight, A., and Stilwell, J. (1996) *Labour Market Forces and NHS Provider Costs: Final Report,* Warwick: Institute for Employment Research.

Wilson, R., Davies, R., Green, A., Owen, D., and Elias, P. (2002) *Spatial Variations in Labour Costs: 2001 Review of the Market Forces Factor,* Department of Health and Institute for Employment Research, University of Warwick.

Wingfield, D., Fenwick, D. and Smith, K. (2005) 'Relative Regional Consumer Price Levels in 2004', *Economic Trends*, 615, February, 36–45.

6

Performance pay and collective bargaining: a complex relationship

Paul Marginson

The rise of performance pay systems

The rise of performance payments systems (PPSs) over recent years is widely presumed to entail negative consequences for the capacity of trade unions to regulate levels of, and increases in, pay through collective bargaining (Heery, 2000). Yet, outside of the public sector (Marsden, 2004a), remarkably little is known about the actual relationship between performance pay and collective bargaining – whether the former undermines, leaves in place, or prompts a reconfiguration of the latter. Much of the relevant literature (e.g., Hendry et al., 2000) ignores the role of unions, and therefore the implications for collective bargaining. This chapter addresses what is a significant gap.

The defining feature of PPSs is an explicit attempt to shift from time and seniority to performance-related criteria, whether focused on the individual employee, work group, establishment, and/or company as a whole. Four types of PPS are conventionally identified: bonuses, including piece-work and payments-by results (PBR), where there is a direct relationship between pay and employees' output; merit or performance-related pay based on management appraisal; profit-related pay schemes, which entitle employees to a share of the company's business success; and skills- or competency-based pay. Whereas the first three are 'output-based', the fourth is 'input-based' (Cox, 2005). In the case of the first three therefore, the proportion of employee earnings which is 'at risk' to variations in performance is increased. This is consistent with the central role accorded to reward management in the human resource management (HRM) literature, which emphasises both individualisation and explicit links to business performance (e.g., Lawler, 1990). The first type is long established, whereas, reflecting the rise of HRM, forms of the second based on performance review or appraisal along with the third and fourth types are phenomena that are more recent.

The recent growth of PPSs is an international phenomenon (van het Kaar and Grünell, 2001). In Britain, the panel data from the 2004 Workplace Employment Relations Survey (WERS) recorded an increase in the use of individual or group performance-related pay schemes from 20 per cent to 32 per cent of continuing workplaces between 1998 and 2004 (Kersley et al., 2006). And the proportion of workplaces in the economy's trading sector with profit-related pay, which had risen rapidly in the second half of the 1980s (Millward et al., 2000), remained constant at 40 per cent, despite the abolition in 2000 of favourable tax arrangements (Kersley et al., 2006). This coincided with a continued decline in the proportion of workplaces covered by collective bargaining over pay, which fell from 30 to 22 per cent over the same period, and from 17 to 11 per cent of workplaces in the private sector. In 2004, the proportion of employees in the workplaces concerned amounted to 39 per cent for the economy as a whole and 26 per cent in the private sector (Kersley et al., 2006). Even where collective bargaining remained in place, much of it appeared ritualistic and with limited impact on pay outcomes (Forth and Millward, 2002). At first sight, the growth of performance pay would seem to be related not only to the demise of collective bargaining, where it continues, but also to trade union weakness.

Of the various types of PPS, it is the rapid diffusion of performance-related pay based on management appraisal which has been seen as posing the sharpest challenge both to trade unions and to established conventions for collective pay bargaining (Heery, 2000). Indeed, one of the main managerial goals underpinning this type of PPS has been identified by Kessler and Purcell (1995) as the marginalisation of trade union involvement in pay setting. In contrast, the effects of profit-related pay on collective pay bargaining have been seen as more benign; Pendleton (1997) suggests that it could be complementary to, rather than corrosive of, existing arrangements since its premise is more to do with participation than incentivisation (see also Pendleton in chapter 12.) The implications of a growing emphasis on PPS for collective pay bargaining in the United Kingdom may therefore be less straightforward than seems at first sight, being open to differing possibilities.

Cross-national research to date has generated mixed results on whether there is convergence in the types of PPS being implemented (Brown and Heywood, 2002; Long and Shields, 2005). The interface with collective bargaining institutions has also remained largely unaddressed. The context elsewhere in western Europe is framed, as in the United Kingdom, not only by increased economic openness and competition, but also by varying forms of 'organised decentralisation' within different national industrial relations systems in which, unlike the United Kingdom, multi-employer collective bargaining over pay remains a cornerstone (Traxler et al., 2001). A cross-national, comparative focus can address the capacity of collective bargaining in different institutional and legal settings to regulate pay levels and increases in a context of sustained growth in PPSs.

The chapter starts by reviewing the management objectives associated with, and union responses to, different types of PPS. In considering the implications for union involvement, and for collective negotiations over pay, the second section argues that the relationship between PPSs and collective bargaining is open to a range of possibilities. The third section presents a comparison between banking and machinery equipment, drawing on evidence from UK companies which continue to recognise trade unions and focusing on the extent and ways in which PPS is subject to collective bargaining. The effects of the differing institutional arrangements for collective bargaining found amongst European countries are illustrated in the fourth section through a comparison of machinery and equipment in three countries: Austria, Norway, and the United Kingdom. The chapter concludes that the implications of PPSs for collective bargaining are shaped by the type of scheme involved, the level at which it operates, sectoral characteristics, and cross-country differences in the institutions underpinning collective bargaining.

Management objectives, trade union responses, and union involvement

Management objectives

The managerial objectives underpinning different types of PPS, and union responses to PPSs, will shape the implications for collective bargaining. Surveying the literature, five sets of possible management rationales can be identified. Arranged in an overlapping continuum from 'soft' to 'hard' objectives (Arrowsmith et al., 2007), these objectives include:

- *Stakeholder reward*: a demonstration of employees sharing in company success and a concern to maintain employee loyalty and identification with the organisation, and possibly motivation. Profit-related pay or bonus is the primary example (Hyman, 2000; Pendleton, 1997).
- *Performance management*: in which the PPS is designed to reinforce the communication of business goals and their operationalisation into team and individual objectives (Armstrong and Baron, 2005; Kessler and Purcell, 1995). Merit pay is the main example, linked as it is to line managers' appraisal of individual employee performance against agreed targets, goals and desired behaviours, and where the effect can be renegotiation of performance standards (Marsden, 2004a).
- *Productivity*: in which the PPS is designed to make labour both more productive and adaptable. Traditional PBR and contemporary individual, group, and

site bonus systems are the most common means to incentivise staff (Brown, 2002). Specific schemes can be used to support targeted business initiatives like sales drives; underpin teamwork and customer service; and to retain key staff. Input-based schemes, such as skills or competency pay, have similar objectives (Cox, 2005).

- *Cost-control*: flows from the recognition that labour costs are an important element in total costs (Kessler and Purcell, 1995). A shift from base to per-formance and non-consolidated pay can contain the level of costs and dampen overall increases in the paybill. Some bonuses are designed to be largely self-financing, whilst under profit-related pay costs, to some extent, fluctuate in line with returns.

- *Industrial relations*: performance pay, especially discretionary and individu-alised forms, can reduce union influence by narrowing the scope of collective bargaining over earnings (Kessler and Purcell, 1995). The weakening of trade unions might be a goal in itself, or a subsidiary goal to those indicated above, or indeed an effect rather than a purposeful objective.

Trade union responses

Whilst the implications of this last set of goals are clear for trade unions, other man-agerial goals can also entail challenges for unions. For example, the scope for the exercise of managerial discretion under appraisal-based performance pay raises issues of fair treatment and procedural justice (Kessler, 2001). Better targeting of expenditure on pay can place across-the-board settlements, and the principle of the 'common rule' which underpins them, in jeopardy (Marsden, 2004b). In gen-eral, Heery (2000) identifies five main reasons informing trade union scepticism over, and at times opposition to, PPSs. First, such schemes can represent a threat to the security and stability of members' earnings. Second, PPSs can possibly have perverse effects – for example, individual performance pay can demotivate some employees and undermine team work. Third, PPSs can widen differentials between individuals, between teams, and between segments of the workforce in different parts of the business, and also between male and female employees. Fourth, individual-based schemes in particular can be divisive, undermining the capacity of unions to develop collective organisation and goals amongst members. Fifth is the threat to the union's procedural role as the collective bargaining agent of employees, because greater discretion is granted to management over pay.

Because it threatens to combine all five of the above, individual performance or merit pay has been a particular focus for union hostility. The grounds for union antagonism are underlined by evidence that firms that have de-recognised unions have moved furthest in developing individual performance pay (Brown et al., 1998). Yet, despite opposition in principle, 'in many cases union policy towards payments systems of this kind are marked by ambivalence' (Heery, 2000: 66). So long as trade unions see an opportunity to jointly regulate schemes, they are likely to seek accommodations with management (Kessler, 1994).

In practice, faced with a growing emphasis on individual performance pay, unions have sought to influence the design, functioning, and outcomes of such schemes through processes of collective consultation and negotiation. In the public services, for example, collective agreements have established a framework for such schemes, albeit following significant industrial disputes in some instances and initial unilateral implementation by local management in others (Marsden, 2004a). The effect has been a formalisation of management practice which has limited the scope for the exercise of management discretion and made the operation of schemes more transparent.

In contrast, profit-related pay has attracted comparatively less union antagonism: a fear that it may expose a greater proportion of employee's earnings to risk being tempered by the realisation that it promises a return 'on top' of what might be secured through conventional collective bargaining. Indeed large unionised firms are more likely to have such schemes than their non-unionised counterparts (Pendleton, 1997). Where it has arisen, union opposition to profit-related pay has stemmed from the lack of opportunity to jointly regulate such schemes, which tend to be viewed by management as non-negotiable (Baddon et al., 1989).

For management, union involvement offers the potential advantages of 'voice', identifying employee concerns and resolving the numerous, well-documented practical problems which schemes can entail (Kessler, 2001), and 'legitimacy' in the process of implementing and operating schemes, including a 'guarantee' that management will not act opportunistically and subsequently renege on the terms of schemes (Heywood, 2007).

Much, therefore, depends on the type of PPS under consideration, and the context in which it is introduced and operated. Hence, although at first sight performance pay sits uneasily with established practices of collective bargaining over pay, the relationship between the two is open to a range of possibilities. Some types of PPS, introduced in certain contexts, may indeed have the effect of undermining collective bargaining. Yet in other contexts, the introduction of similar schemes may lead to a reconfiguration of collective bargaining, with for example negotiation occurring over the financial 'pot' available for pay increases and/or the framework, procedures, and distributional outcomes of a PPS. A third possibility is that PPSs may sit alongside, and leave unaffected, established collective pay bargaining arrangements. In short, the relationship between PPSs and collective bargaining is not pre-determined, and is shaped by a range of contingencies. These include the types of scheme involved, sectoral context in the shape of technologies and the nature of product and labour markets and the institutional arrangements which characterise different countries' collective bargaining systems. The findings presented in the next two sections highlight the saliency of these three contingencies.

A two-sector comparison

A study of banking and machinery and equipment in the United Kingdom, as undertaken by the author with colleagues (Marginson et al., 2007), involves a comparison between a manufacturing and a service sector which both have levels of union density and collective bargaining coverage above the median for the private sector. According to the 2003 Labour Force Survey (LFS) (the most recent available at this level of disaggregation), collective bargaining coverage was 43 per cent in banking and 30 per cent in machinery and equipment, against a private sector average of 22 per cent at that time. Given the focus of the study on the largest workforce group in machinery and equipment, there was also a contrast between white-collar employees in banking and blue-collar employees in machinery equipment. The distinction between blue-collar wage and white-collar salary systems remains a significant feature of UK payments systems, despite movement towards harmonised remuneration systems in some organisations (Druker, 2000).

In terms of markets, machinery and equipment are highly exposed to international competition, whereas the important retail segment of banking has remained more sheltered. Profit margins in machinery and equipment are under continuous pressure, whilst banking remains highly profitable. Even so, the deregulation of financial markets and arrival of new modes of delivery for banking services have wrought profound changes in the sector, including an intensification of competition within the domestic market (Storey et al., 1999).

These profound changes have triggered an overhaul of payments systems in banking to incentivise performance, rather than to reward long service and experience. The use of both merit (appraisal-based performance) pay and bonus has become increasingly common, and the sector is a pace-setter in terms of the diffusion of PPSs. According to a 2004 survey of 35 pay settlements in banking, 80 per cent of organisations used an all-merit approach to determine employee pay increases, compared to 68 per cent in 1997 (IRS, 2004). The use of bonuses is also widespread in banking: the New Earnings Survey (NES) indicates that 30 per cent of employees were in receipt of bonus payments in 2003. According to the Annual Survey of Earnings and Hours (ASHE), bonuses accounted for just over 10 per cent of banking employees' earnings in 2004. The 2004 WERS found that financial services had the highest incidence across all sectors of performance-related pay (which includes merit pay), utilised in 82 per cent of workplaces with ten or more employees, and profit-related bonus, found in 67 per cent (Kersley et al., 2006: 189–193).

In machinery and equipment, although there is little evidence of widespread diffusion of new forms of performance pay in recent years, there is a tradition of workplace bargaining over piece-work and PBR bonus systems which characterised engineering a quarter of a century ago (see, for example, Brown, 1973; Lerner et al., 1969). Indeed, the most striking recent development in pay for blue-collar workers in this, and other parts of manufacturing, has been the decline of traditional, output-based payments systems (Druker, 2000). As in banking, this reflects major changes in production systems and work organisation, entailing a growing emphasis on team-working, under which the costs involved in operating these traditional systems have come to outweigh the benefits (Freeman and Kleiner, 2005). Data from the LFS indicate that these forms of PPS have all but disappeared: in 2004, less than 1 per cent of employees in machinery and equipment were in receipt of piece-work and PBR bonus. More generally, the incidence of all forms of PPS in machinery and equipment has declined over recent years; the NES indicates that the proportion of manual employees in the sector covered by incentive pay (which includes all forms of performance pay except Inland Revenue-approved profit sharing schemes) fell from 26 per cent to 19 per cent between 1994 and 2003. The proportion of earnings accounted for by PPSs is modest, at just under 5 per cent according to ASHE. Findings from the 2004 WERS are not disaggregated within manufacturing, where one-quarter of workplaces reported using output-based schemes and 38 per cent reported having profit-related pay. There is, however, little recent evidence on the extent to which these schemes continue to be a focus for collective bargaining.

Reviewing findings from six company case studies in each of the two sectors (see Marginson et al., 2007), there are evident not only differences but also some similarities. An important difference concerns the profile of the PPSs[1] found in banking, where the cases were drawn from the important retail segment (which is widely unionised), as compared to machinery and equipment. Similarities are apparent in the management rationales underpinning the use of different types of PPS and in the extent to which different types of PPS are subject to collective consultation or negotiation. There is both difference and similarity in union responses and union involvement in the two sectors.

Profile of PPS

Performance pay loomed larger, and operated at more levels, in the payments systems of the banks than of the machinery and equipment companies. The six banks had schemes operating at various group, sub-unit, team and individual levels, which comprise both bonus payments and – with one exception – individual merit pay. Just one of the machinery and equipment companies operated schemes at more than one level; and the predominant type of PPS was company performance (profit-related) bonus. In machinery and equipment, individual performance pay was utilised at just one company, and even here, its operation was contingent on the payment of an inflation-matching, across-the-board increase. Consistent with broader trends, former piece-work systems in the two companies concerned had been negotiated out in recent years. Comparing the proportion of earnings for which bonus payments accounted, a greater proportion of pay was 'at risk' in the banks than in the machinery and equipment companies where, with one exception, the amounts involved were modest.

There would seem to be a greater preference for simplicity in machinery and equipment than in banking, in both the design and scope of a PPS: first, in eschewing appraisal-based merit schemes and preferring – usually – one type of bonus; and second in terms of standardisation, with schemes built around relatively aggregate and 'objective' criteria, and inclusive of the non-managerial workforce. The schemes in machinery and equipment also tended to be more recent, or more recently revised, than in banking. This may reflect a greater degree of environmental uncertainty, evidenced by more instances of financial difficulty and/or changes of ownership or management.

Managerial rationales

There were similarities between the two sectors in the managerial objectives attached to different types of PPS. The provision of incentives was not managers' main goal in respect of company performance bonuses and merit pay, but it was a key goal for localised performance bonuses in both sectors. Cost-control objectives were identified in respect of various schemes in the banks, and company performance bonuses in both sectors. Soft development goals were in evidence concerning merit pay, but had been increasingly overlaid by 'harder' performance management goals. The importance of company performance bonuses in communicating business and corporate objectives was underlined by managers in both sectors; merit pay systems in the banks were also seen as enabling management to drive home business messages. The stakeholder reward goal was prominent in the rationales advanced in both sectors for company performance bonuses. Hard, union exclusion goals were not, however, immediately apparent in any of the companies.

Union responses

Consistent with other studies (Heery, 2000) there was ample evidence of union dislike of the principles and premises of individual merit pay in both sectors. The crucial difference was that despite the rhetoric of conference resolutions calling for standardised pay settlements, the finance sector unions had had to accommodate to the practical realities of the introduction and operation of such schemes. Over time, they had been able to progressively secure influence over the procedural apparatus and substantive outcomes of schemes (see below). Antagonism towards merit pay found in most, but not all, of the machinery and equipment companies was also reflected in the marked preference for a PPS based on 'objective' rather than 'subjective' criteria amongst union representatives in the sector.

Yet, the findings also demonstrate that trade unions are not necessarily opposed to PPSs. Insofar as schemes offer additional earnings opportunities for members, provide the opportunity to engage more closely with members (e.g., in securing procedural justice under merit pay schemes in banking), or hold the promise of improving site performance and thereby site viability and employment security (in machinery and equipment), unions could see advantages flowing from PPSs.

A shared priority for union negotiators in both sectors was to maximise increases in basic pay. Where there were merit pay arrangements, this translated into pressure to ensure that the ratings accorded to the great majority of staff who were deemed average performers or above were translated into pay increases which at least matched the cost of living. In the case of bonuses, most of the schemes were viewed by union representatives, as well as managers, as having been introduced 'on top of' basic pay. It was only in the two cases (one in each sector) where the scale of the bonus was such that it was seen by the union as potentially or actually threatening the magnitude of any increase in basic pay that union concerns crystallised.

Consultation and negotiation

Union involvement in regulating PPSs through consultation and negotiation varied markedly according to the type of PPS. Key dimensions of the banks' merit pay schemes, including the size of the overall pay pot and its distribution between rating bands, were the focus of negotiation. And there was a tacit understanding between management and union that the outcome would deliver increases which would at least match inflation for the great majority of the workforce. The effect was that amongst the banks this form of performance pay had become pretty standardised. In addition, the mechanisms and functioning of merit pay schemes were the subject of extensive consultation with the finance unions.

In general, bonus payments were less frequently the focus of negotiation or even consultation. Insofar as there was negotiation over bonus schemes, it occurred over those that were more local in nature. This was the case for the team and individual bonuses which accounted for a significant proportion of earnings for certain staff in two of the banks and for the factory productivity bonus at one of the machinery and equipment companies. The payments involved in the three cases represented a significant proportion of earnings, helping to explain why the union was able to bring them within the ambit of collective bargaining.

Elsewhere, bonus schemes were not the subject of negotiations. Amongst the banks, management provided information about company bonus schemes and consulted over aspects of these. In machinery and equipment, consultation over aspects of schemes – and union influence in shaping a few of their parameters – was evident for those company performance bonuses which were site-specific. Consultation over supra-site performance bonuses, relating to group and divisional performance, was, however, conspicuous by its absence. In general, the discretionary nature of company performance bonuses was underlined by managers in both sectors. So too was the unitarist nature of the discourse which underpinned them. This was reflected, for example, in statements by managers at two of the machinery and equipment companies: respectively, 'employees should share in the success of the company' and 'all staff contribute to [company] performance'. Their effect was to establish a management-determined element of pay that was largely beyond the scope of collective bargaining. It was, then, in respect of this type of PPS that an indication of union exclusion might be detected. This was most apparent where, in the context of tight margins, tensions between management and union over the respective emphasis to be given to increasing basic pay and funding (company performance) bonus spilled over into industrial conflict, as occurred at one of the machinery and equipment companies (see also Cox, 2005).

Explaining the differences

The differences between the two sectors, particularly in terms of the significance of performance pay for earnings and the nature and multiplicity of the schemes adopted, can be explained in various ways. Firms in machinery and equipment operate in more internationalised markets, which contribute to lower margins and profits than in the banks. This means that efforts to meet employee concerns over real basic pay leaves less to play with over forms of performance pay such as bonuses. In contrast, banks have been better placed to use bonuses and profit-related schemes to drive their culture-change initiatives and to incentivise and reward staff without adding to fixed costs. The growth of these non-consolidated forms of PPS has also helped contain the overall pay pot. At the same time, increases in consolidated appraisal-based pay have been held down, leaving less scope for dispersion in merit pay schemes. In turn, low dispersion enables employers to accommodate trade union concerns over individualisation whilst maintaining the performance-management systems underpinning appraisal-based schemes intact.

There are relevant differences at workplace level, too. Bank branches, for example, are customer-facing service operations, where individual employees can influence levels of sales. In machinery and equipment, work is more highly integrated and collective; a growing emphasis on team-working is reflected in a shift away from individual incentivisation. This means there is more scope and rationale for localised and individualised incentive and reward schemes in the banks.

Differences between shopfloor wage systems and white-collar salary systems are salient too. The principle of the 'rate for the job' has always been more firmly rooted in machinery and equipment than in banking, along with higher levels of union organisation and traditions of workplace bargaining over pay. Management in machinery and equipment may be more reluctant to invoke the challenge to this collective principle which individual merit pay represents, as well as seeing less need to do so, than is the case in banking.

Overall, although unions can block management proposals to introduce PPSs, as at one of the machinery and equipment companies, their more general impact, if any, is in moderating schemes through negotiation and consultation. In both sectors, unions have largely managed to resist the individualisation of pay outcomes, and the introduction of performance pay has not undermined collective bargaining in the sense of its core focus on delivering inflation-based increases to basic pay. Yet the proportion of employee earnings that is determined without collective bargaining has grown. In terms, then, of the implications of PPSs for collective bargaining, the findings confirm that the relationship between the two is indeed open to a spectrum of possibilities. They also demonstrate that these 'variable' implications are shaped by the nature of PPSs, the level at which they operate, and by sectoral characteristics. These influences are returned to in the conclusion.

Developments in three countries compared

Findings from parallel studies undertaken in two other countries, Austria and Norway,[2] enable the impact of differing institutional arrangements for collective bargaining on the relationship between PPSs and collective pay bargaining to be assessed. This is done by reviewing findings from a comparative analysis of the sector-level investigations and company cases studies, six in each country, in machinery and equipment which the author jointly undertook with colleagues from the Austrian and Norwegian research teams (see Nergaard et al., 2007).[3] Between them, the countries represent three main variants of the collective bargaining systems found amongst European countries. Specifically, they involve differing configurations of two main features: (1) multi- or single-employer bargaining; and (2) single or dual channel employee representation.

Austria represents the pattern found in the Germanic-Dutch countries, with multi-employer bargaining and dual channel representation. Bargaining at local (enterprise) level, which falls within the competence of works councils, is governed by formal provisions exhaustively specifying its scope. These derive from both sector collective agreements and labour law. However, the dual channel system makes it difficult to synchronise bargaining between levels, because of coordination problems between trade unions and works councils. Collective bargaining coverage is almost universal (98 per cent).

Norway represents the Nordic pattern, with multi-employer bargaining, single channel representation, and formal provisions in the central agreement which lay out general principles governing the scope and limits of local (enterprise) levels. Synchronisation between levels is facilitated by the co-ordination capacity of unions. Collective bargaining coverage is high (70 per cent). The United Kingdom represents the Anglo-Irish pattern of single-employer bargaining and single channel representation (now also characteristic of several central east European countries). Collective bargaining coverage is comparatively low (35 per cent).

These differing configurations might be expected to influence the nature and collective regulation of PPSs. Thus, comparing single- with multi-employer bargaining, lower collective bargaining coverage under the former exposes companies recognising trade unions to competition from those where employers are able to design and implement payments systems unilaterally. Insofar as these entail performance pay, PPSs in firms with collective bargaining may be more employer-driven and performance pay may have greater quantitative significance in earnings under single-, than under multi-employer bargaining. The absence of a sector-level framework, which could be extended to apply to PPSs, may also result in greater variation in company-level schemes under single-employer bargaining.

Comparing dual channel representation systems with single channel representation systems, under the former unions have less possibility of influencing company-level pay systems through informal means such as policy guidelines. Hence, they may be more intent on using sector agreements to define the scope of PPS arrangements to apply at company level. In turn, this may result in more limited development of PPSs than under single channel arrangements and employers may be more tempted unilaterally to introduce a PPS at company level under dual channel arrangements. Under single channel arrangements unions at sectoral level may afford more leeway to company-level union organisations precisely because there is the possibility of exercising informal influence on local union responses to PPSs.

Comparing the implications of multi- as compared to single-employer bargaining, PPSs in machinery and equipment in the United Kingdom were – as anticipated – noticeably more employer-driven than in Austria and, especially, Norway. The PPSs were rarely integrated into collective bargaining in the United Kingdom, but frequently this was the case in company-level negotiations in Norway. In Austria, the sector level agreement recently provided for a new PPS to be implemented by 2010; at company level, works councils used their codetermination rights to protect or negotiate out existing PBR-type schemes. But once account was taken of different types of PPS, an alternative interpretation can be offered. Individual merit pay, which was the focus of negotiation in several of the Norwegian companies, was hardly found in either the Austrian or UK companies. Conversely, the predominant type of PPS amongst the UK companies – company performance bonus – was not the subject of negotiation in those cases where it occurred in Austria and Norway. This suggests the possibility that single-employer bargaining encourages different types of PPS to those promoted under multi-employer bargaining.

The two further expectations were, however, not confirmed: the diversity of PPSs in machinery and equipment in the United Kingdom was no greater than in Austria or Norway; and the quantitative significance of PPSs in the same sector in the United Kingdom was, on average, no greater than in the other two countries. The first finding points to the operation of processes of sectoral isomorphism, with employers being influenced by practice in other, leading, companies. Surprisingly, although machinery and equipment companies are competing in highly internationalised markets, these isomorphic processes seemed not to reach across borders. The exception was in two multinational companies whose operations were studied in two countries (the United Kingdom and Austria or Norway), where similar schemes had been implemented in both the countries concerned in each case. The second finding might stem from the priority which employers in all three countries place on meeting employees' basic pay expectations. Given tight margins, noted earlier for the UK cases but which equally prevailed in Austria and Norway, the sums available for PPSs are constrained, irrespective of bargaining arrangements.

Comparing the effect of single or dual channel representation arrangements across the two multi-employer bargaining countries, the expectations outlined above were in large part confirmed. Unions in Austria, where the sector agreement covering machinery and equipment had, as mentioned above, provided for a new PPS, have sought to establish parameters for the development of such PPSs at company level. In Norway, the central agreement permits a range of PPSs so long as their implementation is consistent with certain general criteria. Unions in Norway are also more engaged with company-level PPSs in machinery and equipment, through processes of information and consultation, as well as negotiation, than their works council counterparts in Austria. The latter tend to be involved only insofar as they have codetermination rights (which apply to some types of PPS, including piece-work and individual performance pay, but not to others). In this respect, the situation in the United Kingdom is more similar to that in Norway. Furthermore, reflecting the more constrained scope for PPS specified under the Austrian sector than the Norwegian central agreement, the unilateral introduction of employer-determined PPSs was – as anticipated – more evident in the former than in the latter.

The findings underline the impact for the relationship between collective bargaining and PPSs of variations in two key dimensions of the institutional arrangements underpinning collective bargaining in different parts of Europe.

Implications and conclusions

The spread of new forms of performance pay has variable implications for collective bargaining; implications which are shaped by the type of PPS, the level at which they operate, sector and the institutions underpinning collective bargaining in different countries. Variously: collective bargaining can embrace PPSs alongside established conventions for negotiating increases in basic pay; collective bargaining can be reconfigured in the face of the challenges posed by particular forms of PPS for trade unions and their members; and management can successfully place some PPSs beyond the scope of collective bargaining, thereby loosening unions' purchase on overall earnings.

Are PPSs a threat to unions?

Expectations in the literature, that individual merit pay potentially represents the most significant threat to traditional collective bargaining over wages (Heery, 2000;

Kessler and Purcell, 1995) and that recent forms of bonus, particularly those which are profit-related, might be more benign in their effects (Pendleton, 1997), are not straightforwardly confirmed by the findings above. Where appraisal-based pay is widespread, as in UK banking, unions have proven able to redraw the lines of collective negotiation around the size of the available pay pot and its distribution. Combined with their ability to secure greater transparency and consistency in the functioning of schemes, unions in banking have obtained a degree of standardisation of outcomes.

In contrast, bonuses are less likely to be subject to collective negotiation. In part, this is because management view them as a discretionary business tool; they want the flexibility to be able to vary bonus criteria and outcomes to reward or incentivise as appropriate. In part also, unions are wary of becoming formally embroiled in the negotiation of bonuses (unless they become a significant component of earnings), for two reasons. First, the priority is achieving consolidated increases to basic pay, often in difficult circumstances given the wider competitive environment faced by firms. Bonuses may be welcomed as additional earnings, provided they do not subvert this priority. Second, bonuses, by their very nature, involve variable sums; anything beyond a reactive mode to members' concerns might condemn unions to the criticism normally reserved for management when bonus earnings fall.

Nonetheless, there is a clear distinction between local sales- or productivity-based bonuses, and those which are linked to company performance. The former are markedly more likely to be subject to union negotiation or, at least, extensive consultation. The impact of these local schemes on weekly or monthly earnings can be substantial; also, in contrast to profit-related arrangements, there is a mechanistic link between workload and reward outcomes. Whether individual or collective, local productivity bonuses are at the frontier of the wage-effort bargain. It was such considerations which led unions to seek to regulate piece-work and PBR schemes through the workplace negotiations which characterised an earlier era (Brown, 1973).

The prevalence of profit-related, company performance bonuses in Britain, despite the withdrawal of fiscal incentives in 2001, is perhaps unexpected. Although these may appear complementary to established arrangements for collective pay bargaining, the findings above suggest that their effects might actually be insidious for unions. They help underpin a unitarist management discourse, based on the identification of common interests around business objectives, and raise the possibility that 'pain' might have to be shared, in the shape of restructuring and work intensification, as well as the fruits of business success.

Differences between sectors in the range of PPS utilised, their quantitative significance for earnings and the implications for collective bargaining were demonstrated in the comparison between banking and machinery and equipment in the United Kingdom. Sector-specific reasons for these differences were identified in the third section above. Yet there was also less diversity in PPS practice within both sectors than might have been anticipated, given the company-centric nature of the institutions which regulate the employment relationship in Britain. This suggests that agency influences, such as choice of PPS and of the amount of earnings to be placed at risk, operate within sectoral boundaries which are shaped by technologies, product- and labour-market environments, and traditions (and relative strength) of union organisation (Arrowsmith and Sisson, 1999).

The cross-national dimension

Turning to the cross-national dimension, the chapter finds a marked difference between the capacities of collective bargaining to regulate PPSs between countries with single- and multi-employer bargaining systems. This is fundamentally because the scope which exists for competition between different regimes for pay setting – collectively bargained, unilaterally determined by management or, less frequently, individually negotiated with employees – which is ever present under single-employer bargaining arrangements, such as Britain's, is effectively absent under multi-employer bargaining arrangements[4] (Traxler, 2003). In the context of PPSs, developments in unionised environments under single-employer bargaining are prone to be driven by those in non-unionised firms. This is altogether less likely under multi-employer bargaining. The distinction between multi- and single-employer bargaining is, however, not the only relevant one from a European, cross-country perspective.

The findings from the previous section also confirm that in countries with multi-employer bargaining the forms which 'organised decentralisation' (Traxler et al., 2001) takes exercise an important bearing on the continued capacity of employers' organisations and, more particularly, trade unions to influence pay and other developments at company level (Marginson and Sisson, 2004). In particular, the relevance of the distinction between single and dual channel representative arrangements for the capacity of collective bargaining to regulate PPSs has been demonstrated (see also Ilsøe et al., 2007). Extending the canvass to Mediterranean countries, such as Spain, where unions have an organisational presence and status within companies, but where there are weaker formal provisions governing the relationship between collective negotiations at sector and company levels, a further scenario becomes apparent (Traxler et al., 2007). Trade unions lack the capacity of their Nordic counterparts to synchronise across levels and unilateral management initiatives introducing new forms of PPSs are more widespread. Confirming a central tenet of industrial relations analysis, institutions really do matter.

Acknowledgements

The chapter derives from joint work with Jim Arrowsmith on ESRC funded project (RES 000–23–0453). Molly Gray made an important contribution to the project fieldwork. The comparative analysis has benefited from discussions at a series of workshops with colleagues based at the University of Vienna, Fafo (Oslo) and the Autonomous University, Barcelona / University of Barcelona undertaking parallel projects in Austria, Norway and Spain, respectively.

Notes

1. Input-based forms of performance pay, such as skills- and competency-based pay, were not included within the scope of the study.
2. The Austrian and Norwegian teams were based at the University of Vienna, led by Franz Traxler, and the FAFO research institute in Oslo, led by Jon Erik Dølvik. A further parallel study is being undertaken in Spain, by a team jointly based at the Autonomous University of Barcelona and the University of Barcelona, but the company case studies are yet to be completed at the time of writing.
3. Comparative findings on banking are presented in Arrowsmith et al. (2007) and Traxler et al. (2007).
4. This is so long as the multi-employer agreements concluded have high levels of coverage of both firms and the workforce.

References

Armstrong, M. and Baron, A. (2005) *Managing Performance: Performance Management in Action,* London: CIPD.

Arrowsmith, J., Bechter, B., Nicolaisen, H., and Nonell, R. (2007) 'The Management of Variable Pay in Banking', Paper to the 8th European IIRA Congress, Manchester, 3rd–6th September.

Arrowsmith, J. and Sisson, K. (1999) 'Pay and Working Time: Towards Organisation-Based Systems?', *British Journal of Industrial Relations,* 37, 1, 51–75.

Baddon, L., Hunter, L., Hyman, J., Leopold, J., and Ramsay, H. (1989) *People's Capitalism?* London: Routledge.

Brown, D. (2002) 'Bonus and Variable Pay: Lessons from the UK', *Compensation and Benefits Review,* 34, 6, 24–30.

Brown, M. and Heywood, J. (eds) (2002) *Paying for Performance: An International Comparison,* Armonk, NY: M.E.Sharpe.

Brown, W. (1973) *Piecework Bargaining,* London: Heinemann.

Brown, W., Deakin, S., Hudson, M., Pratten, C., and Ryan, P. (1998) *The Individualisation of Employment Contracts in Britain,* Employment Relations Research Series No. 4, London: DTI.

Cox, A. (2005) 'The Outcomes of Variable Payments Systems', *International Journal of Human Resource Management,* 16, 8, 1475–1497.

Druker, J. (2000) 'Wages Systems' in Druker, J. and White, G. (eds) *Reward Management,* London: Routledge.

Forth, J. and Millward, N. (2002) 'Pay Settlements in Britain', NIESR Discussion Paper 173, London: National Institute for Economic and Social Research.

Freeman, R. and Kleiner, M. (2005) 'The Last American Shoe Manufacturers', *Industrial Relations*, 44, 2, 307–330.

Heery, E. (2000) 'Trade Unions and the Management of Reward' in Druker, J. and White, G. (eds) *Reward Management*, London: Routledge.

Hendry, C., Woodwards, S., Bradly, P., and Perkins, S. (2000) 'Performance and Reward: Cleaning Out the Stables', *Human Resource Management Journal*, 10, 3, 46–62.

Heywood, J. (2007) 'A Comparative View of Unions, Involvement and Productivity', Miegunyah Public Lecture, University of Melbourne, August.

Hyman, J. (2000) 'Financial Participation Schemes' in Druker, J. and White, G. (eds) *Reward Management*, London: Routledge.

Ilsøe, A., Madsen, J. S., and Due, J. (2007) 'Impacts of Decentralisation: Erosion or Renewal?', *Industrielle Beziehungen*, 14, 3, 201–222.

IRS (2004) 'Pay in Finance Banking on Brighter Prospects', *Irs Employment Review* 804, 23 July, 32–35.

Kersley, B., Alpin, C., Forth, J., Bryson, A., Bewley, H., Dix, G., and Oxenbridge, S. (2006) *Inside the Workplace*, London: Routledge.

Kessler, I. (1994) 'Performance Related Pay: Contrasting Approaches', *Industrial Relations Journal*, 25, 2, 122–135.

Kessler, I. (2001) 'Reward System Choices' in Storey, J. (ed.) *Human Resource Management: A Critical Text*, 2nd ed., London: Thomson.

Kessler, I. and Purcell, J. (1995) 'Individualism and Collectivism in Theory and Practice: Management Style and the Design of Pay Systems' in Edwards, P. (ed.) *Industrial Relations*, Oxford: Blackwell.

Lawler, E. (1990) *Strategic Pay: Aligning Organisational Strategies and Pay Systems*, San Francisco: Jossey Bass.

Lerner, S., Cable, J., and Gupta, S. (eds) (1969) *Workplace Wage Determination*, Oxford: Pergamon.

Long, R. and Shields, J. (2005) 'Performance Pay in Canadian and Australian Firms', *International Journal of Human Resource Management*, 16, 10, 1783–1811.

Marginson, P., Arrowsmith, J., and Gray, M. (2007) 'Undermining or Reframing Collective Bargaining? Variable Pay in Two Sectors Compared', Paper to the 2007 Pay and Reward Conference, Manchester, 29th March.

Marginson, P. and Sisson, K. (2004) *European Integration and Industrial Relations*, Basingstoke: Palgrave.

Marsden, D. (2004a) 'The Role of Performance-Related Pay in Renegotiating the "Effort Bargain"', *Industrial and Labor Relations Review*, 57, 3, 350–370.

Marsden, D. (2004b) 'Unions and Procedural Justice: An Alternative to the Common Rule', *Cep Discussion Paper CEPDP0613*, London: Centre for Economic Performance, LSE.

Millward, N., Bryson, A., and Forth, J. (2000) *All Change at Work?* London: Routledge.

Nergaard, K., Dølvik, J., Marginson, P., Bechter, B., and Arasanz Díaz, J. (2007) 'Engaging with Variable Pay', Paper to the 8th European IIRA Congress, Manchester, 3rd–6th September.

Pendleton, A. (1997) 'Characteristics of Workplaces with Financial Participation: Evidence from the Workplace Industrial Relations Survey', *Industrial Relations Journal*, 28, 2, 103–119.

Storey, J., Wilkinson, A., Cressey, P., and Morris, T. (1999) 'Employment Relations in UK Banking' in Regini, M., Kitay, J., and Baethge, M. (eds) *From Tellers to Sellers: Changing Employment Relations in Banks*, Cambridge: MIT Press.

Traxler, F. (2003) 'Bargaining, State Regulation and the Trajectories of Industrial Relations', *European Journal of Industrial Relations*, 9, 2, 141–161.

Traxler, F., Arrowsmith, J., Molins, J., and Nergaard, K. (2007) 'Organised Decentralisation: The Backbone of Multi-Level Bargaining?', Paper to the 8th European IIRA Congress, Manchester, 3rd–6th September.

Traxler, F., Blaschke, S., and Kittel, B. (2001) *National Labour Relations in Internationalised Markets*, Oxford: OUP.

van het Kaar, R. and Grünell, M. (2001) 'Variable Pay in Europe', Dublin: EIRO. http://www.eurofound.europa.eu/eiro/2001/04/study/tn0104201s.html

7

Regulating pay: the UK's national minimum wage

James Arrowsmith

In the neoclassical mythology of free markets, pay is, or should be, the product of the forces of supply and demand. Individuals and their employers agree to a rate and form of remuneration in the context of a wider 'labour market' governed by the relationship between the supply of labour and its derived demand. The process will also be influenced by micro-level differences in human capital and the marginal productivity of labour. In this impersonal, self-regulating account of pay-setting, pay is variable both at once and over time between sectors, and organisations within sectors, according to organisational performance, and within organisations according to individual (or team) performance. If it is not, then markets are not operating efficiently, and adverse consequences are predicted in terms of efficiency and unemployment.

In reality, there are two main types of deviation from perfect markets, and both involve forms of regulation. 'Market failure' largely results from practical impediments to the operation of markets, such as information and mobility constraints and the transaction costs of monitoring. Larger firms might therefore utilise not just markets, but hierarchies, to internalise the regulation of pay (Williamson, 1975). This can involve career ladders and devices such as above market-clearing 'efficiency wages'[1] to retain, develop, and motivate employees, particularly skilled workers, within 'internal labour markets' (Doeringer and Piore, 1971). Though employers may desire variable forms of pay to incentivise discretionary effort – what Flanders (1970, pp. 72–73) termed the 'managerial function' of pay, as against the 'market function' of recruitment and retention – pay variation is likely to be bounded in practice by the priority of risk-averse workers with real earnings, as well as social equity concerns (Wells, 1985). The development and implementation of company strategies over pay can thus be a complex and difficult balancing act, as Chapters 3 and 5 in this volume attest.

The second form of deviation results from 'market interference'. This comes mainly from trade unions, which in orthodox economic theory organise labour to assert monopoly power for the purpose of rent-sharing,[2] or from the state in the form of employment law. Again, in principle, neither necessarily serves to disadvantage employers. 'Collective bargaining' might form part of sophisticated employers' strategies of internal pay management. Minimum wages and other forms of employment regulation might generally be well received as placing a floor under 'unfair' competition. Yet employers rarely embrace trade unions voluntarily nor, where they are present, actively seek to involve them as stakeholders (Lucio and Stuart, 2005; Storey, 1992). Private-sector collective bargaining is in decline and, where it remains, its impact on pay outcomes has diminished in importance (Forth and Millward, 2000). Equally, employers tend to be hostile to labour law on the grounds of bureaucracy and cost (Dickens and Hall, 2003, pp. 149–50; Pollert, 2007, pp. 118, 130–311). The role of collective bargaining in the regulation of pay is addressed in Chapters 4 and 7. This chapter focuses on the most explicit and controversial form of state regulation of pay, statutory minimum wages. In particular, it examines the objectives, operation and effects of the UK National Minimum Wage (NMW), which was introduced in 1999 and is the first national pay floor in UK history. Its relevance was enhanced by the reduction in significance of collective bargaining over pay and the expansion of the private service sector, in which much low pay is concentrated. Furthermore, though introduced at a cautiously low rate, the level of the NMW soon accelerated (by 49 per cent between its effective date of April 1999 and the October 2006 uprating) to purchase a significant 'bite' in many sectors.

The NMW thus represents a very useful experiment to test competing expectations of what a minimum wage can do. One of the justifications made for a NMW was that it would help rectify the real 'market failure' of unequal bargaining power between employers and vulnerable employees, which resulted in exploitative rates of pay. The government also advanced efficiency as well as fairness claims for the NMW, arguing that it would increase the supply and stability of labour, prompt more-productive working practices, and reduce 'unfair' competition. In contrast, employers feared that any significant increases in labour costs arising from the NMW would lead to reduced profitability, investment and job cuts, especially in competitive, labour-intensive sectors. Nearly a decade on, there is plenty of research to examine what actually happened.

Next the chapter examines the operation, evolution and enforcement of the NMW. The following section reviews the evidence concerning the NMW's economic impact, and the implications this has for theory. Finally some conclusions are drawn: first, I argue that the NMW remains an important symbol of the legitimacy of market interference, though the case is more proven on grounds of fairness than efficiency. Second, its most significant current challenge is consolidation and enforcement given relatively steep increases in the rates and changes in the composition of the labour market. Third, the experience of the NMW raises important theoretical questions. In principle, minimum wages are a key test of the functioning of a 'competitive' market, as low-wage work tends to be governed by few institutional constraints. Yet analysis of the impact of the NMW provides strong evidence that 'the competitive model may not be a complete description of the low-paid labour market' (Metcalf, 2004, p. C86). This is not just because of practical imperfections in the operation of 'free markets' but because, even in the low-pay sectors, notions of fairness infuse and affect the operation of supply and demand. Markets for labour are, in reality, social rather than merely economic constructs (Rubery, 1997).

Background

The precursors of the NMW

Governmental regulation of pay in Britain can be traced to Tudor times. Concerns about price inflation led to various local attempts to stipulate wage maxima in the sixteenth century, culminating in the Statute of Artificers 1563 (Woodward, 1980). This permitted local Justices of the Peace 'to limit, rate, and appoint the wages ... of artificers, handicraftsmen, husbandmen, or any other labourer, servant, or workman' while 'respecting the plenty or scarcity of the time'. However, by the end of the eighteenth century, the effect of agrarian enclosures shifted the priority to the amelioration of poverty. The most notable intervention here was the so-called 'Speenhamland' system of poor relief. This was a means-tested sliding scale of wage supplements introduced by local magistrates in response to rising food prices. It was not a nationwide system and was used only temporarily, particularly in the south of England and in times of unrest. The 1834 Poor Law Amendment Act ended the practice because it subsidised poverty pay and encouraged indolence. Workers would henceforth have to turn themselves over to the workhouse to qualify for relief.

With industrialisation, arguments for fairness and efficiency were added to alleviation of the worst instances of poverty to make a case for minimum pay regulation. A Resolution of the House of Commons in 1891 required all government contractors to 'pay rates of wages and observe hours of labour' no less favourable than those commonly recognised or prevailing generally. This was renewed by Parliament and became known as the Fair Wages Resolution.

The next significant development came in 1909 with the Trade Boards Act, which set up essentially bipartite boards with the power to fix minimum wages in four low-paying, unorganised manufacturing sectors. The Act was introduced under a Liberal government by Winston Churchill as President of the Board of Trade, who was influenced by reports of the evils of 'sweated labour' and the experience of similar initiatives in Australia and New Zealand. In Parliament, Churchill famously made the case for regulation in the following terms (Callaghan and Jones, 1993, p. 20):

> It is a serious national evil that any class of His Majesty's subjects should receive less than a living wage in return for their utmost exertions. It was formerly supposed that the working of the laws of supply and demand would naturally regulate or eliminate that evil ... But where you have ... no organisation, no parity of bargaining, the good employer is undercut by the bad and the bad employer is undercut by the worst ... We believe that decent conditions make for industrial efficiency and increase rather than decrease competitive power.

The boards were re-named Wages Councils (or Wages Board in agriculture) in 1945 when the system underwent major expansion to embrace a range of service, as well as other manufacturing, sectors. However, their impact was mixed in the full-employment years of the long boom. After 1979, they represented an affront to the Conservative government's free-market ideology.

In the 1980s, official policy was based on the idea that state regulation of private contracts should be minimized. It was also held that 'market rigidities' caused inefficiency and unemployment, as workers 'priced themselves out' of jobs. A range of measures were therefore introduced – restricting trade union rights, privatisation and 'contracting out', lowering welfare benefits, subsidising unemployed 'trainees' – to increase labour-market 'flexibility' and its correlate of low-paid work (Brosnan and Wilkinson, 1988). The Fair Wages Resolution was rescinded by the Thatcher administration in 1983 (along with a renunciation of the comparable ILO Convention number 94) and, following successive restrictions, all the wages councils except the agricultural boards were terminated in 1993 (Dickens et al., 1993; Rubery and Edwards, 2003).

The abolition of the wages councils left the United Kingdom unique amongst major developed nations in having no general system of minimum-wage protection. In 1997, when Labour was returned to power, 17 of the then 29 OECD member countries had a statutory minimum-wage system, with most of the others (e.g., Germany, Austria, Italy, and the Scandinavian countries) having national or sectoral minima applied via collective bargaining.

The origins of the NMW

The origins of the NMW lay in trade union and Labour party responses to the weakening and ultimate abolition of the wages councils, in a context of increased pay inequality and trade union decline. Traditionally, the union movement opposed state wage regulation on 'voluntarist' grounds. State intervention was seen as reducing incentives to unionise for the low paid, and risked compressing pay scales and awards for higher-skilled union members. Wages councils, however, were tolerated as they applied to sectors largely beyond trade union reach and because they bore an ostensible duty to promote collective bargaining.

By the mid-1980s, when the voluntarist settlement had completely unravelled, such arguments were no longer credible. Large parts of manufacturing as well as the growing service sectors were increasingly characterised by declining trade union membership and recognition, and low pay. The Trades Union Congress (TUC) endorsed the principle of a NMW in 1986, and it became part of Labour's election manifesto in 1992. That commitment amounted to a minimum wage of £3.40 per hour, based on a formula of half full-time male median hourly earnings. This met with considerable business hostility and political derision, and by the 1997 election, the Labour party proposed to postpone the details until after the election. The government would take advice from a new independent body which would consult extensively with business and industry and make recommendations taking account of the economic circumstances of the time. In the event, establishing this body, the Low Pay Commission (LPC) was one of the first acts of the Labour government, coming just two months after it achieved office.

There was predictable opposition to the prospect of a NMW from the Conservative party and representatives of small firms and employers in low-paying sectors. They argued that a minimum wage would raise costs for many employers, leading to reduced investment and job losses. Indeed, the NMW did represent a totemic break with the labour-market approach that the Conservatives had pursued throughout their previous 18 years in office. In contrast, Labour's view was that the state was entitled to regulate pay, not just on ameliorative grounds; such 'interference' was good for business too. Combining arguments based on social justice with strongly pro-business sentiments, the government's case was the very model of 'new' Labour's approach to employment policy. Not only would a NMW reduce poverty, inequality, and exploitation but it would also stimulate innovation, investment in human resources, and incentivise work.

The 'Fairness at Work' white paper, which introduced the government's employment legislation programme in May 1998, stated that:

> Together with tax and benefit reforms, the minimum wage will help to promote incentives for individuals to find and make the most of jobs. It will ensure greater fairness at work and remove the worst exploitation. It will promote competitiveness by encouraging firms to compete on quality rather than simply on labour costs and price. (Cm 3968, p.12)

A more complete case for the NMW was set out in the Government's submission to the LPC in October 1999:

> The NMW is part of the Government's commitment to a modern knowledge-driven economy, promoting competitiveness by introducing minimum standards. It is the right policy in terms of both fairness to the lowest paid and economic success for the country. By setting a minimum level below which pay must not fall, the NMW prevents short-sighted employers from paying poverty wages to undercut competitors – a strategy which is seldom successful in the long term. Very low wages result in high turnover of staff, unskilled and untrained workers, low productivity and dissatisfied customers.... By outlawing

exploitatively low pay levels, the NMW is designed to help minimise in-work poverty and, alongside other Government initiatives to 'make work pay', is attracting more people to work. The NMW should also make a significant contribution to equal opportunities by improving the relative earnings of women and ethnic minorities. (Department of Trade and Industry, 1999, pp. 5–6)

The case for statutory minimum-wage regulation therefore represented an ideological shift in the regulation of employment and was based on positive economic as well as social grounds. At the same time, however, anticipation of potentially negative economic consequences placed strong boundaries about what was considered acceptable in terms of social 'fairness' (Thornley and Coffey, 1999).

Operation and enforcement of the NMW

The LPC

The LPC is an independent non-departmental public body set up under the National Minimum Wage Act 1998 to advise the Government about the NMW. It has nine members, consisting of three employers' and employee representatives, plus two independent experts and an independent chair. Its original remit was to recommend the form and level of the new NMW, bearing in mind any implications for the UK economy and competitiveness. However, it secured permanent status in 2001, with new terms of reference including responsibility for a programme of research. Nearly 100 research projects have been commissioned since 1999, and the LPC also undertakes a thorough analysis of economic and labour-market data.

The LPC continues to make recommendations concerning NMW uprating, and any other revisions and reforms, in the light of evidence and submissions received from interested parties. Setting the NMW is thus an interpretive rather than formulaic process distinguished by a formal distance from government, though the government submits its own representations and, of course, makes any final decisions.

NMW rates

The NMW was introduced to cover all workers, excluding only the genuinely self-employed. The rate is calculated on an hourly basis inclusive of earnings incentives such as piece-work but excluding additional payments such as shift-work premia and overtime pay. As customer 'gifts', tips cannot count towards the NMW except when administered through the payroll. There is a small daily offset (£4.30 per day from 1 October 2007) where accommodation is provided. This is the only benefit in kind that counts towards the NMW and was designed to safeguard the position of workers in sectors like hospitality where live-in accommodation is widespread. However, the offset remains low to discourage employers from charging high rents so that they can pay their workers less. Overall, defining the criteria was a potentially complex exercise, though to some extent mitigated by the fact that low-paid workers generally have simpler, as well as inferior, pay and benefits arrangements (White, 1999).

There are now actually three NMW rates. The main 'adult' rate was initially set at £3.60 per hour for workers aged 22 and over, with a 'development' or 'youth' rate of £3.00 for those aged 18–21 inclusive. In 2004, a new rate of £3.00 was introduced for workers aged 16 and 17. Originally, the development rate could also be used for workers aged 22 and over during their first six months in new employment, provided they received accredited training of at least 26 days during this period. This facility was abolished in October 2006, though the apprentice and accredited training exemption was extended to those over 26. The 18–21 rate continues to be available, and was made exempt from the Employment Equality (Age) Regulations 2006 (see Chapter 8).

Until recently, evidence showed that most employers had little interest in utilising the lower rate (Heasman, 2003). Small employers in particular tended to be unaware or confused by it. In any case most preferred to pay a standard rate on grounds of equity and simplicity – the exception being hairdressing where the youth and development rates were linked to apprenticeship (Cronin and Thewlis, 2004). However, more employers are now making use of the 18–21 rate as adult rates increase (LPC, 2007, p. 201).

Table 7.1 provides details of the rates and their increases, together with indicators for inflation and earnings growth to demonstrate the relative acceleration of the NMW over a number of years. As a result, the 'bite' of the adult NMW – its ratio to the median hourly wage – has increased from 47.6 per cent in April 1999 to around

Table 7.1   NMW rates 1999–2007

Date (1)	Main rate (£)	% change	18–21 rate (£)	% change	16–17 rate (£)	% change	RPI	AEI
1999	3.60	–	3.00	–	–	–	–	–
2000	3.70	2.8	3.20	6.7	–	–	3.0	4.6
2001	4.10	10.8	3.50	9.4	–	–	1.8	4.3
2002	4.20	2.4	3.60	2.9	–	–	1.7	4.4
2003	4.50	7.1	3.80	5.6	–	–	2.8	3.8
2004	4.85	7.8	4.10	7.9	3.00	–	3.0	3.9
2005	5.05	4.1	4.25	3.7	3.00	0.0	2.8	4.1
2006	5.35	5.9	4.45	4.7	3.30	10.0	3.2	3.8
2007	5.52	3.2	4.60	3.4	3.40	3.0	4.5	3.6

Note: RPI is the all-items annual average Retail Price Index change for that year (2007 = first six months); AEI refers to the Average Earnings Index figure, which excludes bonuses and is for March each year. Note (1): The 1999 rates were introduced in April, otherwise rates refer to the upratings made in October of that year (the first increase to the 18–21 rate was made in June 2000 but all subsequent revisions have occurred in October).

Source: DTI/BERR, ONS.

53 per cent in October 2006 (LPC, 2007, p. 7). The United Kingdom now has one of the highest minimum-wage rates in Europe, either in nominal or purchasing-power terms (Regnard, 2007). This has led to mounting business concerns. In response to the 2006 increase the CBI said that 'the minimum wage is starting to have a damaging impact on competitiveness' as 'more and more companies are finding it difficult to absorb the rise' (Dennis, 2006, p. 33). The British Chambers of Commerce warned that the rise 'will have an adverse effect on employment' and the British Retail Consortium said that 35,000 jobs might be cut in the wake of the increase, which it claimed would add £1.13 billion to costs in the industry (ibid.). The LPC has thus recently intimated that the era of significant above-inflation increases is over, at least for the time being.

Enforcement

Attention has now shifted to enforcement, not least as the higher rates offer employers more incentive to evade the legislation. Over 25,000 workers were found to have been underpaid a total of £3.29 million in 2005–2006, an increase of over 14,000 cases on the previous year. Official estimates from the Annual Survey of Hours and Earnings (ASHE) show that there were 336,000 jobs paid below the national minimum wage in Spring 2006, amounting to 1.3 per cent of all jobs in the United Kingdom. People in part-time work – mainly women – were almost three times as likely (at 2.6 per cent) as full-time workers to be paid less than the minimum wage. Though these figures are inclusive of jobs exempt from the NMW, at the same time they do not capture non-compliance in the informal economy, which is significant in sectors like agriculture, clothing, and restaurants (Ram et al., 2004).

As a result, the enforcement of the NMW has become stricter and, since 2005, better targeted in low-paying sectors such as hairdressing, childcare, and hotels. Originally, the emphasis was to secure compliance by widespread publicity to employers and low-paid workers. In its first evidence to the LPC in 1999, the government said that it 'has always recognised that the policy will only be successful if it is "self-enforced", that is if it is widely known, and voluntarily complied with' (Department of Trade and Industry, 1999, p. 15). However, it was also clearly recognised that non-compliance might be a product of recalcitrance rather than ignorance. Unusually, the NMW was underpinned by a dual process of enforcement, which acknowledged both its importance and the vulnerability of many workers to whom it applied. Workers would be able to make a complaint relating to the NMW to employment tribunals (and to prosecute in the civil courts for payment of arrears), or to contact compliance officers based in HM Revenue and Customs (HMRC).

There are 16 regional compliance teams involving over 100 officers around the United Kingdom. A telephone helpline is also operated by the HMRC. This received more than 61,000 calls between 2005 and 2006, an increase of 7 per cent on 2004–2005 and 15 per cent on 2003–2004. The location of the inspection agency within HMRC was emblematic of the government's intent. It also facilitates enforcement in proactive mode because cases are also generated based on tax returns. The Revenue is widely viewed as 'an effective and efficient enforcer' (Simpson, 2004, p. 38).

Compliance officers are able to inspect workplaces and issue enforcement and penalty notices to employers. The former demands payment of the NMW, including arrears, the latter is effectively a fine amounting to twice the hourly adult NMW rate per worker to whom the failure to comply relates for each day of that failure to comply. Penalty notices are issued if an enforcement notice has been disregarded by a specified number of days. The ultimate sanction for non-compliance is criminal prosecution and a fine of up to £5,000 for each offence (2007). The HMRC stated in its 2007 Departmental Report that it had its first criminal cases against repeat and major offenders under consideration, and the first prosecution was subsequently brought against an employer for non-disclosure of information and obstruction.

The penalty system was tightened in January 2007 when the deadline for complying with penalty notices was reduced and the minimum penalty was increased over 20-fold. Further changes mean that employers will no longer be able to pay arrears without a fixed penalty fine (Department of Trade and Industry, 2007) and it is proposed that they will also have to pay interest to affected employees. Nevertheless, the LPC still believes that there remains 'no effective deterrent to non-compliance and no real disincentive for firms contemplating evading the minimum wage requirements' (LPC, 2007, pp. 215–216).

Part of the problem is that the enforcement system depends in large part on low-paid workers being willing and able to make complaints against their employer. However, the limited nature of any collective dimension to employment relations in the low-pay sectors, especially in small firms, reduces workers' ability to exercise their statutory rights (Edwards, 2007). Compliance officers have also been reluctant to use existing powers because of the resource implications (Croucher and White, 2007).

Given these concerns, government funding for monitoring and policing the NMW increased by 50 per cent in 2007. However, much of this is likely to be absorbed by a mounting workload reflecting not just increases to the NMW rates, but an expanding population of migrant workers in low-paid and casual employment (Roninson, 2002). By the end of 2006 (legal) migrant workers made up to 12.5 per cent of the United Kingdom working population, up from 7.4 per cent a decade earlier, with a forecast net inward growth of 190,000 per year (Home Office/DWP, 2007). Migrants are disproportionally represented in low-paying occupations (LPC, 2007, p. 155), where they have had the effect of suppressing wage rates through substitution and competition (Dustmann et al., 2007). More to the point, they are less likely to be informed of their statutory rights and are vulnerable to a range of practices incompatible with the NMW such as non-payment of wages, excessive deductions, and long and unrecorded working hours (Zaronaite and Tirzite, 2006).

Impact of the NMW

Empirical research

The impact of the NMW can be measured in many ways. Economically, both advocates and opponents of the NMW anticipated various implications for labour costs and profits; investment and employment; labour supply and turnover; hours and intensity of work; and work organisation and productivity. Important social criteria include effects on poverty and inequality. There is now a wealth of research into the impact of the NMW, much of it sponsored by the LPC, to which we cannot do justice here. Three areas of interest, however, stand out and these are briefly examined in this and the following sections.

First, the NMW has had an increasingly positive impact on wage inequality, particularly between the sexes. Second, successive LPC reports have highlighted that the NMW has not been a cause of unemployment. Third, academic research finds little evidence of a wider positive impact in terms of offsetting compensations such as up-skilling or investment in new technology. Overall, it seems that the experience of the NMW has generally been benign; with important exceptions, most affected firms have so far been able to absorb or pass on any increases in costs in a context of sustained economic growth.

The introduction of the NMW, even at its initially low rate, immediately benefited around 4 to 5 per cent of workers by an average earnings increase of 10 per cent, with a more significant gain still measured at the level of the household (Metcalf, 2002). The hourly wages of the lowest paid subsequently rose by more than the increase for median-paid workers, in contrast to the period before the NMW, though the overall impact on income inequality was mitigated by the substantial growth of high earnings and a limited spillover to other low-paid workers (Butcher, 2005; Dickens and Manning, 2004).

A more substantial effect has been to reduce wage inequality between the sexes. Women are three times more likely than men to be in low-paid jobs, especially in part-time work in sectors like retail, cleaning, and caring (Heasman, 2003). Early research found 'only moderate evidence of any substantial decline in the overall gender pay gap following the NMW' (Dex et al., 2000; Robinson, 2002, p. 439). However, the acceleration of the NMW rates meant that the pay gap between female and male adult hourly median earnings declined from 15.7 per cent in 1999 to 10.8 per cent in 2006 or from 19.7 per cent to 16.8 per cent when using the mean (LPC, 2007, p. 134).

At the same time, aggregate labour-market statistics demonstrate 'no discernable impact of the minimum wage on employment' (LPC, 2007, p. 45), even in low-paying sectors. This reflects the strong performance of the UK economy as a whole. Gross domestic product grew by an average 2.8 per cent per annum between 1997 and 2006, with unemployment falling from over 7.5 per cent to around 5.5 per cent over the same period. Strong demand permits firms to pass on increases in costs, though there is also evidence that the NMW had an adverse effect on profitability. The possibility cannot be ruled out, therefore, that the NMW may have had an impact on job creation, if not negatively in terms of direct job losses.

Draca et al. (2006) found that the NMW reduced profits by 23 per cent in the average care home (where 38 per cent of workers had their wages increased as a result of the NMW) and by 8 to 11 per cent in affected firms elsewhere (see also Machin and Wilson, 2004). As a heavily regulated sector, care homes had little scope to change prices or quality of work, yet employment was not significantly affected, and there were no signs that this contributed to firm closure. Compensating improvements to productivity or efficiency were also noticeably absent despite the magnitude of the shock. Similar results were observed for affected firms across the economy, suggesting that the main impact of the NMW was to redistribute 'excess' profits to low-paid workers.

Research in other low-paying firms and sectors sheds further light on the process of adjustment to the NMW. In a survey of horse riding schools, responses were polarised by size and performance as smaller, struggling firms sought to claw back cost increases through cutbacks in training and other non-financial benefits (Morris et al., 2005). This was more difficult in other sectors like hospitality and retail, where training either is an intrinsic requirement of the job or required by other regulations (Langlois and Lucas, 2005). Hospitality employers were relatively sanguine as economic growth and urban regeneration contributed to higher demand and prices, and tightening labour markets meant that pay increases were to some extent necessary in any case (Williams et al., 2004). This also helped explain limited efforts to offset the NMW by improving productivity or overall product or service quality (Adam-Smith et al., 2003).

Druker et al. (2005) also found a dichotomous impact in hairdressing. Most firms were 'reactive', and sought to pass on any increased costs via prices and/or cutting back on training young recruits. Some were 'innovative' or 'proactive', but this reflected market position and growth more than the NMW, which affected relatively few of their staff. Existing market conditions were also relevant in clothing and textiles, where increased competition from eastern Europe and Asia already threatened the viability of many firms (Lucas and Langlois, 2003). Many employers chose to abandon piece-work in response to the NMW, and sought to increase monitoring, discipline, and workloads as a result (Heyes and Gray, 2001). Even here, though, not all workers were affected, leading to a differential impact between firms (Undy et al., 2002).

In general, then, the early impact on costs was limited, with the implementation of paid holiday under the Working Time Regulations seen as much more significant for employers in low-pay sectors than the NMW (Heyes and Gray, 2004). As Mason et al. (2006, p. 112) commented on their 2003 survey of small employers, 'the

NMW has had limited effect on the small business sector ... It is truly an example of a dog which did not bark, at least so far'. Nevertheless, successive upratings of the NMW did increase costs for many employers, offering a pretext or opportunity to introduce a variety of productivity-enhancing practices.

Case-study research helps to explain the structural constraints limiting this course of action. For example, a study of 36 small firms drawn from six low-paying sectors (cleaning, clothing and footwear, hospitality, residential care, retail, and security) found that employers' so-called 'high road' options were constrained by three related sets of factors (Grimshaw and Carroll, 2006). First was the pressure on prices and costs reflecting dependence on dominant customers or intensive competition, including from foreign or illegal operators. This encouraged highly Taylorised forms of work organisation and meant that there were limited resources available to invest in new techniques, even if management wanted or knew how to change. Management views concerning staff motivation and abilities were the second factor. Third was limited training provision, and a preference for informal methods, linked to fears of staff poaching, as well as affordability concerns.

These findings echo research carried out by this author with colleagues. A longitudinal investigation of 55 hotels, catering, and clothing small firms found constraints linked to limited resources, managerial idiosyncrasies, and the limited scope to organise work differently or to intensify work (Gilman and Arrowsmith, 2001; Ram et al., 2002). As Arrowsmith et al. (2003, pp. 448, 452–453) said:

> efforts to cope with increased costs through labour substitution or better labour utilisation (work reorganisation, training, capital investment) were limited ... Top-down pressure for wider change was limited by access to capital, a difficult trading environment and a narrow scope to actually do the work differently. Bottom-up pressures were defused in part by employee ignorance and the absence of collective organization, but also in some cases by compensating factors to do with working-time flexibility and personal proximity and relations with management.

In this account, absorbing the NMW was facilitated by a degree of 'informality' in workplace employee relations, in terms of individualised and opaque pay arrangements and notions of broader reciprocity between managers and staff (Gilman et al., 2002). Earlier research by others found that employers anticipated responding to the NMW with a range of cost-minimisation (55 per cent) or quality-enhancement (33 per cent) 'strategies' (Brown and Crossman, 2000). This research by the author and colleagues, however, found that such reactions were largely unnecessary. This was because the NMW did not originally provide sufficient regulatory shock, and also because of the indeterminacy and informality of employment in small firms which enabled much of the envisaged impact to be absorbed or sidestepped. As a result, it is not surprising that the introduction of the NMW had more 'fairness' than 'efficiency' effects (Arrowsmith and Gilman, 2004).

Theoretical implications

The initial NMW increased wages in at least 1.2 million jobs, rising to two million, and a similar number have had their pay influenced by the NMW as employers use it as a benchmark to avoid being labelled a 'minimum wage employer' (Dennis, 2007; Incomes Data Services, 2006). Yet the NMW has had very little deleterious impact on inflation or employment (Metcalf, 2007). This is contrary to the expectations of orthodox economic theory, which assumes that product and labour markets are competitive and that firms are price-takers over wages. In these circumstances, minimum wages artificially hike labour costs and lead to unemployment. The higher the wage floor, the bigger the problems for businesses and society as a whole. Since low pay is most commonly a feature of low-skilled employment, wage regulation particularly adversely affects vulnerable groups such as young labour-market entrants and women returners. Milton Friedman (1975) went so far as to describe minimum-wage law as a form of discrimination against the low skilled, claiming that 'the consequences of minimum wage rates have been almost wholly bad, to increase unemployment and to increase poverty'.

This view was most convincingly challenged by the work of Card and Krueger (1995) in the United States of America. Using empirical data from different states in the same low-paying sectors, they concluded that relatively high minimum wages had no significant negative implications for employment. Research from other countries demonstrated similar findings, with the caveat that young workers were slightly more exposed to unemployment risk (Dolado et al., 1996).

This was broadly explained in terms of employers' monopsony power relative to labour, which provides employers with some discretion over wages. Some employers pay wage rates below what would otherwise be market equilibria, whereas others choose to pay relatively higher wages to reduce labour turnover and increase motivation. In this sense, minimum wages merely provide a corrective to market failure for those firms paying below what would be the market rate. Any effect would be to reduce profits rather than employment, though essentially only up to the point that the market rate was reached. According to one former member of the LPC, this view was influential in shaping its 'trial and error' approach whereby an initially cautious rate was established and uprated in a pragmatic process of evidence-based experimentation.

The problem with the monopsony approach, however, is that 'it helps to rationalise certain findings that would be anomalous within conventional neoclassical theory, but it does not itself explain the anomaly' (Edwards and Gilman, 1999, p. 22). Whereas it refers to imperfections such as information and mobility barriers that prevent wage levels reflecting the relative efficiency of labour, in reality the problem is more structural and profound, arising from the unequal interdependency of employment. Labour, unless in possession of particularly valuable or scarce skills, is usually much more dependant on its employer than vice versa. At the same time, labour is not like any other commodity; it expends discretionary effort and may acquire tacit knowledge over the job, requiring various forms of motivation and control.

Furthermore, employees are usually engaged on an open-ended basis and with a loosely specified contract to reflect the dynamic nature of the world of work. Employment is thus not just a market, but a personal and authority relationship. It is also a relationship in which there may be broad mutual interest in the success of the enterprise, but scope for conflict over its goals, means, and allocation of rewards (Edwards, 1986). It is this balance between cooperation and conflict, as much as any market forces or frictions, which results in firms having different systems and levels of pay. In this sense, pay indeterminacy merely reflects the indeterminacy of the employment relationship itself.

These observations are nothing new to industrial relations or sociological approaches to pay which focus not just on the economic 'laws' of supply and demand but on political and social forces within the workplace and beyond. In this tradition, most theories of wages are seen to 'have overstressed coherence and functionality and underplayed both the persistence of conflict and contradictions and the scope for discretionary, random or opportunistic decisions' (Rubery, 1997, p. 338). Yet it was the economist Richard Lester who, in coining the term 'range of indeterminacy' over half a century ago, pointed out the importance of not just the material, but the 'human relations' characteristics of a job (Lester, 1952).

Labour mobility and pay reflect not just market factors but a variety of institutional, historical, and psychological considerations that have a bearing on perceptions of trust, fairness, and security. In these circumstances, 'it is naive and chimerical to talk of "the competitive wage", "the equilibrium wage", or "the wage that clears the market"' (ibid., p. 500). This critique of orthodox economics exposes both the limits of the monopsony approach and of its orthodox critics (e.g. Lal, 1995), who seem to assume that there can be no exploitation of labour, or that if it does occur it will best be corrected, left alone, by some invisible hand of the market.

The idea of a range of indeterminacy helps explain how some firms can sustain low rates of pay whilst erstwhile similar competitors favour higher rates. It also extends to pay differences *within* firms, particularly small firms where pay is often set informally and workers may have only limited knowledge of wider rates and components of pay (Gilman et al., 2002).

According to the latest WERS survey, only 5 per cent of employees in organisations with 10–99 employees are covered by collective bargaining (Kersley et al., 2006, p. 180). In contrast, by far the most important mechanism for pay-setting was unilateral determination by management, with some scope for individual negotiation. It is therefore not surprising that the NMW had limited impact on pay differentials in those low-pay sectors dominated by small firms. Equally, pressure from high-paying jobs, firms and sectors to restore differentials was suppressed not just by the initially low rates of the NMW, but also by a general weakening of collective bargaining.

Conclusion

This chapter has charted the objectives, operation, and effects of the UK's NMW, which forms one of the most significant pieces of employment legislation in recent history. Not only was it the first standard and universalistic attempt at wage regulation by the state (the only concession being age variation as a limited proxy for skill) but its assertion of the legitimacy of market interference, emphasis on the complementarity of fairness and efficiency goals, and the espoused social partnership of the LPC all represented an ideological break with the past – or, perhaps more accurately, a return to some form of pre-Thatcherite consensus.

Nearly ten years on, the principle of the NMW now seems firmly established and accepted by former political and business opponents. In large part, this reflects a generally favourable economic context that has permitted progressive increases without too many adverse economic effects. Overall, the NMW significantly increased the pay of the lowest-paid workers but resulted in few job losses or any wider effects in terms of employment practices in firms. It remains to be seen whether this continues given the increasing 'bite' of the NMW and a changing context of rising inflation and faltering economic growth. The prospect of a regulatory shock remains, and this will be manifested in different ways in different contexts. Some firms will be able to take the 'high road' of teamwork, investment in technology, and training, whereas others will have to cut costs and intensify work where possible. The potential effects of the NMW on worker retention and motivation, amongst other things, therefore remain contingent.

Just as pressing for policy makers, however, is the problem of how to stand still. Compliance is already being eroded, partly as large-scale migration puts downward pressure on pay whilst fuelling informal working in highly competitive and low-margin sectors (Jones et al., 2006). The primary challenge for the NMW is thus whether its enforcement mechanisms are sufficient to safeguard the 'fairness' effects already achieved.

A final, and more fundamental, observation is that the experience of the NMW draws attention to limitations in conventional wage theory. It has been noted that 'far from being profit-maximisers, firms ... are using relatively simple rules of thumb when setting wages', using quartile 'focus points ... rather than maximise the return per worker' (Lam et al., 2006, pp. 69–70, 77). This only partly reflects barriers to the operation of perfect markets such as transaction costs and obstacles to information and labour mobility. It also reflects the indeterminacy of pay arising from the peculiarities of labour as a factor of production, and the power of mimicry as a force for legitimation (Arrowsmith and Sisson, 1999). Workers retain much free will in the expenditure of labour-power and are likely to possess interests and concerns (such as equity, status and maintaining living standards) that need not readily coincide with those of the firm. Likewise, employers can have ambiguous or competing interests over pay in terms of labour costs, recruitment and retention, and motivation.

Pay is thus a contested and shifting terrain reflecting not only balances of power but also custom and practice and employers' willingness to experiment. In this context, it is not surprising that the regulation of pay has few deterministic effects.

Notes

1. The efficiency wage hypothesis argues that wages, at least in some markets, are determined by more than simply supply and demand. Specifically, it points to the incentive for managers to pay their employees more than the market-clearing wage to increase their productivity or efficiency. This increased labour productivity pays for the relatively higher wages.
2. The rent-sharing hypothesis is that employees are able to raise their wages by threats and that firms are compelled to share some of their profits with the employees.

References

Adam-Smith, D., Norris, G., and Williams, S. (2003) 'Continuity or Change? The Implications of the National Minimum Wage for Work and Employment in the Hospitality Industry', *Work, Employment and Society*, 17, 1, 29–47.

Arrowsmith, J. and Gilman, M. (2004) 'Small Firms and the National Minimum Wage', in Marlow (eds) *Managing Labour in Small Firms* London: Routledge.

Arrowsmith, J., Gilman, M., Edwards, M., and Ram, M. (2003) 'The National Minimum Wage and Employment Relations in Small Firms', *British Journal of Industrial Relations*, 41, 3, September, 435–456.

Arrowsmith, J. and Sisson, K. (1999) 'Pay and Working Time: Towards Organisation Based Systems?', *British Journal of Industrial Relations*, 37, 1, 55–75.

Brosnan, P. and Wilkinson, F. (1988) 'A National Statutory Minimum Wage and Economic Efficiency', *Contributions to Political Economy*, 7, 1–48.

Brown, D. and Crossman, A. (2000) 'Employer Strategies in the Face of a National Minimum Wage: An Analysis of the Hotel Sector', *Industrial Relations Journal*, 31, 3, 206–219.

Butcher, T. (2005) 'The Hourly Earnings Distribution before and after the National Minimum Wage', *Labour Market Trends*, 113, 10, October, 427–435.

Callaghan, B. and Jones, R. (1993) 'Wages Councils and Abolition: The TUC Perspective', *International Journal of Manpower*, 14, 5, 17–28.

Card, D. and Krueger, A. B. (1995) *Myth and Measurement: The New Economics of the Minimum Wage*, Princeton: Princeton University Press.

Cronin, E. and Thewlis, M. (2004) *Qualitative Research on Firms' Adjustments to the Minimum Wage: Final Report to the Low Pay Commission*, London: IRS Research.

Croucher, R. and White, G. (2007) 'Enforcing a National Minimum Wage: The British Case', *Policy Studies*, 28, 2, 145–161.

Dennis, S. (2006) 'Minimum Wage Increased by Inflation-Busting 5.9 Per Cent', *IRS Employment Review*, 845, April, 31–33.

Dennis, S. (2007) 'Employers' Views on the National Minimum Wage (1)', *IRS Employment Review*, 866, March, 17–20.

Department of Trade and Industry (1999) *The Government's Evidence to the Low Pay Commission*, London: DTI.

Department of Trade and Industry (2007) 'National Minimum Wage and Employment Agency Standards Enforcement: Consultation Document', London: DTI.

Dex, S., Sutherland, H., and Hoshi, H. (2000) 'Effects of Minimum Wages on the Gender Pay Gap', *National Institute Economic Review*, 173, 80–88.

Dickens, L. and Hall, M. (2003) 'Labour Law and Industrial Relations' in Edwards, P. (ed.) *Industrial Relations: Theory and Practice*, Oxford: Blackwell, 124–156.

Dickens, R. and Manning, A. (2004) 'Has the National Minimum Wage Reduced UK Wage Inequality?', *Journal of the Royal Statistical Society*, 167, 4, 613–626.

Dickens, R., Gregg, P., Machin, S., Manning, A., and Wadsworth, J. (1993) 'Wages Councils: Was There a Case for Abolition', *British Journal of Industrial Relations*, 31, 4, December, 516–529.

Doeringer, P. and Piore, M. (1971) *Internal Labour Markets and Manpower Analysis*, Lexington, MA: D. C. Heath.

Dolado, J., Kramarz, F., Machin, S., Manning, A., Margolis, D., and Teulings, C. (1996) 'Minimum Wages: The European Experience', *Economic Policy*, 23, 319–372.

Draca, M., Machin, S., and van Reenen, J. (2006) 'Minimum Wages and Firm Profitability', *CEP Discussion Paper no. 715*, February.

Druker, J., White, G., and Stanworth, C. (2005) 'Coping with Wage Regulation: Implementing the National Minimum Wage in Hairdressing Businesses', *International Small Business Journal*, 23, 1, 5–25.

Dustmann, C., Frattini, T., and Preston, I. (2007) 'A Study of Migrant Workers and the National Minimum Wage and Enforcement Issues That Arise', *Report for the Low Pay Commission*, London: Low Pay Commission.

Edwards, P. (1986) *Conflict at Work*, Oxford: Blackwell.

Edwards, P. (2007) 'Justice in the Workplace: Why It Is Important and Why a New Public Policy Initiative Is Needed', *Work Foundation Provocation Series*, 2, 3, London: Work Foundation.

Edwards, P. and Gilman, M. (1999) 'Pay Equity and the National Minimum Wage: What Can Theories Tell Us?', *Human Resource Management Journal*, 9, 1, 20–38.

Flanders, A. (1970) *Management and Unions: The Theory and Reform of Industrial Relations*, London: Faber.

Forth, J. and Millward, N. (2000) *'Pay Settlements in Britain'*, NIESR Discussion Paper no. 173, London: National Institute of Economic and Social Research.

Friedman, M. (1975) 'Living within Our Means', Interview, The Open Mind, 12 July. http://www.theopenmind.tv/tom/searcharchive_episode_transcript.asp?id=494 (accessed 25 July 2007)

Gilman, M. and Arrowsmith, J. (2001) 'Modernising the Workplace? Labour's New Employment Relations Agenda', *Competition and Change*, 5, December, 291–310.

Gilman, M., Edwards, P., Ram, M., and Arrowsmith, J. (2002) 'Pay Determination in Small Firms in the UK: The Case of the Response to the National Minimum Wage', *Industrial Relations Journal*, 33, 1, 52–67.

Grimshaw, D. and Carroll, M. (2006) 'Adjusting to the National Minimum Wage: Constraints and Incentives to Change in Six Low-Paying Sectors', *Industrial Relations Journal*, 37, 1, 22–47.

Heasman, D. (2003) 'Patterns of Low Pay', *Labour Market Trends*, 114, 4, April, 171–179.

Heyes, J. and Gray, A. (2001) 'The Impact of the National Minimum Wage on the Textiles and Clothing Industry', *Policy Studies*, 22, 2, 83–98.

Heyes, J. and Gray, A. (2004) 'Small Firms and the National Minimum Wage: Implications for Pay and Training Practices in the British Private Service Sector', *Policy Studies*, 25, 3, 209–225.

Home Office/ Department for Work and Pensions (2007) *The Economic and Fiscal Impact of Immigration: A Cross-Departmental Submission to the House of Lords Select Committee on Economic Affairs*, London: The Stationary Office.

Incomes Data Services (IDS) (2006) 'Viewpoint: The Impact of the NMW in 2006 and Prospects for 2007', IDS Pay Report 967, December, 2–3.

Jones, T., Ram, M., and Edwards, P. (2006) 'Shades of Grey in the Informal Economy', *International Journal of Sociology and Social Policy*, 26, 9/10, 357–373.

Kersley, B., Alpin, C., Forth, J., Bryson, A., Bewley, H., Dix, G., and Oxenbridge, S. (2006) *Inside the Workplace: Findings from the 2004 Workplace Enployment Relations Survey*, London: Routledge.

Lal, D. (1995) *The Minimum Wage: No Way to Help the Poor*, London: Institute of Economic Affairs.

Lam, K., Ormerod, C., Ritchie, F., and Vaze, P. (2006) 'Do Company Wage Policies Persist in the Face of Minimum Wages?', *Labour Market Trends*, 114, 3, March, 69–81.

Langlois, M. and Lucas, R. (2005) 'The Adaptation of Hospitality and Retail Firms to the NMW: A Focus on the Impact of Age-Related Clauses', *Industrial Relations Journal*, 36, 1, 77–92.

Lester, R. A. (1952) 'A Range Theory of Wage Differentials', *Industrial and Labor Relations Review*, 5, 4, July, 483–500.

Low Pay Commission (LPC) (2007) *National Minimum Wage: Low Pay Commission Report 2007*, London: The Stationary Office.

Lucas, R. and Langlois, M. (2003) 'Anticipating and Adjusting to the Introduction of the National Minimum Wage in the Hospitality and Clothing Industries', *Policy Studies*, 22, 1, 33–50.

Lucio, M. M. and Stuart, M. (2005) '"Partnership" and New Industrial Relations in a Risk Society: An Age of Shotgun Weddings and Marriages of Convenience?', *Work, Employment and Society*, 19, 4, 797–817.

Machin, S. and Wilson, J. (2004) 'Minimum Wages in a Low-Wage Labour Market: Care Homes in the UK', *Economic Journal*, 114 (March), C102–C109.

Mason, C. M., Carter, S., and Tagg, W. S. K. (2006) 'The Effect of the National Minimum Wage on the UK Small Business Sector: A Geographical Analysis', *Environment and Planning (C: Government and Policy)*, 24, 99–116.

Metcalf, D. (2002) 'National Minimum Wage: Coverage, Impact and Future', *Oxford Bulletin of Economics & Statistics*, 64, Supplement 1, December, 567–582.

Metcalf, D. (2004) 'The Impact of the National Minimum Wage on the Pay Distribution, Employment and Training', *Economic Journal*, 114 (March), C84–C86.

Metcalf, D. (2007) '*Why Has the British National* Minimum Wage Had Little or No Impact on Employment?', *CEP Discussion Paper No. 781*, April.

Morris, D., Collier, T., and Wood, G. (2005) 'Effects of Minimum Wage Legislation: Some Evidence from Small Enterprises in the UK', *International Small Business Journal*, 23, 2, 191–209.

Pollert, A. (2007) 'Britain and Individual Employment Rights: "Paper Tigers, Fierce in Appearance but Missing in Tooth and Claw"', *Economic and Industrial Democracy*, 28, 1, 110–139.

Ram, M., Edwards, P., Gilman, M., and Arrowsmith, J. (2002) 'The Dynamics of Informality: Employment Relations in Small Firms and the Effects of Regulatory Change', *Work, Employment and Society*, 15, 4, 845–861.

Ram, M., Edwards, P., and Jones, T. (2004) 'Informal Employment, Small Firms and the National Minimum Wage', *A Report for the Low Pay Commission*, September.

Regnard, P. (2007) 'Minimum Wages 2007', *Statistics in Focus*, 71/2007, Luxembourg: Eurostat.

Robinson, H. (2002) 'Wrong Side of the Track? The Impact of the National Minimum Wage on Gender Pay Gaps in Britain', *Oxford Bulletin of Economics and Statistics*, 64, 5, 417–440.

Roninson, V. (2002) 'Migrant Workers in the UK', *Labour Market Trends*, 110, 9, September, 467–476.

Rubery, J. (1997) 'Wages and the Labour Market', *British Journal of Industrial Relations*, 35, 3, 337–366.

Rubery, J. and Edwards, P. (2003) 'Low Pay and the National Minimum Wage', in Edwards, P. (ed.) *Industrial Relations: Theory and Practice*, Oxford: Blackwell, 447–469.

Simpson, B. (2004) 'The National Minimum Wage Five Years On: Reflections on Some General Issues', *Industrial Law Journal*, 33, 1, 22–41.

Storey, J. (1992) *Developments in the Management of Human Resources*, Oxford: Blackwell.

Thornley, C. and Coffey, D. (1999) 'Notes and Issues: The Low Pay Commission in Context', *Work, Employment & Society*, 13, 3, 525–538.

Undy, R., Kessler, I., and Thompson, M. (2002) 'The Impact of the National Minimum Wage on the Apparel Industry', *Industrial Relations Journal*, 33, 4, 351–364.

Wells, P. (1985) 'The Aggregate Supply Curve: Keynes and Downwardly Sticky Money Wages', *The Journal of Economic Education*, 16, 4, 297–304.

White, G. (1999) 'Pay Structures and the Minimum Wage', Occasional Paper No. 3, London: Low Pay Commission.

Williams, S., Adam-Smith, D., and Norris, G. (2004) 'Remuneration Practices in the UK Hospitality Industry in the Age of the National Minimum Wage', *Service Industries Journal*, 24, 1, 171–186.

Williamson, O. E. (1975) *Markets and Hierarchies*, New York: Free Press.

Woodward, D. (1980) 'The Background to the Statute of Artificers: The Genesis of Labour Policy 1558–1563', *Economic History Review*, 33, 1, 32–44.

Zaronaite, D. and Tirzite, A. (2006) *The Dynamics of Migrant Labour in South Lincolnshire*, Spalding: South Holland District Council.

8

Pay equity: gender and age

Susan Corby

This chapter focuses on gender equality and pay and on age equality and pay, primarily adopting a legal perspective. These two discrimination strands are the subject of this chapter because although under European and UK law it is unlawful to discriminate on the grounds of sex, race, disability, religion and belief, sexual orientation and age, only in respect of gender and age are there *specific* provisions in directives, statutes, and/or regulations on the pay aspect of discrimination. Pay is defined in accordance with Article 141 of the Treaty of Rome: 'the ordinary basic or minimum wage or salary and any other consideration, whether in cash or in kind, which the worker receives directly or indirectly, in respect of his employment, from the employer.'

The contention of this chapter is that the equal pay laws and the age laws are fundamentally flawed and legal changes are needed to foster pay equity. Accordingly, proposals for reform are put forward ranging from relatively modest ones, such as ending the exemptions under the Age Regulations, to relatively radical ones, such as an employment inspectorate to include pay equity.

This chapter is divided into four main parts: gender equality and pay; the author's research; age equality and pay; and proposals for reform. In the first part, gender equality and pay, the chapter considers definitions of equality and how those definitions relate to the legal framework, the problems with the legislation which include lack of legal aid at employment tribunals and other limitations of the law. Then in the second part, the findings from the author's research are explored: these suggest that women often do not know how their pay compares to that of their male colleagues and are unaware of their legal rights. In the third part, the chapter turns to the provisions on age. As the age laws only came into force in 2006, there is little or no experience of their impact or case law at this juncture. Accordingly, the bulk of this chapter focuses on gender equality and pay. In the final part, various reform proposals are discussed.

Gender equality and pay

This first part, gender equality and pay, covers four main areas: the gender pay gap and the reasons for it; definitions of equality and the legal framework; the special position of the UK public sector; and the problems with the law.

The gender pay gap

There is a wealth of evidence on the gender pay gap. According to the Office for National Statistics (ONS) the UK gender pay gap, as measured by the hourly earnings of full-time employees excluding overtime hours, was 12.6 per cent in April 2007 at the median, while the mean was 17.2 per cent (Office for National Statistics, 2007).

There are a number of theoretical explanations for the gender pay gap: economic, sociological, and institutional, all of which have been critiqued. These include human capital theory: on average women are less productive than men either due to their innate abilities or acquired skills; crowding theory: women tend to be crowded into certain sectors and a relatively narrow range of occupational groups, either through custom and cultural values or through prejudice and/or discrimination by employers, who only hire women if they can do so at a wage discount. Such jobs are labour intensive, have low productivity, and wages are accordingly low. A variation on this is the dual labour market theory, the segmentation of jobs into primary and secondary sectors: discrimination and crowding results in women being prevented from entering the primary sector (see Anderson et al., 2001; Miller et al., 2004 for a fuller discussion of these theories).

Another economic explanation of the gender pay gap is preference theory which relates to women's choices, not employers' discrimination: employers have a degree of monopsony[1] in respect of women who prioritise home over work, because such women tend to *prefer* certain work in terms of hours and/or location and thus have restricted employment options (Hakim, 1991, 2002).

Employment relations academics reject economic explanations of the gender gap which, they say, is largely explained by sociological and institutional factors. Women's work is undervalued, so the jobs they fill are low paid and they bear an unequal burden of family responsibilities. Moreover, the pay gap is associated with employer characteristics such as where one works, the pay setting arrangements, and the design of payment systems, not human capital. Indeed, the earnings gap widens between men and women, even before graduate women take time off work for family formation (Grimshaw and Rubery, 2007).

To sum up, there is evidence of a significant gender pay gap and there are many explanations for it. Moreover, the gender pay gap persists despite laws on equal pay, to which this chapter now turns.

Equality and the law

Equality between men and women or between workers of different ages can be conceived in a number of ways. One approach conceives of equality as consistency and like being treated as like. It derives from a liberal ideology that asserts the individual's right to universally applicable standards of justice, a right that applies to all, for instance men/women and old/young workers. It has been termed formal or procedural equality (Fredman, 2002; Hepple et al., 2000). Equality as consistency has two main characteristics: first, it requires a comparator whose relevant circumstances are not materially different from the complainant. Second, the principle of consistency of treatment is satisfied regardless of whether an individual benefits as a result, so there can be levelling down (for instance, by removing a benefit), as well as levelling up (by extending a benefit) provided the complainant and comparator are treated the same (Hepple et al., 2000).

Alternatively, equality can be conceived as equality of opportunity or starting gate equality. Distortions in the market have to be removed to ensure that everyone is at the starting gate, though the most meritorious will win the race. So, for instance, flexible working arrangements and generous maternity provisions are introduced to ensure that women are not disadvantaged by child care/child bearing, but promotion is on merit. This, however, assumes that 'merit' is neutral, rather than embodying the values of the dominant culture (see Fredman, 2001 for a fuller discussion).

A third approach conceives equality as equality of results. The first two models emphasise cause and provide redress for the individual, but the third model focuses on effect and outcome for the many. If the third approach is used, there will not be equality until the gender pay gap is eliminated (Fredman, 2001, 2002).

The legal framework

Equal pay law is grounded in the like treated as like approach: equality as consistency. It is unlawful to pay men and women differently in three situations: when a person is employed on the same or broadly similar work as a person of the opposite sex; when a person is employed on work rated as equivalent to that of a person of the opposite sex as measured by an analytical job evaluation scheme; or when a person is employed on work of equal value to that of a person of the opposite sex. In other words a woman[2] can claim equal pay with a man even if she and her comparator perform different jobs; so, for instance, a female cook and a male carpenter, will be rated as equal if the demands of both their jobs, such as the effort, skill, and decision making required to perform them, are equal.

A comparator of the opposite sex can only be drawn from someone in the same employment, or, if this is a private sector case, from an associated employer[3] or if the terms and conditions of the claimant and comparator derive from a single source.[4] Where an employment tribunal finds that the work of the claimant and comparator are equal or of equal value, the employer can mount what is called a genuine material factor defence. In other words, the employer gives a reason for the difference in pay that is not gender based. In England and Wales a successful claimant can win six years' back pay (five years in Scotland).

The UK public sector

Many UK public sector organisations have instituted analytical job evaluation schemes as a basis for gender equality, using a like as like approach. For instance, the National Health Service (NHS) introduced a new job evaluated pay system Agenda for Change, to cover all NHS staff except doctors and dentists and the most senior managers (Department of Health, 2004). Civil Service departments have also introduced new pay systems based on analytical job evaluation schemes, as have universities (Joint Negotiating Committee for Higher Education Staff, 2003) and some local authorities (Sherman, 2007).

The UK public sector is also under an obligation to promote equality of opportunity, that is starting gate equality, in the form of a gender equality duty. That duty, introduced in April 2007, has two main aims: to impose a requirement to promote equality through impact assessment and consulting stakeholders and to impose an enforceable duty to eliminate discriminatory structures by proactive and anticipatory action. The duty covers public authorities (and private sector organisations which provide goods and services to public bodies) which are required to have 'due regard' to the need to eliminate discrimination that is unlawful under the Equal Pay Act (Equal Opportunities Commission, 2007, para 2.67).

This duty moves beyond the fault-based model of equal pay law with its reliance on individuals making complaints in an adversarial legal system and with remedies designed to compensate the individual after the event. Thus under the gender duty, the duty bearer, even though not responsible for creating discrimination, becomes responsible for eliminating structures, policies, and practices that are found to have an adverse impact on the protected group. So equality moves away from equality as consistency towards equality as proactively removing barriers and thus to equality as equality of opportunity (Fredman, 2002).

Problems with the law on equal pay between men and women

The limitations in the law have already been signalled and this chapter now considers a number of problems, both theoretical and practical. First, the Equal Pay Act (1970) (EqPA) incorporates, at least to some extent, gendered assumptions prevalent in society about the value of jobs and, particularly where job evaluation is used, it reflects norms, rather than sets them; see Wright (2007) for a full discussion.

Second, it is individualistic; there is no provision for class actions as in the United States, where legal action can be taken on behalf of a class of women and largely depends on statistics, not individual detriment. Such class actions have the potential to cost organisations much money (Waldemeir, 2007) and reflect the fact that gender pay discrimination is often not just a question of individual justice but affects groups and is systemic.[5] Moreover, individual enforcement goes hand in hand with an adversarial approach and this often poisons the atmosphere and results in defensive reactions, rather than proactive responses (Hepple et al., 2000).

Another problem arises because the EqPA covers contractual issues and the Sex Discrimination Act covers non-contractual issues (even though European law does not make this distinction) and, as a result, claimants may bring a claim under the 'wrong' jurisdiction; for instance, when it is not clear whether a bonus is contractual or discretionary.[6]

A further problem arises over the so-called 'genuine material factor' defence, the employer's reason for a difference in the pay of men and women performing equal work. The courts have differed in their view as to the test the employer has to satisfy and the evidence needed.[7]

Another complication is that the ambit of the equal pay laws is constrained as to with whom the claimant can compare. Although, as noted above, a claimant can use a comparator who has a different employer where both the claimant's and comparator's pay derive from 'a single source', the UK courts have interpreted this stringently. For instance, male civil servants working for one government department which had its own pay regime were not entitled to compare their work with that of female civil servants who worked in another government department which had its own, different pay regime, notwithstanding that the claimants and their comparators were in the common employment of the Crown.[8]

Another issue currently of concern is the extent to which service-related pay scales are compatible with equal pay for men and women, given that seniority based pay systems normally have a disparate impact on women (because they have more time out of the labour market for child-bearing, work part-time, etcetera). Even though many employers have stopped using very long pay scales, gender differentials may not be eliminated if women are slotted in towards the bottom of a new pay band, and men towards the top, in reflection of their previous pay positions.

The European Court of Justice, in a case concerning like work,[9] considers that length of service goes hand in hand with experience, but says that employees may challenge service-related pay where they provide 'evidence capable of giving rise to *serious doubts* as to whether recourse to the criterion of length of service is, in the circumstances appropriate' (author's emphasis). In such a case, the employer will be required to provide detailed justification. As Rubenstein (2006) maintains, however, it is not clear what comprises serious doubts (see Rubenstein 2006 for a fuller discussion).

In short, equal pay law is complex, particularly where the comparison is based on work of equal value (not like work, or work rated as equivalent under a job evaluation scheme). Moreover, this complexity has meant that some cases, particularly where a reference to the European Court of Justice (ECJ) is involved, have taken many years to complete (Incomes Data Services, 2004). Yet there is no legal aid at tribunals. It is, therefore, unusual for litigants in person to be able to take advantage of the legislation (Bellamy and Cameron, 2006).

The Equality and Human Rights Commission (EHRC) can fund legal representation, but it has not the resources to do so for every claimant that approaches it, so it chooses cases strategically, primarily on whether a point of law needs to be tested. Trade unions can finance claims on behalf of members but trade union density is only 28 per cent overall and 17 per cent in the private sector (Grainger and Crowther, 2007). While no-win-no-fee lawyers have been active on behalf of claimants in the National Health Service and local government, their presence is less common elsewhere.

The new gender duty on public bodies is, on the face of it, welcome. The public body has to take proactive steps with the objective of making 'equality a central goal of [public bodies'] day-to-day activities' (O'Cinneide, 2005, p. 228). Thus the duty, which is enforced by the EHRC via compliance notices, has the potential to be a powerful tool to ensure that equal pay issues are brought to the forefront of public authorities' concerns.

A note of caution at this juncture, however, must be sounded. First, the duty only imposes an obligation on public bodies to give 'due regard' to equality, to balance the importance of equality against other considerations (O'Cinneide, 2005).

Second, although at the time of writing the Government has just announced that it will require public bodies to report on gender equality, it has not yet specified details (Harman, 2008). Third, the Government, in imposing the duty, has not prescribed any specific course of action to tackle gender pay discrimination. It merely requires public authorities to assess the impact of policies and practices, and 'to consider the need to have objectives that address the causes of any differences between the pay of men and women that are related to their sex' (Equal Opportunities Commission, 2007, para. 3.40). The duty does not require public authorities to carry out an equal pay review, even though such a review (which entails comparing the pay of men and women doing equal work including work of equal value, identifying and analysing any pay gaps, and eliminating gaps that cannot satisfactorily be explained on grounds other than sex), is recommended in a statutory Code of Practice (Equal Opportunities Commission, 2003).

Third, there is a danger that at least some public bodies will focus on procedural compliance rather than outcome (O'Cinneide, 2003a) as has happened with the race equality duty introduced in 2003 (Hepple, 2006). Fourth, while the gender duty is proving a powerful lever for change in Northern Ireland, the Greater London Authority, the Scottish Parliament and the Welsh Assembly, where it applied well before 2007 (when the gender duty on *all* public bodies came into effect), there has been considerable political support in those places. Accordingly, its value will only be tested when it is 'applied in less favourable political waters' (O'Cinneide, 2005, p. 232).

Gender pay research

Having considered the legal position, this chapter now turns to this author's research with colleagues in 2005, co-financed by the South East England Development Agency and the European Social Fund (Corby et al., 2005). Already this chapter has identified one reason why the equal pay laws are often not used, namely litigants' lack of representation at employment tribunals, but this research identified other reasons.

Methodology

The research was carried out using two methods. First all employers who had 50 or more employees in the south east of England were sent a questionnaire in 2005. This produced 454 usable responses (a 13 per cent return), with private manufacturing being over-represented in the responses (31 per cent compared to 16 per cent overall in the region) and the public sector and private services being under-represented. The questionnaires were analysed by SPSS version 12.1.

Second, interviews were carried out with people in 40 organisations: the manager responsible for human resources (HR) and two women, a senior and a junior female employee (defined by their position in the organisation's hierarchy), 120 interviews in all. The organisations for interview were selected to provide a mix of size (number of employees), location, and sector/industry. The interviews were taped, transcribed, and analysed according to broad themes.

The main limitation of this data was that the manager responsible for HR was asked to provide two female employees to be interviewed. That could bias the findings towards positive attitudes to the employer. All the interviews, however, were confidential and anonymous.

Findings

This research was part of a wider study into gender and the labour market in south east England, covering employers' gender policies and practices and attitudes to equality and the views of female employees, including any perceived barriers. For the purpose of this chapter, however, only the findings relating to gender pay equity are considered.

The questionnaires revealed that by and large respondent employers did not know whether or not their pay systems were gender neutral. For instance, less than one in five of our respondent employers who had performance-related pay monitored outcomes by gender. Also, the majority of our respondent employers had not carried out an equal pay review, so they did not know if or where there were gender pay gaps.

Some HR managers had not carried out such a review because they feared the amount of work involved. For instance, one said, 'I don't feel like suggesting it because I'd have to do it and there's so much other stuff going on.' Another said, 'I think we costed it; it was going to take one [full time equivalent] six months.'

Other managers responsible for human resources (HR) misunderstood the concept of an equal pay review. The questionnaire asked those who said that they had carried out an equal pay review (36 per cent) what had been the result, and responses, such as 'pay adjusted to align with the external market', suggested that at least some respondents had confused an equal pay review with a pay review and this was confirmed by interviews.

For instance, a HR manager in advanced manufacturing, who had noted on the questionnaire that the organisation had carried out an equal pay review, admitted in the subsequent interview that 'it wasn't a gender pay review. It was a pay review regardless of gender. In a sense gender doesn't make a difference and we ignore it.' Nor did the questionnaires suggest that there was any legal imperative to take action on gender. Only 18 employers (4 per cent) said that they had been involved in litigation in the past three years in respect of the Equal Pay Act and Sex Discrimination Act.

This research puts forward three main explanations for the fact that equal pay laws were rarely used. First, private sector pay structures were very often opaque and lacked any clear rationale so comparisons were not visible or easily identifiable, even in medium-sized enterprises (between 50 and 250 employees). A comment by an HR manager in a private care home with 200 employees was typical. She said, 'We're influenced by NHS pay scales and what people want and what they expect to get; but no formal structure... a knee jerk reaction.' Similarly, an HR manager in private services with 250 employees said, 'We look at what our competitors pay. We kind of go from there... There's nothing formal. There's nothing laid out.' An HR manager in manufacturing with 80 employees said, 'it's a bit kind of stick your finger in the air; see which way the wind is blowing'.

This lack of rationale and opacity was reflected in the interviews with female employees: generally, they were ignorant of what their colleagues were paid or the rationale for pay, particularly where there was not collective bargaining. Indeed, some interviewees, both HR managers and female employees, reported that their organisations specifically enjoined secrecy over pay, a finding consonant with research from the Chartered Institute of Personnel and Development (CIPD). The CIPD found that 'about one third of employers stipulate that staff do not discuss pay and conditions with their colleagues' (Woodward and Curtis, 2007, p. 8).

Even where there were no explicit stipulations, the research found that there was a culture of not discussing one's pay with others. Typical comments by female employees were 'Mine's definitely lower. I can't prove it... I've no idea. I might be wrong.' 'I would imagine the pay is still higher for men. I get that feeling.' Similarly, a compliance officer at a firm of solicitors said that she was 'stunned' when she asked for a pay rise and received a hefty 25 per cent. Although grateful for the rise, she had no idea how it had been calculated (Corby et al., 2005). None of these women knew that they could use the statutory equal pay questionnaire to obtain relevant information.

A second reason why equal pay laws were not used was that the majority of managers responsible for HR, but who were not HR professionals, together with many of the women interviewed, were largely ignorant of the law; they were mistakenly of the view that equal pay meant only like work and not work of equal value and also that only contemporaneous comparators could be used. For instance, a female production controller had succeeded her husband and was well aware of what he had been paid and so knew exactly how much less she was being paid, while a female finance manager in manufacturing knew that the man she had succeeded had been paid more than her; but neither realised that they could compare themselves with a predecessor.[10]

Third, where women knew or suspected what other contemporaneous people were paid for similar work, they did not want to 'rock the boat', often because their employer was flexible about the hours they worked and they were grateful for that. They made a choice about what was reasonable in relation to the available possibilities and available information, rather than making their choice on what was optimal on the basis of full information.

To summarise, many managers had not sought to discover whether there was gender pay inequality; private sector pay structures were often inchoate and unsystematic and female employees largely were often not fully aware of their legal rights and of their colleagues' pay.

Age discrimination

The first and second parts of this chapter examined the legal position and workplace practices in respect of gender and pay. The third part covers age and pay, considering first the legal position, particularly the exemptions, and employers' practices.

The law

The law on equal pay between men and women is over 30 years old and there has been much experience in using it, as well as independent research. In contrast, the age discrimination legislation is the newest kid on the block and research on age and pay has been relatively sparse. The Employment Equality (Age) Regulations, which stem from a European directive (EC2000/78), only took effect on 1 October 2006.

While the Regulations cover all aspects of age in employment, this chapter concentrates on pay (adopting the EU definition of pay – see above).

The Age Regulations, like the EqPA are grounded in a like as like approach, equality as consistency. Unlike the EqPA, however, the Age Regulations contain both specific and across-the-board exemptions. Specifically, for instance, there are numerous exemptions relating to occupational pensions provisions and the statutory redundancy scheme, whose payments are based on age and service, are exempt, as are enhanced redundancy provisions made by the employer, albeit only where the employer's formula closely mirrors the statutory scheme (Incomes Data Services, 2006).

A further example of a specific exemption relates to the age-based provisions of the national minimum wage (NMW). This exemption, moreover, extends to an employer's pay structure based on the age bands in the NMW, even where workers are paid in excess of the NMW to which they are entitled, provided that there is no pay differentiation on age grounds within an NMW age band, and provided that the young workers are not paid more than the adult NMW (Incomes Data Services, 2006).

The NMW's age-related pay rates are based on the assumption that young workers can be distinguished from older workers and that age is a proxy for skill. Lucas and Nair Keegan (2007), however, who carried out research into 16- and 17-year-old workers in the hospitality sector in north Wales, question this. Establishments in this sector typically did not have any systematic basis for determining pay and managers' presumption that young workers lacked the skill and training of older workers and/ or performed smaller jobs could not be objectively verified (see Chapter 7 for a fuller discussion of the NMW.)

As to across-the-board exemptions, Regulation 32 provides a blanket exemption to service-related pay and benefits for up to and including five years. Service can be calculated as the length of time the worker has been working for the employer in total, or doing work of a particular type and certain absences can be discounted from the calculations (Incomes Data Services, 2006).

At the time of writing, it is unclear whether the ECJ will consider this blanket exclusion lawful. Interestingly, the ECJ was of the view that a blanket exclusion of those aged 52 and over from German fixed term work legislation did not comply with the directive.[11] Despite the fact that member states enjoy broad discretion under the directive in their choice of measures for attaining their objectives (in that case the integration of older workers), the ECJ stressed that this discretion is always subject to the principle of proportionality, which requires every derogation from an individual right to reconcile the principle of equal treatment with the aim of the legislation.

Even after five years, service-related pay and benefits may still be provided by the employer under Regulation 32(2) and the test is low: an employer can justify this if it 'reasonably appears' to him that the provision 'fulfils a business need ... (for example, by encouraging the loyalty or motivation, or rewarding the experience of some or all of his workers)'. This can be contrasted with the test of justification elsewhere under the Age Regulations: an employer can only justify a provision, criterion, or practice if a proportionate means of fulfilling a legitimate aim has been adopted. In short, the test for age-related pay and benefits of more than five years is weak. As Sergeant (2006, p. 22) says:

> This seems to be a wholly subjective test and will surely be very difficult to challenge. All such benefits are likely to be justifiable in terms of rewarding experience. Even this test, however, is removed for service related differences of five years or less.

Pensions, too, are covered by a lengthy list of exemptions to be found in Schedule 4 of the Regulations. For instance, it remains lawful to provide benefits only to members who have completed a minimum period of pensionable service not exceeding two years and to provide entitlement to benefits under a defined benefits scheme according to length of pensionable service. (Pensions are discussed in Chapter 10.)

Practice

This chapter now turns from the Age Regulations to employers' practices. A study based on a representative survey of 2,087 establishments in Britain with at least five employees found that age is rarely a criterion for benefits. Only 2 per cent of establishments made the length of annual leave dependant on age and the equivalent figure for sick pay was 1 per cent (Metcalf and Meadows, 2006).

Pay related to service (which is a proxy for age) was more common than pay related to age itself. According to the UK Government in evidence to the ECJ in the Cadman case, 36 per cent of UK employees are remunerated on the basis of length of service. Metcalf and Meadows, however, found that only 5 per cent of establishments had pay scales with service-related increments of more than five years. Moreover, service-related increments were less common than performance-related increments or merit based non-incremental pay systems.

Similarly, research by McNair and Flynn (2005), who carried out case study research into 14 organisations, found that pay and benefits were rarely age related, except in respect of private health insurance, and that long, service-related, incremental pay scales were found usually only in the public sector.

Proposals for reform

As seen above, the gender/pay and age/pay laws are problematic. Dickens (2007) suggests that this is because the government gives priority to employers' views on economic efficiency and competitiveness, rather than social justice and this has resulted in a piecemeal legislative approach. Against that background, various proposals for reform are briefly discussed in this fourth and final part of the chapter, beginning with suggested improvements to the legislation and then to the enforcement mechanisms.

Changes to the legislation

Dealing first with improvements to the EqPA, one proposal centres on pay awareness. As noted above, the author found in her research that employers often ask employees not to discuss their pay with others and pay structures are often not transparent. An employee thinking of bringing a claim can ask key questions of their employer, using a statutory equal pay questionnaire, but this risks the employee being labelled as a trouble maker.

The Government has proposed outlawing clauses in contracts banning employees from revealing their salaries to colleagues and will make it unlawful to stop employees discussing their pay (Harman, 2008). Often, however, there is just a culture of secrecy. Accordingly, it is proposed that once a year all employers of, say, over 20 employees (the cut-off point for trade union recognition claims) should automatically publish their pay and bonus rates along with job titles. To avoid data protection problems the pay data could be provided in monetary bands, as with directors' pay in annual reports, with a gender breakdown and giving age bands. If such a proposal were adopted, the United Kingdom would be in tune with a European Union directive (2002/73/EC): this requires member states to 'encourage' employers to provide their employees with regular information on equal treatment for men and women.

Other proposals for changes to the EqPA centre on tightening the genuine material factor defence and allowing a claimant to use a hypothetical comparator. Under the EqPA, an *actual* comparator has to be used, but women who work in highly segregated workplaces often do not have an *actual* appropriate comparator (Women and Work Commission, 2006). Under the other discrimination acts and EU law, a claimant can construct a *hypothetical* comparator.

Another proposal centres on class and representative actions. As noted above the EqPA is individualistic, but sometimes there are many individuals bringing claims in relation to the same pay structure particularly in local authorities and the NHS, for instance school dinner ladies comparing themselves with male road workers and female health care assistants comparing themselves with male porters. Currently, employment tribunals, faced with these multiple claims have to rely on the co-operation of the parties in identifying test cases and being prepared to submit them as a bundle of claims and to accept the outcome of the decision. Claims, however, still have to be treated separately in relation to settlement or withdrawal.

An alternative would be the approach followed by some other legal systems of so-called representative or generic actions: a body, such as the EHRC or a trade union, could identify a group of employees in one or more workplaces who were all adversely affected by unequal pay. That body, as proxy claimant, would then submit a claim on behalf of the group, whose names would be notified to the employer and the tribunal and the eventual decision would apply to all in the group (Gibbons, 2007; TUC, 2007).

Another option would be to have binding arbitration by a standing arbitration board, as the Local Government Employers propose in the face of equal pay claims by local authority workers estimated to cost many millions of pounds (Brodie, 2006). Alternatively, there could be arbitration by the Central Arbitration Committee, which had until 1986 an obligation under the EqPA to examine discriminatory collective agreements referred to it by a union, an employer or the secretary of state and order a levelling up, where appropriate, so that the disadvantaged group could catch up. It is not clear, however, whether such arbitration could prevent individuals from exercising their rights under EU law and thus, notwithstanding any arbitration, prevent them from pursuing individual claims.

As to the Age Regulations, the blanket exemption for pay and benefits of five years or less is hard to justify if one seeks to change workplace practices, rather than allow them to continue. Similarly, there seems intellectually to be scant grounds for a lower test of justification where the employer provides age-related pay and benefits of five years or more, than where the employer discriminates on other matters as regards age.

Enforcement

Therefore, the first step is to strengthen the laws, but that is not enough. Any law essentially stands or falls on its enforcement.

Ayres and Braithwaite (1992) point out that there is a range of corporate behaviour in response to legal regulation. Some employers will abide by the law because they are law abiding or out of a sense of social responsibility. Others carry out what in effect is a cost/benefit analysis and only comply if it is economically rational to do so. Accordingly, Ayres and Braithwaite maintain that there should be a hierarchy of enforcement measures starting with persuasion and self-enforcement, then individual legal claims, progressing to sanctions against employers and revocation of licence at the apex.

Adapting this to pay equity and looking at a range of enforcement measures, this chapter therefore proposes what McCrudden (2007) calls reflexive regulation, in other words mandatory self-enforcement. This encourages organisations to 'own' the policies and procedures that they devise, but with sanctions if they fail to do so. Under this head is the proposal for mandatory equal pay reviews as an essential tool for identifying employers' gender pay anomalies.

Research by Adams et al. (2006) suggests that the voluntary approach to equal pay reviews that the government has adopted has had a limited impact: only 12 per cent of 872 organisations with 25 or more employees had carried out a voluntary equal pay review. As noted above, employers were unwilling to carry out such reviews, or did not understand what they were, and as the Institute of Employment Rights has argued: 'without mandatory equal pay reviews there will be no significant reduction in the gender pay gap in the short to medium term' (Institute of Employment Rights 2004, p. 2).

Interestingly, the Conservative party has proposed that an organisation should carry out a mandatory equal pay review where it has lost an equal pay claim at a tribunal (Conservatives, 2007), that is, where there is evidence of pay discrimination that warrants a systemic approach. Though this may be welcome, its effect will be limited and *post hoc*.

The Equal Opportunities Commission, which has long called for mandatory equal pay reviews, proposes offering employers 'a carrot'. Where an employer has carried out an equal pay review, there should be a protected period or moratorium during which the employer could implement changes to the pay system, and no equal pay claims may be brought. That, however, could fall foul of EU law, as it would prevent individuals exercising their rights, if only for a period (Equal Opportunities Commission, 2005).

Also under the head of reflexive regulation are public duties. Although we noted some concerns about the duty on public bodies to promote gender equality, on balance the duty (and there are similar duties for disability and race) is welcome as it entails a proactive approach. It should, therefore, be extended to age. At present, there is in effect a discrimination hierarchy, with gender being covered by more far reaching laws than age, which is at the bottom of the hierarchy. So as a first step, the duty should be reformulated to include age. (At the time of writing, the government has announced plans for this.) As a second step, it should be extended to the private sector. In Northern Ireland, *all* employers have a duty to take measures to ensure a fair proportion of Catholics and Protestants in their workforce (O'Cinneide, 2003b).

Reflexive regulation is one enforcement approach; individual claims are another, but there needs to be some means of aiding claimants financially so that they can enforce their rights. The Equality and Human Rights Commission (EHRC) can legally assist individuals, but as noted above it has limited resources and so can only help some claimants. One option, therefore, would be to increase the budget of the EHRC. Another option would be to provide legal aid when there are complex matters of fact – in practice most pay equity cases. This could be achieved by removing original jurisdiction from employment tribunals and giving it to the Employment Appeal Tribunal, where there is legal aid. See Justice (1987) for a full discussion.

Although UK unions have traditionally ensured that employers comply with the law, their record on equal pay is mixed as they have competing interests.[12] Against that background there needs to be some external enforcement body. Admittedly the EHRC can undertake so-called formal investigations into suspected discriminatory practices, but it is likely that its main focus will be persuasion, as was the EOC's (a predecessor of the EHRC). So an employment inspectorate seems the best option.

Brown (2006, p. 76) writing on the national minimum wage (NMW) has praised its enforcement methods: not only persuasion and publicity and individuals being able to take claims to an employment tribunal, but also there is enforcement through an inspectorate: compliance officers of HM Revenue and Customs (HMRC). HMRC inspectors are 'energetic, ingenious and generally respected' and as a last resort they can use the criminal law (see chapter 7). The Working Time Regulations too are enforced by inspection by a state agency, the Health and Safety Executive, whose inspectors can prosecute in the criminal courts, as well by individuals taking claims to tribunals. Similarly, there are enforcement officers under the Gangmasters Licensing Authority.

Thus, there are different inspectorates for different employment law rights, but currently most employment law rights are not covered by an inspectorate, including those relating to discrimination and pay equity, though such an all-embracing employment inspectorate would be particularly useful in non-union workplaces.

Furthermore, an employment inspectorate would reflect the interrelationship of employment rights. For instance, gender pay equity laws interrelate with laws covering maternity and paternity leave and the right to request flexible working. An employment inspectorate could, for instance, look at the scope of an equal pay review, or how pay information is communicated, when visiting an organisation on other matters such as the Working Time Regulations. Brown comments (2006, pp. 76–77):

> Almost all other countries have independent labour inspectorates that, to a greater or lesser extent, seek out employers who breach labour standards, and that take up cases on behalf of aggrieved employees. Britain's labour market regulation is defective in this respect.

Of course, whether or not inspection by a government agency has an impact is largely dependant on the number of inspectors and thus government funding; but it is in the interests of business to prevent under-cutting by rogue employers who do not comply with labour standards and it is in the interests of government to encourage economic efficiency through the employment of women and workers of all ages and to provide greater fairness in the labour market. In short, the government has an interest in establishing an adequately funded employment inspectorate. Interestingly, the European Commission (2000, p. 11) has said that it will explore the possibilities of improving the functioning of legal remedies in respect of equal pay legislation, including calling on member states 'to reinforce the role and powers of the labour inspectorate bodies'.

Summary and conclusions

This chapter has concentrated on the role of the law in providing for pay equality in respect of gender and age. It has highlighted weaknesses in the equal pay legislation, such as the lack of legal aid and the absence of any provision for class actions, although pay discrimination is often systemic, affecting groups not individuals.

The chapter has also drawn on the author's own research findings which indicate that women do not exercise their rights to equal pay because of lack of knowledge of what their colleagues are paid and of what their legal rights are. Also, they often do not want to risk being labelled a trouble maker. Finally various proposals for reform were examined, both relatively modest ones, such as ending the exemptions in the age regulations, and more radical ones such as the proposal for an employment inspectorate.

It concludes, however, with a note of caution. The law, whether concerned with pay equity or other matters, is only one of many environmental factors which shape employment and social norms, and legislation alone cannot hope completely to provide for equality. As the eminent labour lawyer Otto Kahn Freund (1954, p. 43) said: 'the first duty of a lawyer about to discuss the legal framework of industrial relations is to warn his readers not to overestimate its importance'.

Notes

1. Monopsony occurs where demand (in this case for labour) comes from one source.
2. The Equal Pay Act applies to both men and women and men can claim equal pay with women, as well as vice versa. In practice, however, nearly all the claims are brought by women. Hence this chapter (like the Act itself) uses the feminine for simplicity.
3. A company which the claimant's employer controls or where both the claimant's and comparator's companies are controlled by a third person.
4. Armstrong and ors v. Newcastle upon Tyne NHS Hospital Trust [2006] IRLR 124 CA.
5. The Commission for Equality and Human Rights can conduct formal investigations where they believe that systemic practices in an organisation are discriminatory, but it is too early to know to what extent it will use its powers.
6. See Hoyland v. Asda Stores Ltd [2006] IRLR 468 CS. The Discrimination Law Review taking place at the time of writing may obviate this problem by proposing a single equality act.
7. Glasgow City Council and ors v. Marshall and ors [2000] ICR 196 HL; Villalba v. Merril Lynch and Co Inc and ors [2006] IRLR EAT.
8. Robertson and others v Department of the Environment, Food and Rural Affairs [2005] IRLR 363 CA.
9. Cadman v. Health and Safety Executive [2006] IRLR 969 ECJ.
10. Macarthys Ltd v Smith [1980] ICR 672 ECJ.
11. Mangold v. Helm [2006] IRLR 143 ECJ.
12. GMB v Allen and others UKEAT/0425/06.

References

Adams, L., Carter, K. and Shafer, S. (2006) 'Equal Pay Reviews Survey 2005', *Working Paper Series*, 42, Manchester: Equal Opportunities Commission.

Anderson, T., Forth, J., Metcalf, H. and Kirby, S. (2001) *The Gender Pay Gap*, London: Women & Equality Unit, Cabinet Office.

Ayres, I. and Braithwaite, J. (1992) *Responsive Regulation: Transcending the Deregulation Debate,* Oxford: Oxford University Press.

Bellamy, K. and Cameron, S. (2006) *Gender Equality in the 21st Century: Modernising the Legislation,* London: Fawcett Society.

Brodie, M. (2006) 'Equal Pay Crisis in Local Government', *Diversity at Work,* 22, April, 23–24.

Brown, W. (2006) 'The Low Pay Commission', chapter 6 in Dickens, L. and Neale, A. (eds) *The Changing Institutional Face of British Employment Relations,* Alphen aan den Rijn, Netherlands: Kluwer Law International.

Conservatives (2007) *Fair Play on Women's Pay,* London: Conservative Party.

Corby, S., Stanworth, C., and Green, B. (2005) *Gender and the Labour Market in South East England: Employers' Policies and Practices,* London: University of Greenwich.

Department of Health (2004) *Agenda for Change: What Will It Mean for You?,* London: Department of Health.

Dickens, L. (2007) 'The Road is Long: Thirty Years of Equality Legislation in Britain', *British Journal of Industrial Relations,* 45, 3, 463–494.

Equal Opportunities Commission (2003) *Code of Practice on Equal Pay,* Manchester: Equal Opportunities Commission.

Equal Opportunities Commission (2005) *Response to the Women and Work Commission, Part Two: Closing the Gender Pay Gap,* Manchester: Equal Opportunities Commission.

Equal Opportunities Commission (2007) *Gender Equality Duty: Code of Practice,* Manchester: Equal Opportunities Commission.

European Commission (2000) 'Towards a Community Framework Strategy on Gender Equality 2001–2005', *Communication on Gender,* 335 final, Brussels: Commission of the European Union.

Fredman, S. (2001) 'Equality A New Generation?', *Industrial Law Journal,* 30, 2, 145–168.

Fredman, S. (2002) *Discrimination Law,* Oxford: Oxford University Press.

Gibbons, M. (2007) *A Review of Employment Dispute Resolution in Great Britain,* London: Department of Trade and Industry.

Grainger, H. and Crowther, M. (2007) *Trade Union Membership 2006,* London: Department of Trade and Industry.

Grimshaw, D. and Rubery, J. (2007) 'Undervaluing Women's Work', *Working Paper Series,* 53, Manchester: Equal Opportunities Commission.

Hakim, C. (1991) 'Grateful Slaves and Self-Made Women: Fact and Fantasy in Women's Work Orientations', *European Sociological Review,* 7, 2, 101–121.

Hakim, C. (2002) 'Lifestyle Preferences as Determinants of Women's Differentiated Labour Market Careers', *Work and Occupations,* 29, 4, 428–459.

Harman, H. (2008) *The Framework for a Fairer Future – The Equality Bill,* Cm 7431, London: The Stationery Office.

Hepple, B. (2006) 'The Equality Commissions and the Future Commission for Equality and Human Rights', chapter 9 in Dickens, L. and Neale, A. (eds) *The Changing Institutional Face of British Employment Relations,* Alphen aan den Rijn, Netherlands: Kluwer Law International.

Hepple, B., Coussey, M. and Choudhury, T. (2000) *Equality: A New Framework, Report of the Independent Review of the Enforcement of UK Anti-Discrimination Legislation,* Oxford: Hart Publishing.

Incomes Data Services (2004) 'Streamlining the Equal Value Procedures', *Diversity at Work,* 5, November, 11–16.

Incomes Data Services (2006) 'Age Discrimination', *Employment Law Supplement*, London: Incomes Data Services.

Institute of Employment Rights (2004) *Written Evidence to the Women and Work Commission*, London: Institute of Employment Rights.

Joint Negotiating Committee for Higher Education Staff (2003) *Framework Agreement for the Modernisation of Pay Structures*, London: JNCHES.

Justice (1987) *Industrial Tribunals: A Report of a Committee Chaired by Bob Hepple*, London: Justice.

Kahn-Freund, O. (1954) 'Legal Framework' in Flanders, A. and Clegg, H. A. (eds) *The System of Industrial Relations in Great Britain*, Oxford: Blackwell.

Lucas, R. and Nair Keegan, S. (2007) 'Young Workers and the National Minimum Wage', *Equal Opportunities International*, 26, 6, 573–589.

McCrudden, C. (2007) 'Equality Legislation and Reflexive Regulation: A Response to the Discrimination Law Review's Consultative Paper', *Industrial Law Journal*, 36, 3, 255–266.

McNair, S. and Flynn, M. (2005) 'The Age Dimension of Employment Practices: Employer Case Studies', *Employment Relations Research Series*, 42, London: Department of Trade and Industry.

Metcalf, H. and Meadows, P. (2006) 'Survey of Employers' Policies, Practices and Preferences Relating to Age', *Research Report 325/ DTI Employment Research Series* 49, London: Department for Work and Pensions.

Miller, L., Neathey, F., Pollard, E. , and Hill, D. (2004) 'Occupational Segregation Gender Gaps and Skills Gaps', *Working Paper Series*, 15, Manchester: Equal Opportunities Commission.

O'Cinneide, C. (2003a) 'Extending Positive Duties across the Equality Grounds', *Equal Opportunities Review*, 120, August, 12–16.

O'Cinneide, C. (2003b) 'Making Use of Positive Duties: the UK Experience', chapter 4 in Costello, C. and Barry, E. (eds) *Equality in Diversity: The New Equality Directives*, Dublin: Irish Centre for European Law.

O'Cinneide, C. (2005) 'A New Generation of Equality Legislation? Positive Duties and Disability Rights', chapter 12 in Lawson, A. and Gooding, C. (eds) *Disability Rights in Europe*, Oxford: Hart.

Office for National Statistics (2007) *Annual Survey of Hours and Earnings 2007*, London: ONS.

Rubenstein, M. (2006) 'Highlights: December 2006', *Industrial Relations Law Reports*, 35, 905.

Sergeant, M. (2006) 'The Employment Equality (Age) Regulations 2006: A Legitimisation of Age Discrimination in Employment', *Industrial Law Journal*, 35, 3, 209–227.

Sherman, J. (2007) 'Men Are to Pay a High Price for Sexual Equality', *The Times*, 12 March.

TUC (2007) 'Government Must Act on Council Equal Pay', *Press Release*, www.tuc.org.uk/equality/tuc-1316-f0.cfm (accessed 30 March 2007).

Waldemeir, P. (2007) 'Wal-Mart Loses Attempt to Block Sex-Bias Lawsuit', *Financial Times*, 7 February, 21.

Women and Work Commission (2006) *Shaping a Fairer Future*, London: Department of Trade and Industry.

Woodward, W. and Curtis, P. (2007) 'Tories Risk Row with Business Backers over Plans to Close Pay Gap', *The Guardian*, 5 February, 8.

Wright, A. (2007) '"Modernising" Away Gender Pay Inequality? Some Evidence from the Local Government Sector on Using Job Evaluation', paper presented to the *Performance and Reward Conference*, Manchester, 29 March.

9

Executive rewards – 'don't you just give them loads of money?'

Jon Dymond and Helen Murlis

Introduction

At parties we are often asked 'and what do you do?', resisting the urge to respond that we are rocket scientists or actors, a reply that 'I advise companies on how to set pay for their executive directors' provokes at worst a look of blank incomprehension, at best the response 'Don't you just give them a lot of money?' Whilst our temporary social discomfort might be relieved if we simply agreed that that is what we do, we would be doing the field of executive reward a disservice.

In practice of course executive reward consultants do not simply 'give them a lot of money', but the reasons people have this perception are both interesting and revealing and the assumption that this is what we do is perhaps not an entirely unfair one. In this chapter, it is our intention to consider whether or not this perception has any grounds in fact, to consider the factors that have influenced executive reward as it is today and to explore the evolution of pay at the top and in doing so to express some candid opinions about where executive reward has gone wrong.

The plan of this chapter is as follows: first, we consider why executive reward is such an emotive subject and the factors that have contributed to its growth. Next, we examine the components of executive reward and ask whether executive reward will change. Then we look briefly at chief executive officers (CEOs) in the public sector, before concluding with a plea for a more systematic approach to top pay.

Why is executive reward such an emotive subject?

The subject of executive reward is often highly emotive. Barely a day goes by without a journalist or columnist commenting, usually in derogatory terms, on the 'fat cat' rewards available to executive directors. Broadly speaking they comment on the size of rewards available; and a perception that there is a 'rewards for failure' culture where 'golden parachutes' can run into millions of pounds worth of value. Examples of press comment taking this line are legion; typical of the genre is the article in the *Financial Times* in early 2008 titled 'Bankers' pay is deeply flawed' (Rajam, 2008).

The size of executive rewards

Although the methods for calculating how much an executive director is paid can vary, it is clear that executive directors earn more, very much more than most of us. According to the Annual Survey of Hours and Earnings (Office for National Statistics, 2007) full-time males at the median (and most chief executives are male too) earned £498 per week in April 2007, less than £26,000 a year. Chief Executive Officers (CEOs) of companies with a market capitalisation of over £1 billion earn around £2 million a year. To some people this amount is simply 'too much'. For the public, many commentators and, rather worryingly, many corporate governance analysts at investment institutions, a lack of understanding about what it is a CEO or an executive director actually does to warrant their pay, other than 'be the boss', contributes to this disbelief. To be fair, companies have often been lamentably poor at describing the nature and challenges of the boss's job and the sense of injustice felt by employees within companies let alone by the broader public is perhaps only to be expected. Leaving aside the argument from personal incredulity for the moment, the other factor which contributes to this sense that the amounts being earned are too high is a perception that we could all do an executive's job if only we had the opportunity. By contrast, although some of us wonder how the captain of a premier league professional football team earns £5 million a year, most of us acknowledge that we couldn't possibly play as well as he can. The main reason for this incongruity is perhaps that, for most of us, until very recently, the potential route to the top executive suite was unclear whereas an inability to move forward without tripping over our own feet made it clear that the route to sporting stardom was blocked. In companies, the reasons for your not being promoted to become the boss were much, much less clear. Perhaps the increased and better-communicated investment by some companies in talent management and leadership development, will, in time, change the perception that, to borrow from the Nike advertisement for a moment, we can all 'just do it'.

The 'rewards for failure' perception

The one subject most likely to provoke an emotional verbal Vesuvius from business journalists is rewards for failure. A perception that executives are paid monstrous sums even if they have destroyed shareholder value, sacked thousands, or been found guilty of overcharging customers, remains firmly embedded in the British psyche despite the reports of Cadbury (Financial Reporting Council, 1992), Greenbury (Study Group on Directors' Remuneration, 1995), Hampel (Committee on Corporate Governance, 1998), Higgs (2003) and the Director's Remuneration Report Regulations (2002), which all addressed rewards for failure.

While companies continue to do such a poor job of explaining the legal and contractual issues involved in explaining why they pay what they do, and whilst they themselves are unclear about what each element of executive reward is actually for, this perception is unlikely to change.

Have we lost perspective on executive reward?

It is our contention that the emotions which executive reward provoke has led many to lose perspective on the subject. In the grand scheme of the things that a company does, the amounts of money executive directors receive are not as grotesque as we might think, as Figure 9.1 shows.

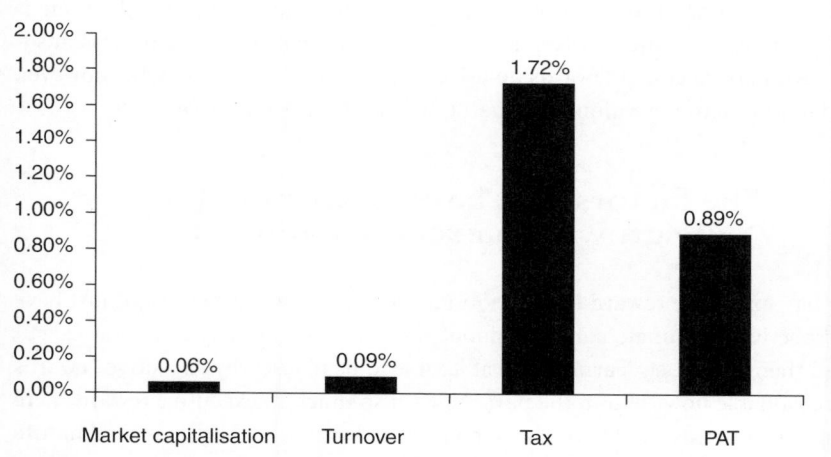

Figure 9.1   FTSE 350 pay as a percentage of market capitalisation, turnover, tax paid, and Profit After Tax (PAT)

Source: Hay Group, 2007a.

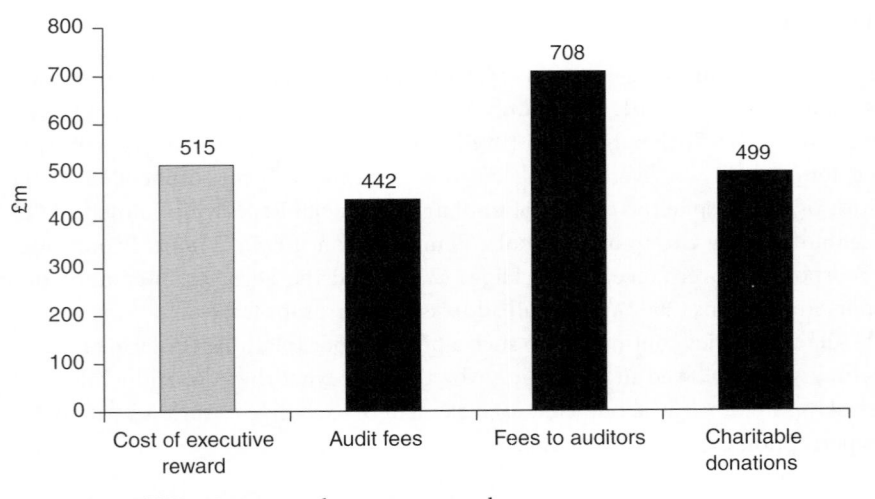

Figure 9.2 FTSE 100 pay vs. other company outlays

Source: Hay Group, 2007a.

Executive reward accounts for less than 1 per cent of the profit after tax (PAT) generated by the FTSE 350, and as illustrated in Figure 9.2, FTSE 100 companies give nearly as much to charities as they do to their own executive directors and, perhaps more surprisingly, give even more to their auditors.

Whilst it is important that companies spend this money properly, from an investor's point of view, the actual amounts doled out to executive directors are so small as to be immaterial in absolute terms. This does not mean that the issue is insignificant; after all, there are equity considerations relating to relative, not absolute rewards and executive rewards do affect executive behaviour. Maybe, however, we need to rein in our emotions and maintain a sense of perspective.

The factors that have contributed to the growth in executive reward

For all that, executive reward is an emotional subject on which we might just have lost perspective, legitimate concerns about the growing gap between what executives and their employees earn should at least lead us to ask why executive rewards are more valuable now than in the past. As with so much in executive reward there is no one answer. Several factors have contributed including the changing nature of companies and therefore of executive's jobs; the modern 'star' culture; agency theory; the talent shortage; and pay disclosure. These factors have all had an impact on the shape of modern executive reward and form the essential backdrop to the sections of this chapter looking at the different elements of executive reward.

The changing nature of companies

Arguably, the tasks and challenges facing the modern top executive are more complicated and difficult than they were in the past. Over the past 50 years, the structure of companies has changed significantly. Historically, executives of large companies were in effect managers of relatively stable monopolies or oligopolies, there was less competition for both customers, and capital and workforces were often less well educated as well as highly unionised and therefore could effectively be managed en masse through collective bargaining. It was a world of 'command and control'. In contrast, modern companies need to operate in a globalised economy, competition is more intense, barriers to entry are lower than they were and employees are more questioning and educated and require credible leadership able to engage people in their vision. In such an environment the job of being an executive is more difficult. We believe that it requires a broader range of skills, deeper knowledge, and perhaps most importantly a broader strategic vision than previously. Arguably, all of these additional skills need to be paid for and the result has been that executive reward levels have climbed accordingly.

Star culture

The past fifty years or so has seen the establishment of a 'star culture' and the creation of the cult of the celebrity chief executive officer (CEO). The modern obsession with stars, idols, and talismanic individuals has spread to business. For reasons which are not entirely as facile as our fascination with the comings and goings of C-list celebrities, investors and boards of directors have lionised certain executives and encouraged a 'no price is too high' culture in the boardroom. A distinctive star CEO can deliver competitive advantage in an increasingly competitive world and is therefore worth paying more for and in some cases, far more. At least that is how the argument used to run, and indeed has run, for perceived saviours, such as Stuart Rose at Marks and Spencer. However, like many a Hollywood celebrity, some of these star CEOs have fallen out of favour; Luc Vandevelde, who was also interestingly at Marks and Spencer, being an example. Nevertheless, the star CEOs and their big pay packages are likely to remain a feature of corporate life. The reason for this is largely that companies and, in particular, company boards do not want to take a risk handing stewardship of a company to a relatively 'unproven' executive. Indeed, investors too are more suspicious than they might perhaps admit at the appointment of an 'unknown' to senior posts and tacitly support a factor which drives up executive reward levels.

Agency theory and its critiques

Perhaps the main factor in rising levels of executive reward is agency or principal-agent theory. In classical economics, the CEO and the firm owner are the same. In today's large companies the firm is owned by the shareholders and the CEO, who does not necessarily share the interests of the shareholders, is the leading manager. According to agency theory, shareholders must structure the CEOs compensation arrangements to reward behaviour that increases shareholder wealth, so reducing conflicts of interest (see Gomez-Mejia and Balkin, 1992).

Essentially agency theory arose because economists from the 1930s onwards studied companies and noticed that managers tended to be risk averse and engaged in behaviours which were not necessarily conducive to maximising long-term shareholder value. They looked to enhance their public profile, to build 'empires' and to spend large sums on corporate offices at the expense of investing for value. In other words, there was 'rent extraction' as managers were able to design their own risk free reward packages. Furthermore, Galbraith (1967) argued that managers of corporations had become bureaucrats and had more in common with civil servants.

In the different economic climate of the 1980s investor agitation was on the rise as companies sought to improve their returns by restructuring and refocusing on value, it was recognised that executives needed to be paid more like entrepreneurs than like bureaucrat managers. In short, executives needed to align their interests with those of shareholders and behave more like principals than agents. Accordingly, executives in the United States of America (USA) and, to a lesser extent, the United Kingdom (especially following changes in tax in 1984), began to be paid in share options which, at least in theory, would reward executives for increasing shareholder value. The introduction of the share option as a major component of executive reward led to an explosion in the value of the rewards managers received as they began to share in the gains that shareholders enjoyed.

Agency theory is relevant to the setting of incentive targets, since the use of trackable performance measures in incentive design is considered a clear means of ensuring that 'agents' focus on the delivery of shareholder value. Others argue, however, that agency theory rarely reflects what happens in practice. They argue that because performance measures are by their nature complex, managers are essentially still able to extract rent (to use economic parlance), restrained only by 'outrage' constraints applied by the media and management consultants (Fatturose et al., 2007).

The talent shortage

According to the laws of supply and demand, if supply falls short of demand, prices should rise. There is undoubtedly a perception in the boardroom that the supply of top executive talent is shrinking and that accordingly prices are increasing. This shortage would appear to explain the increase in executive reward levels.

However, there are many in reward circles who would argue that because we have more people going to business school and companies are increasingly paying attention to their human capital and to maximising people's abilities, the potential the supply of talent is increasing not decreasing and that therefore the price of executive directors should be falling. The argument that the talent pool is deeper than it has ever been is particularly powerful when one considers the market for executives in the USA. We note that US pay levels are far higher than in other countries and yet US companies continue to hire US talent at high prices when there are highly capable executives in other markets (e.g., India, Malaysia) who are now capable of running US companies. We might have expected to see US firms acting as arbitrageurs and plundering other talent markets. In practice, of course, this arbitrage does not happen and it is rare for say, UK nationals to run US companies.

In the UK marketplace, however, it might appear that this kind of arbitrage is happening. Today 25–30 per cent of FTSE 100 companies are run by non-UK nationals (e.g., Marjorie Scardino at Pearson) but it appears that the opportunity to profit from pay differences does not exist and in fact executive pay levels have continued to increase. It does appear then, that the market for executive directors does not conform to the normal laws of supply and demand. Such a simplistic view of the executive reward market place however fails to take account of other factors which drive executive reward. For instance, the supply of potential executive directors or CEOs may indeed be increasing but all that means is that vacant positions can more easily be filled. Typically, boards aim to put the best possible candidate into a job and that candidate will accordingly be paid more than the others – thus pushing pay up. This also happens with internal candidates, but there is the 'head-hunter premium' of typically around 20 per cent of remuneration to consider. This can mean that the cost of moving an already well-paid executive to a new role rises by what it takes to make the package attractive enough to accept the new employer's offer.

Few move for less than 20 per cent – unless it is a major public service role at the end of a successful career, when the individual has probably 'made their money' and is willing to exchange lower pay for public prominence. Even in such cases, external appointees to public sector jobs have obtained higher salaries than internal appointees. According to the Civil Service Commission (2007), externals often achieved starting pay in a senior civil service role considerably in excess of the salaries quoted, while it was not uncommon for internals to achieve salaries at less than the advertised rate.

The need to give high rewards to talent is partially supported by tournament theory. This suggests that the excessive rewards received by CEOs have little to do with what they 'deserve'. Rather the main purpose of such rewards is to send signals to senior managers to motivate them to compete for the number one spot. The analogy is with a trophy and high rewards in golf or tennis competitions. This theory, however, ignores the fact that the CEO is not an independent actor, but interrelates with the top management team (TMT) and that CEO and TMT pay, rather than CEO pay alone is associated with firm performance (Carpenter and Sanders, 2002).

Another possibility is that executives are an example of a 'Veblen good' (Veblen, 1899), a status item where the appeal of the good or demand actually increases as the price rises, as illustrated in Figure 9.3.

Veblen (1899), a sociologist and economist best known for his work on conspicuous consumption, theorised that commodities such as perfumes and fine wines were unusual in that decreasing their price could actually have the effect of decreasing people's preference for buying them because they would no longer be seen as exclusive or high status products. Given that the people doing the 'buying' and 'selling' in the executive talent marketplace are themselves, or have in their past been the very commodities for sale, could it not just be possible that they perceive these commodities as high value and as such pay, and aim to pay, for the highest priced items in the marketplace?

We believe that an alternative and perhaps less unusual hypothesis as to why executive reward levels seems to defy most people's understanding of supply and demand is that we are in the midst of a fundamental shift in attitudes towards work and the cost of labour. As we shift from a skills and 'effort' based economy towards a knowledge based economy it might be the case that the cost of doing business has increased as employees, and particularly talented employees, demand a greater share of the products of their labour: the gross profits generated by companies. This could mean that regardless of the size of the talent pool, executives have become more expensive and, perhaps distastefully for left wing critics of executive reward, are at the forefront of a transfer of value from owners to workers.

Pay disclosure

Although well intended, and some would argue, necessary, the disclosure of the amounts individual executives are paid made compulsory in the early 1990s,

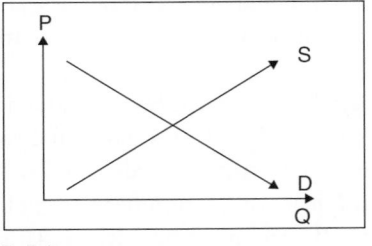

'Classic supply and demand'   'Executive supply and demand?'

P: Price
Q: Quantity
S: Supply
D: Demand

Figure 9.3 Executive supply and demand

might have contributed to increased pay levels. This argument, often put forward by opponents of the disclosure of pay, is that because executives now know what other executives earn and what they earn it for (at least in part), pay levels have increased as these highly competitive individuals demand parity. This argument would be fine but for two reasons. First, prior to the era of compulsory disclosure, companies already had a good idea of what others were paying, courtesy of private surveys such as those produced by Hay Group, Towers Perrin, and the Chartered Institute of Management. Second, that in countries such as France and Germany, where until recently pay levels have not been formally disclosed, executives in different companies earn similar amounts to each other and to those companies in other European countries, such as the UK, where pay levels have been disclosed (Hay Group, 2007b).

The components of executive reward

Base salary

In theory, salary is the fee charged by an employee for his or her services, skills, and abilities. In the case of an executive, however, these skills and abilities are perhaps more difficult to define and understand than they are for other workers. One might expect therefore that the remuneration committees who set executive pay levels would pay particular attention to the nature of their executives' jobs compared to others, especially given that salary is the foundation for an executive reward package. In practice, however, not all remuneration committees use a system that measures this variable accurately. Many companies we have worked with, especially those outside of the FTSE 100 typically set base salary levels by comparing the pay of their directors to those with similar job titles in similar companies. Nevertheless, setting salary levels by position matching alone is in its own right a rather more difficult task than we might at first think.

Setting salary level by reference to other organisations

To set the salary level of the CEO of BP, for example, we might look at the levels of pay at their competitors, at the other oil majors, Chevron, ConocoPhillips, ExxonMobil, Royal Dutch Shell, and Total, and pay the CEO accordingly. Using such a group, however, leaves us with a number of questions, some of which might be:

- Is BP comparable to these companies?
- Could and would our CEO realistically go to work as the CEO at these companies?
- Do these companies pay the way we do in the United Kingdom?
- Are there other companies we should consider?
- What do investors think and expect?

Having considered these questions we might think that

- As an integrated oil company, BP is comparable to the other companies but that they should bear in mind that only one of them has its headquarters in the United Kingdom– and that is half-Dutch.
- Although the CEO could almost certainly move to head up Royal Dutch Shell it is unlikely he could run ExxonMobil, and in any case as a 25-year veteran at BP, he is unlikely to move to a competitor.
- Four of the five comparable companies rely more heavily on share incentives to deliver reward than we do here in the United Kingdom, and by law, US companies have their salary levels effectively capped at $1,000,000 and that affects salary benchmark levels.
- The increasing commercialisation of the National Oil Companies poses a threat to us. We must protect our talent pool, including our CEO from this threat and therefore consider pay in those companies. Furthermore, we think there is the possibility that our CEO could transfer his skills to other sectors. We should therefore consider other major energy companies' pay levels.
- Investors are also interested in pay levels compared to those at other companies in our index, the FTSE 100. We must consider those levels too.

All these variables make it more difficult for remuneration committees to establish an 'appropriate' level of salary. These difficulties are not unique to large companies like BP. In practice, however, because of a lack of time, poor advice, or simple laziness, too many remuneration committees we know often fail to take account of these kinds of questions and as such set salary levels sloppily. This sloppiness also has a knock-on effect: it feeds into the salary data which are then used for comparisons when remuneration committees elsewhere set salary levels.

Executive salary rate increases

One criticism of executive reward is that executives' salaries grow each year at a rate faster than earnings in the general labour market. We have already touched upon reasons for this phenomenon earlier in the chapter, the perceived talent shortage for instance, but some commentators point to these increases as examples of executive greed. We do not think it is greed that has caused this phenomenon, but that it is a result of the imperfect information available to remuneration committees, information which is further corrupted by the lackadaisical approach taken by some of them to salary setting. Different companies set salary levels at different times of year, use different comparator groups to set pay and take account of different factors when setting pay. These differences mean that there is no clear picture of the 'appropriate' level of wage inflation for CEOs available to remuneration committees. Consequently, in our experience, many err on the side of caution and give

CEOs higher than general wage inflation rises recorded either nationally in terms of increases in average earnings or from survey data or research firms like Incomes Data Services or Industrial Relations Services (IRS) to ensure that 'they do not fall behind the market'. This situation is compounded by the general reluctance of remuneration committees to tell an executive that they are in fact performing below 'average' or, in practice, the median, and therefore should receive a below median rise. This reticence, a desire to avoid underpaying executives and a lack of information all contribute to the high rate of salary growth we see for executives, and in fact to the overall growth over time in reward levels.

Contrary to what you might believe if the papers were your main source of information, in recent years the rate of executive salary inflation has decreased. For the past three years or so (i.e., since 2004) salary increases have on average been around the 3 to 6 per cent per annum level (Hay Group, 2007a). The principal reason for this is that investors and their representative bodies, the Association of British Insurers in particular, have focused on salary levels, expecting rises above 10 per cent to be explained. Remuneration committees have accordingly been more conservative. However, this apparently 'good thing' has had some unexpected consequences for annual bonus levels.

Benefits and pensions

Typically, an executive director would expect to receive a full suite of benefits with at least a minimum of life and travel insurance, life assurance, and a pension.

Benefits

The provision of benefits to employees in general is commendable and a normal part of effective reward practice (see Chapter 11). The bulk buying power of companies, where a pound's worth of value can be provided for a cost less than a pound, can be beneficial to both companies and their employees. In the United Kingdom, there has not really been much debate around the provision of benefits to executives. It has to be said that this is a result of restraint on the part of both remuneration committees and executives themselves.

In the USA by contrast, perquisites and benefits have become a high-profile feature of the executive reward debate and highly admired CEOs such as Jack Welch of GE have found their legacy and reputation tarnished by disclosure of the lavish benefits they received and continued to receive even after retirement. Leaving aside any advantageous tax consequences of providing such benefits, the rather feeble argument often put forward by compensation committees, and, shamefully, their advisers, for this state of affairs, is that providing benefits such as chauffeurs, country club membership, private jets, and the like, enables executives to concentrate on the job at hand. To be frank if a one-million-dollar salary does not concentrate the mind on creating shareholder value then we do not know what will. Furthermore, if one can really justify these benefits on these grounds then why not also provide executives with house servants.

Pension

One result of the Directors Remuneration Report Regulations 2002 is that executive pension provision has been forced into the limelight, with pension pots for the average executive director worth around two to three million pounds each. It is perhaps surprising that the issue of pension provision for executives was already not singing and dancing at the front of the executive reward stage. Although a valuable element of executive reward, these schemes were not as controversial as they might have been for the simple reason that pensions are not the easiest things to understand and that at least in structure, if not in funding, provision for executive directors was broadly the same as for other employees. In the late 1990s, many companies reconsidered their occupational pension schemes (see Chapter 10). Most decided that defined benefit (final salary) plans were no longer affordable and as such began to abandon them. With the odd dishonourable exception, pension provision for executives also changed so that newly appointed executives, like other new employees, were excluded from final salary scheme membership, and received contributions to a defined contribution (money purchase) plan as an alternative. Nevertheless, if there is one area where executives can be described as having their noses in the trough it is this one. Higher company contribution rates for executive directors, and, in some companies, the practice of maintaining a defined benefit plan for executive directors only, lends ammunition to the 'don't you just pay them lots of money?' brigade. Justifying pensions intellectually for executives is rather difficult. Salaries are paid for an executive's services; benefits are given because it is tax efficient to provide them, annual bonuses are linked to targets designed to deliver the strategic and operational plan and long-term incentives are provided to align executives with shareholders and to encourage the creation of shareholder value. Figure 9.4 below illustrates the process. The purpose of the pension, however, is less clear. There are really only two viable arguments for executive pensions. First, there is the paternalistic argument that it is responsible for companies to provide employees with provision for old age and that, as employees, executives should receive pensions – especially if they have been with the employer for some time. But, in an age when CEOs in the FTSE 100 earn salaries of over £700,000 per annum does this argument really bear scrutiny – especially for those moving between employers? The second argument is that they 'have' to be provided to reflect 'market practice'. In our opinion, accepting this line of argument without question puts the remuneration committee in no better a position than that of the indulgent parent who dispenses sweets and toys to their children having accepted the 'but Johnny and Susan have one, I want one' line of reasoning.

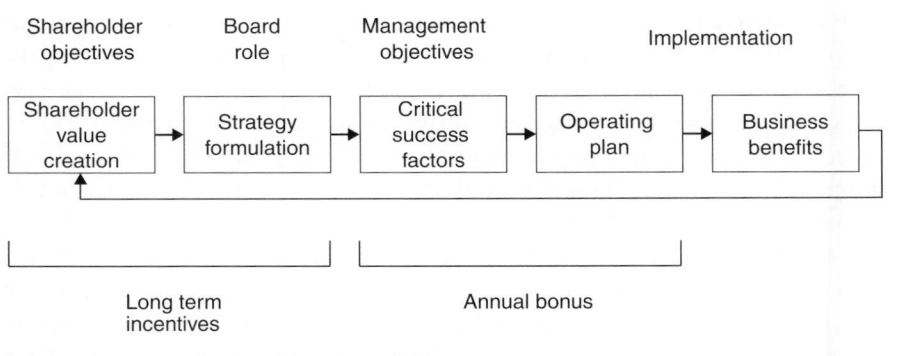

Shareholder objectives	Board role	Management objectives	Implementation

Shareholder value creation → Strategy formulation → Critical success factors → Operating plan → Business benefits

Long term incentives

Annual bonus

Figure 9.4   The elements of executive reward

Of course in practice companies do not explicitly justify the provision of a pension to their executives, it is simply an accepted feature of the reward landscape. Encouragingly, however, 'A day' and the pension cap implemented in 2006 have led some companies to question just why they pay pension to their executives.

Annual bonuses

What are annual bonuses paid for?

Remuneration reports typically inform us that annual bonuses are paid for the achievement of annual objectives. For entirely understandable commercial reasons these objectives are not often clearly described. However, we know that in practice most companies pay an annual bonus for the achievement of a number of financial and strategic objectives set at the beginning of the annual bonus year. Achieving the balance between these objectives is often the most difficult task remuneration committees face. Adding to this difficulty, in recent years remuneration committees have been under pressure explicitly to link annual bonus payments for executives to the achievement of financial objectives, in particular. Although many remuneration committees have always followed this route to performance management and have paid bonuses for the achievement of the annual budget, it can result in something very close to an obsession with the annual budget setting process, even if it does produce externally justifiable results. Of course, structurally the problem with this approach is that non-executives often do not have as good an understanding of the finances and potential performance of the company as executives do, and that, as such, the annual bonus setting process becomes a combative tournament with executives and non-executives battling for their point of view to win out. In our experience, this is both unhealthy for relationships on the board and more pertinently is unhealthy for the process of actually delivering the strategic objectives of the business.

While shareholders deserve and indeed demand to understand why bonuses have been paid, they really do need to remember what the annual bonus should be paid for, that is the achievement of targets, which may be a mix of 'hard' measurable and observable behavioural elements, which drive the strategy of the company. This is not the same as the achievement of earnings growth, EPS improvement, or annual share price performance. These indicators of underlying long-term health should all be rewarded through long-term incentives rather than the annual bonus.

Research by Jon Dymond (2005) indicates that in the pharmaceutical and bio-technology sector a perception that annual bonus payments should be affected by share price performance, or at least that CEOs should not get 'large' bonuses in years the share price fell, resulted in CEO bonus payments effectively tracking total shareholder return performance, rising when total shareholder return (TSR) went up and falling when TSR went down. Yet when TSR went down, remuneration committees compensated CEOs for their lower bonus by making a higher salary increase (which would certainly not conventionally have been the line taken for underperforming employees further down the organisation). If remuneration committees felt performance was good, as indicated by the salary increase, should not they just have paid the annual bonus in the first place? Experience suggests that this kind of perverse behaviour is not unique to this sector and is symptomatic of the difficulty remuneration committees face in trying to please two constituencies, corporate governance experts and executives, whilst wrestling with the underlying market pressure to increase pay levels. Nevertheless, we find many companies now weight annual bonuses to reflect strategic and non-financial targets which are essential to the strategic plan.

Annual bonus levels

Annual bonus maxima and payout levels have increased dramatically over the past five years. The 'on target' bonus for executives in the FTSE 100 is now 50 per cent of salary at the median, yet just five years ago, the maximum available was the same figure. Arguably, these increased bonus payments could be justified if performance had improved in similarly dramatic fashion. In reality, of course this has not happened. Research conducted by the Hay Group shows that as well as the maximum available increasing, the 'minimum' level of annual bonus payment has also increased, as illustrated in Figure 9.5.

The minimum level of annual bonus payment shows the average amount paid out when annual bonus plans actually paid out at all. In the FTSE 350, there was no identifiable minimum level of payment in 1996 but five years later 10 per cent of salary became the minimum payment, and in 2006, the amount paid out at the minimum was approximately 20 per cent of salary. In other words, when bonuses are paid the amount paid out has increased and is increasing at the same time as the maximum available has grown (Hay Group, 2007a)

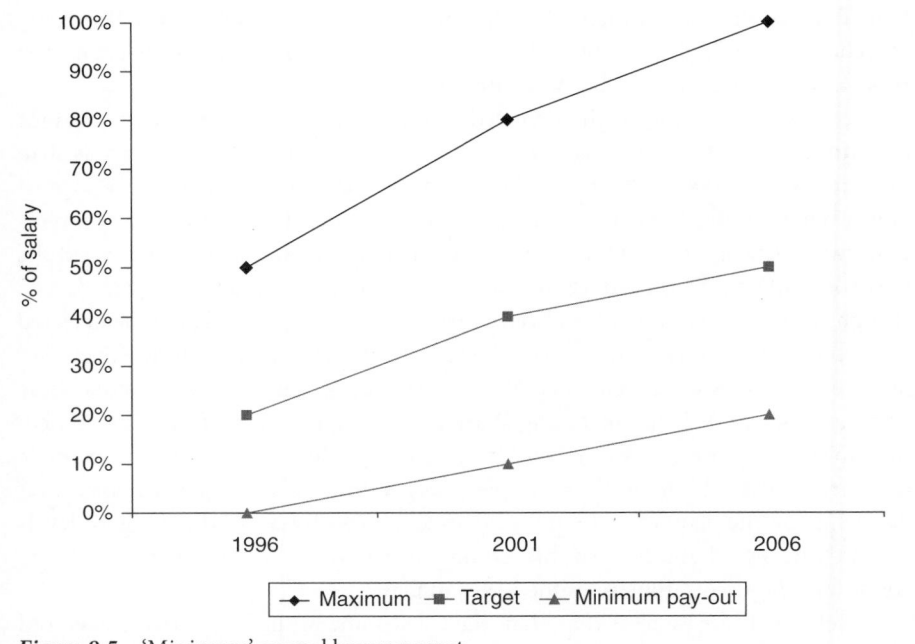

Figure 9.5 'Minimum' annual bonus payout

Source: Hay Group, 2007a.

Our experience suggests that the reasons for these increases are threefold: first, the increased popularity of deferred share bonus plans means that there has to be a meaningful payout for the plans to work, on which more later; second, the pressure to keep executive annual salary increases below 10 per cent applied by institutional shareholders and their representative bodies has led remuneration committees to 'compensate' via the annual bonus; and third, investor pressure to make more of an executive's pay variable than fixed has led remuneration committees to increase the bonus available. To sum up, the performance-related slice of the pie has grown in proportion to the fixed slice, but the pie itself has also got bigger.

Deferred share bonus plans

Anyone looking to blame increased executive reward levels and complexity on executive compensation consultants could start the argument by reference to the explosion in the popularity of deferred share bonus plans over the past few years. Although they can serve a useful purpose, particularly in companies where traditional long-term incentives do not work especially well, such as in the biotechnology sector, their prevalence is out of all proportion to the real need for them. We are not suggesting that executive reward consultants from Warren Buffett's famed firm 'Ratchet, Ratchet & Bingo' (Warren Buffett's 2005 letter to Berkshire Hathaway shareholders) were disingenuous in recommending these plans, rather that the reasons for having one have become rather lost.

The original purpose of the deferred share bonus plan was not to encourage executives to invest in their employer; they could do that anyway, nor was it to provide a link between short- and long-term performance. Rather it was to provide a retention mechanism when, early in the decade, share options were largely underwater (the market price of a share had fallen far below the exercise price of the share option) and, because of shareholder disapproval, could not be re-priced. As a straightforward retention plan or even as a simple deferred reward plan the deferred share bonus plan was, and can still be, excellent. As with long-term incentives however, investors were concerned at the levels of matching available under these plans and demanded that matching share awards should be performance-related. Remuneration committees simply added a minimum hurdle measure, for example that earnings should increase by two per cent per annum. These performance conditions made the plan less retentive and as such executives asked for higher levels of matching award and in turn this led investors to demand tougher performance conditions. Figure 9.6 illustrates the issues in play.

The effect of this today is that plans have lost some of their retentive power and in effect have become another performance-related element of pay. Having lost their original purpose we have to question why share bonus plans are still being enthusiastically embraced and introduced by companies, especially those below the FTSE 100. Could it be the case that we are seeing 'me tooism' on the part of these companies, and that this, combined with the lack of clarity around what the different elements of executive reward are actually for, lends itself to commentators thinking that this element of reward is also an example of unnecessary largesse?

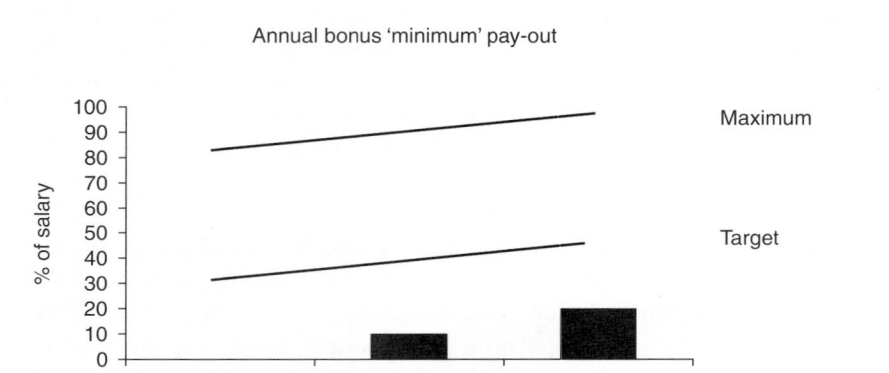

Figure 9.6   The deferred bonus problem
Source: Hay Group, 2007a.

Long-term incentives

The original purposes of long-term incentives are reasonably clear. They were given to executives to encourage growth in long-term revenue, profit, and return on investment. Share incentives, at first share options and then, for those that could afford them, performance-dependent share awards, also served the purpose of aligning the interests of management with shareholders, thus resolving the agency problem. Over time, however, the way executives are rewarded for longer-term performance has changed.

Long-term incentives in the United Kingdom, a history

Concerns over rewards for failure and, almost from their introduction, a perception that executives were getting a free ride from share options that is, they stood to gain if the market as a whole happened to be rising but lost nothing if the share price fell below the exercise price, led many to call for share incentives to have additional performance conditions attached to them. At first, companies responded to these calls by putting minimum performance requirements on the vesting of share option awards. Measures such as a requirement for real earnings growth (above inflation) were put in place to counter the idea that executives stood to make gains regardless of their own performance. Although this did not answer the concern that alignment with shareholders had not really been addressed; for instance, there is no downside for an executive if the share price falls below the exercise price (other than the loss of a potential reward), this remained the status quo for some time.

By the mid 1990s, as more and more UK companies 'went global', attempts to address this downside issue and to prevent rewards for failure, combined with a concern that UK practice was out of step with US and international practice led some companies to introduce Long-Term Incentive Plans (LTIPs). These are plans that provide share awards subject to performance, hence our preference for the term 'performance share plan' (after all, share option plans are a form of long-term incentive plan too). Typically, the performance required for these plans to vest was that total shareholder return performance needed to outstrip that of a group of comparable companies, with varying amounts vesting dependent upon relative position. By 2000, many companies were making awards under both a traditional share option plan, with an EPS growth performance measure, and a performance share plan, with a relative TSR performance measure.

The bursting of the 'dotcom bubble' and more significantly the Profit and Loss account charge for share based incentives arising from IFRS2 (which became accounting practice in 2004) led many companies to conclude that performance share plans offered better value for money than the option plan, and so a migration from options to performance share plans took place. Today, the performance share plan is the vehicle of choice for delivering long-term rewards, but more and more companies have added an earnings performance measure to the previously prevalent relative performance measure, so that both types of performance can be rewarded through the more tax efficient share award vehicle, the LTIP.

Does current long-term incentive practice work?

The original purpose of long-term incentives was to align the interests of management with shareholders and to encourage shareholder value creation. On these criteria current long-term incentive practice does not work as well as it used to, as it actually rewards earnings performance, and performance relative to peers, but does little directly to encourage the creation of shareholder value.

Recent research by the Hay Group, as yet unpublished, shows that on average executives in the FTSE mid-250 can earn seven times more for growing earnings by 1 per cent, even if the share price has not increased, than they can for increasing share price by 1 per cent when the competition have failed to increase theirs at all. In Table 9.1 we can see that EPS growth of 1 per cent garners a reward of £37,000 even if the share price has not increased, whereas efforts to increase share price against the background of a falling market only garners a reward of £5,000.

In our opinion, the earnings focus of current long-term incentive practice is rather worrying. The objective of long-term incentives, to encourage the creation of long-term shareholder value, seems to have been forgotten. Consultants and corporate governance analysts at institutional investors did not intend this to happen, but the demands for increasingly 'difficult' performance conditions on share options, a desire to see options have the same performance conditions as performance share plans and a relentless focus on making TSR related performance conditions 'tougher' has produced this situation.

Under a typical Total Shareholder Return (TSR) related performance share plan executives are rewarded in a rather simplistic way for their performance as Figure 9.7 illustrates.

The problem with this kind of payment curve is that executives receive absolutely nothing for their performance even if they just miss the median position. Is this equitable where the position might have been missed by 1 per cent but the actual return to shareholders was over 100 per cent over the three-year period for which performance was measured? We do not think so. Furthermore, why should being

Table 9.1 The excessive focus of long-term incentives on earnings growth

		No other change	Relative total shareholder return + 1%	ESP + 1%
Change in absolute	+1%	£12,000	£17,000	£49,000
Total shareholder return	0%	£0	£5,000	£37,000

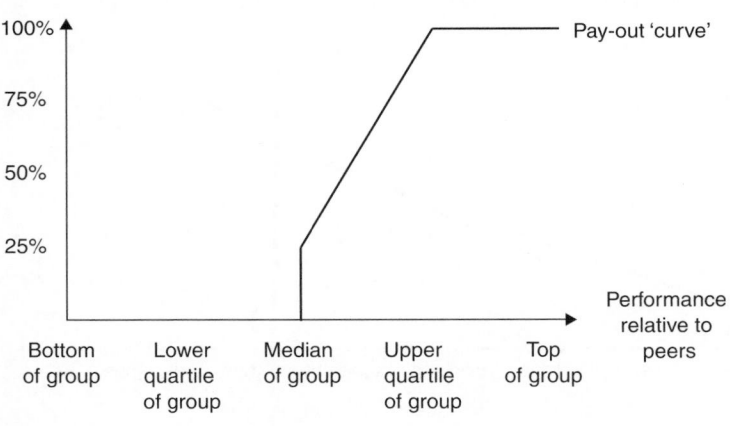

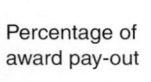

Percentage of
award pay-out

100%

75%

50%

25%

Pay-out 'curve'

Performance
relative to
peers

Bottom   Lower   Median   Upper   Top
of group   quartile   of group   quartile   of group
             of group   of group

Figure 9.7   The typical relative TSR payout curve

top of the group only be worth as much as being at the upper quartile, especially if share price growth has been significantly higher than that achieved by the company at the upper quartile? Given this state of affairs, and the roulette like nature of long-term incentive payouts, it is perhaps unsurprising that executives have long become disillusioned with the structure of their long-term incentives and have shifted focus towards other performance measures such as earnings, which they know, or think they know, they can influence.

Long-term incentive reward levels

In recent years, long-term incentive award levels have levelled out in face value terms at 100 per cent of salary in the FTSE 250 for both performance share and share option awards, and in the FTSE 100 at 150 per cent and 200 per cent of salary for performance share and share option awards respectively. Whether or not these levels are appropriate is debatable; after all there is no absolute measure of 'appropriate' (though we might perhaps ask why it costs at least five times as much to motivate a US executive as it does to motivate a UK one, as other analysis suggests).

What is clear however is that there is some muddle-headed thinking about the relative value of a share option and a share as Figure 9.8 illustrates.

Even if we accept that the different performance conditions attached to share options might be easier to achieve than those attached to performance share awards it seems odd that at market rates of award an executive will only earn as much from their option, as from their performance share plan, if the share price increases threefold.

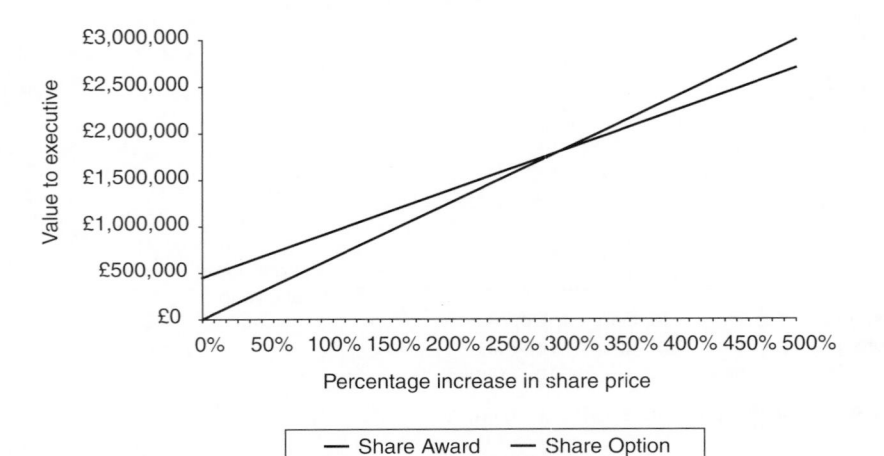

Value of performance share awards made at market rate to FTSE 250 executives
vs
Value of share option awards made at market rate to FTSE 250 executives

Figure 9.8 Value of performance share awards and share option awards made at the average award level in the FTSE 250

Will executive reward change?

Although some companies have put in place unusual and arguably more effective executive reward structures, for example Xstrata and the Berkeley Group, they remain exceptions. Other than when companies face a turnaround or rescue situation, as at Cable & Wireless and Sainsbury's for instance, we rarely see original or different executive reward policies being pursued by remuneration committees. Largely this is because executive reward is stuck in a rut, remuneration committees have been convinced that investors will not take kindly to alternative designs and many HR professionals and executive reward consultants have become transfixed by the power of 'market practice'. However, investors' emphasis on shareholder value and the market pressures which have been pushing up executive reward levels are unlikely to go away and innovative designs may become more and more necessary. Of course, innovation is not in and of itself always a good thing but the limited palette used by remuneration committees to paint today's executive reward programmes is simply not colourful enough to reflect the different shades of company in the listed environment. Unless there is a dramatic change in the environment in which listed companies operate – and it is not that hard to imagine a market crash or directed investment via private equity becoming a more favourable environment than listing – change in executive reward, however, remains unlikely.

If companies remember the history of executive reward, remember what the elements of executive reward are actually for, it is possible, however, that we shall see some innovation in executive reward and in long-term incentive design in particular. Maybe in five years time we will be discussing indexed options or share awards as the solution to the need to prevent a free ride for executives, whilst rewarding absolute share price performance. Maybe we will be discussing how annual bonuses have been simplified and tied to strategic performance rather than to the achievement of accounting figures. Maybe we will be discussing how companies have issued premium priced share options granted at a price that takes into account the cost of capital and the expected return on that capital. Maybe those companies that struggle with long-term incentives will instead focus on long-term rewards. And maybe there'll be more consultants prepared to engage with their client's business rather than their own technical area of expertise.

The public sector

Most of our observations in this chapter relate to the private sector, as this is where the public's concept of a 'loadsamoney' ethos is strongest. But it is worth briefly considering top pay in the public sector, where another divergence of practice between the public and private sectors, to go with those noted elsewhere in this book, is evident. Put simply, by and large the top paid jobs in the public sector attract nothing like the level of cash award as they do in the private sector. The highest paid civil servant, the Cabinet Secretary, for example, has base pay of around £220,000; the top job in the judiciary, the Lord Chief Justice, receives £225,000; while the most senior person in the military, the Chief of the Defence Staff, earns between £209 thousand and £221,000 (Senior Salaries Review Body, 2007). According to Incomes Data Services the highest paid NHS Trust Chief Executive received base pay of £240,000 in 2006 (Incomes Data Services, 2007a). Meanwhile the Prime Minister gets by on £189,000.

One aspect of top pay in the public sector missing from private sector considerations is the political dimension. Governments are wary about the messages sent out to other public sector workers by high pay levels for senior posts, and how they will play with the wider electorate; see, for example, the pressure placed on MPs to accept a lower than recommended pay award in 2007 (*Financial Times*, 2008). This acts to impose something of a 'ceiling' on public sector pay levels. It also leads to a tendency for pay rates to be closely controlled with little scope for flexibility. Posts are often allotted to centrally determined national pay structures, some have spot salaries, some pay ranges with guaranteed progression, and others, such as the senior military, are on performance-related increments. An example might be the new pay structure for 'very senior managers' in parts of the NHS. Under this system, some Trust chief executives receive a spot rate within a pay range determined by the resident population for the area weighted for age and deprivation. Depending on the type of organisation, pay lies between £100,000 and £194,000. Annual increases are made up of a mix of consolidated and unconsolidated awards based on four performance categories. The pay of other board members is a fixed percentage of that of the chief executive determined by role.

Besides levels of base pay, with one or two exceptions (for example, Royal Mail; Incomes Data Services, 2007b) the other striking difference compared to the private sector is either the lack of variable pay arrangements to reward performance altogether, or the comparatively low levels of bonuses that are available where schemes do exist. The bonus pot for the entire senior civil service is just over 7.5 per cent of the paybill, and the average value of bonuses in 2005–2006 was just under £7,000. Meanwhile, the bonus paid to the NHS Trust chief executive referred to above was £20,000 in 2006, or around 8 per cent of base pay. These are tiny proportions compared to those available in the private sector.

To some extent, lower pay rates in the public sector may reflect other factors: in particular, pension scheme arrangements are generally more generous in the public sector. Even so, the lack of access to other private sector cash and non-cash additions such as variable payments, LTIPs, share plans, company cars/allowances, or medical insurance, more than offset the value of the pension benefit.

Whilst undoubtedly controlling costs, artificial limits on the pay of senior public sector employees is causing problems. First, it has compressed pay further down the structure, often making it difficult for the public sector to recruit specialist staff from outside. This has given rise to the external appointments at much higher rates of pay than those available to public sector workers in the same grade. Evidence of a dual labour market is emerging in the civil service, for example, bringing with it problems of equal pay, declining motivation and morale, and incoherent and opaque pay structures. Second, it may restrict the labour pool from which the public sector can recruit its most senior staff. There is no clear evidence on this yet, but the fact that leading barristers can earn considerably more from private practice, for example, could have implications for future recruitment to the judiciary.

Conclusion

Executive reward is an emotive subject and, arguably, the time spent on it or reporting on it (see Figure 9.9) is disproportionate to the economic cost of the rewards themselves.

The way that executives are paid has been influenced by the thinking of economists, academics, entrepreneurs, investors, corporate governance experts, consultants, executives, and ex-executives. Deciding what executives should be paid for operational performance; delivery of strategy; delivery of shareholder value; future performance; past performance; economic performance or accounting performance

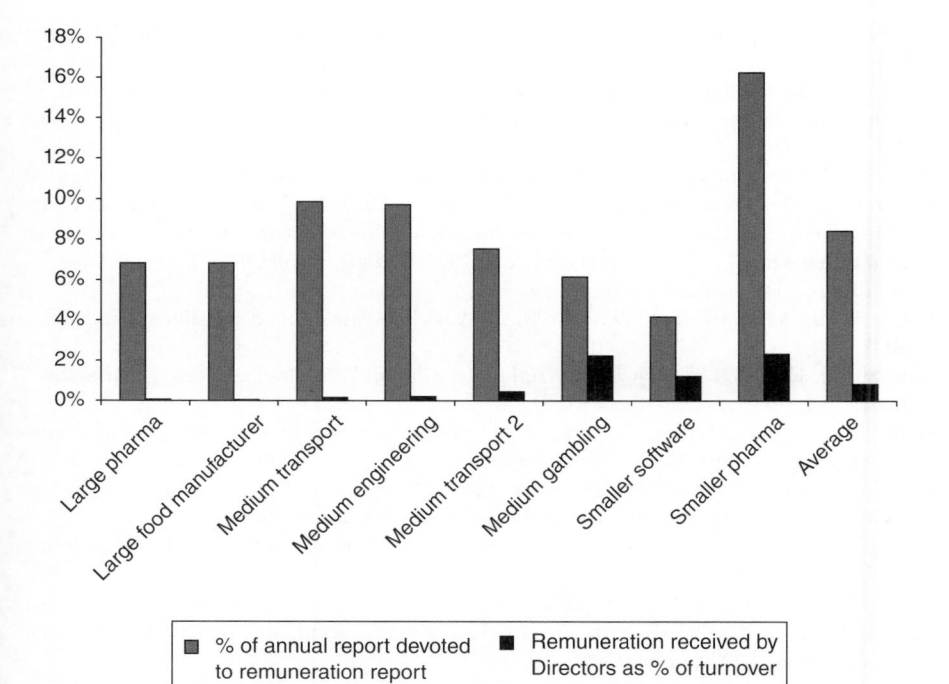

Figure 9.9 Annual report coverage of executive remuneration compared with remuneration costs as a percentage of turnover

is complicated and in the absence of any scientific definition of 'appropriate', deciding the appropriate amount to pay is also difficult. Some of the current issues being debated around executive reward, the influence of private equity on executive pay, for example, and the appropriate ratio of executive to average employee pay, are really not, in our view, the most important subjects.

Reminding ourselves of what executive reward is actually for, what the various elements of executive reward are supposed to do, and ensuring that we do a thorough, rather than a slap-dash, job of establishing the amounts executives deserve to receive, will make it a lot less likely that we get asked at parties 'Don't you just give them a lot of money?

References

Carpenter, M. A. and Sanders, W. G. (2002) 'Top Management Team Compensation: The Missing Link between CEO Pay and Firm Performance?', *Strategic Management Journal*, 23, 367–375.

Civil Service Commission (2007) *Annual Report 2006/07*, London: Civil Service Commission.

Committee on Corporate Governance (1998) 'Final Report', London: Gee. (The 'Hampel Report').

Committee on the Financial Aspects of Corporate Governance (1992) 'Report of the Committee on the Financial Aspects of Corporate Governance', London: Gee. (The 'Cadbury Report').

Director's Remuneration Report Regulations 2002 SI 1986/2002, London: Stationery Office.

Fatturose, J., Skovoroda, R., Buck, T., and Bruce, A. (2007) 'UK Executive Bonuses and Transparency – A Research Note', *British Journal of Industrial Relations*, 45, 3, 518–536.

Financial Reporting Council, United Kingdom (1992) *Cadbury Report: The Financial Aspects of Corporate Governance*, London: Gee.

Financial Times (2008) 'MPs Ordered to Accept Wage Restraints', *Financial Times*, 10 January 2008, 4.

Galbraith, J. K. (1967) *The New Industrial State*, 4th ed., Princeton: Princeton University Press.

Gomez-Mejia, L. and Balkin, D. (1992) *Compensation, Organizational Strategy and Firm Performance*, Cincinnati, OH: South-Western.

Hay Group (2007a) Private briefings, London: unpublished.

Hay Group (2007b) *Top Executive Pay in Europe*, London: Hay Group.

Higgs, D. (2003) *Review of the Role and Effectiveness of Non-Executive Directors*, London: Stationary Office.

Incomes Data Services (2007a) *NHS Boardroom Pay Report 2007*, London: IDS.

Incomes Data Services (2007b) *Executive Pay at Royal Mail*, Executive Compensation Review, 322, December 2007, London: IDS.

Office for National Statistics (2007) *Annual Survey of Hours and Earnings 2007*, London: ONS.

Rajam, R. (2008) 'Bankers' Pay Is Deeply Flawed', *Financial Times*, 9 January 2008, 15.

Senior Salaries Review Body (2007) *Twenty-Ninth Report on Senior Salaries 2007*, Cm 7030, London: Stationery Office.

Study Group on Directors' Remuneration (1995) *Directors' Remuneration: Report of a Study Group Chaired by Sir Richard Greenbury*, London: Gee. (The 'Greenbury Report').

Veblen, T. (1899) *The Theory of the Leisure Class: An Economic Study in the Evolution of Institutions*, New York: Macmillan.

Part III
Benefits issues

10

The pensions revolution

Sue Field, Christian Olsen, and Richard Williams

Introduction

What are the factors that influence and drive changes to occupational pensions schemes within organisations' overall reward structures? In developing any reward structure for its employees, an employer is aiming to attract the right people, develop the right motivation, and produce the right employee actions that will enable the employer to be successful within a commercial environment. This commercial environment, or market framework, is made up of a number of elements. There is the employees' appreciation of the value of the benefit being offered and the employers' perception of the cost of the provision of that benefit. In the case of pensions, there is also the legal structure and, of course, financial aspects such as the level and performance of the financial markets, tax, and the generally accepted accounting practices, all of which can have a bearing on the level and perceived cost of the benefits to be provided. Finally, a further key element is the effect of demographic changes (for example, increasing life expectancy) taking place within society as a whole.

In this chapter, we are going to look at the changes that have taken place in pension benefit provision starting from the late 1970s, with a particular focus on more recent history and with reference to the factors and influences described above. We focus primarily, but not exclusively, on the private sector and on occupational pension provision.

In the late 1980s and early 1990s, final salary pension schemes (which provide a pension based on length of service and on salary near retirement) were considered by many employers, if they considered them in any detail at all, as not being a significant cost, since investment markets had tended to perform well. The authors' experience is that, from the employees' point of view, pensions were almost, for those who had them, taken for granted.

In contrast, the true cost of provision of a pension is now more generally appreciated, in terms of both increasing longevity and of more conservative estimates of projected rates of future investment return. There is now greater clarity about the level and cost of pension provision and a greater understanding of the difference between an aspiration to provide a level of benefit and a cast iron promise that a benefit will actually be provided. In our view, pensions are also now seen by many employers more as part of a commercial contract between them and their employees and less as a product of corporate paternalism.

As we shall see in this chapter, lower cost defined contribution arrangements have become the norm for new employees. As a result, in many industries, there is a disincentive to job mobility for employees who are still in final salary arrangements. Now that final salary pension schemes are on the wane, current press articles, and our experience, suggest that such schemes are appreciated all the more by those employees who are still members.

The outcome may be that well-meant legislation, in an attempt to make final salary pension arrangements clearer, more understandable and more secure, will, when coupled with financial and demographic changes, have been seen to have driven out private sector final salary pension provision altogether. This will result in all the risk, both of longevity and of investment performance, being passed on to employees. Is this to be welcomed? It is certainly clearer, but is the greater uncertainty introduced, however, conducive to a more prosperous economic future for all of us and to greater peace of mind for individual employees?

We will come back to some of these questions after a review of the recent history of pension development in the United Kingdom, the drivers for change and the current state of play. We will then try to predict future trends and to form broad conclusions as to where it might end up in 10 to 20 years time, based in part on developments in other countries.

The history of schemes

Types of occupational pension scheme

A wide range of pension schemes exists in the United Kingdom today with different types, and levels, of risk to members and employers. These are as illustrated in the Figure 10.1.

Until relatively recently the vast majority of occupational pension scheme members in the United Kingdom (including all public sector employees) were in 'final salary schemes' (Watson Wyatt, 2006, p. 3), that is, they were based on a promise that the employer would pay the member a benefit at retirement based on his or her length of service and salary near retirement. While the member may be required to contribute towards the scheme, in this situation the employer bears the entire risk of not being

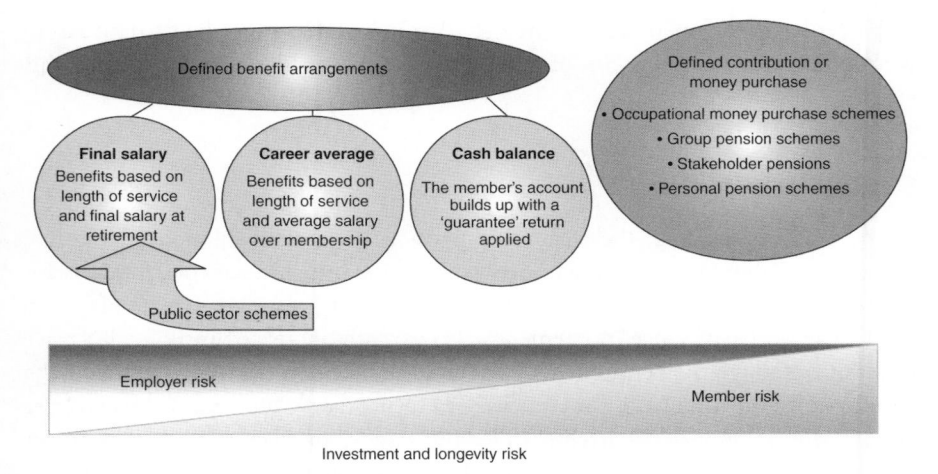

Figure 10.1 Types of pension provision

Source: Report on the Review of the Parliamentary Contributory Pension Fund, Watson Wyatt, 2007a.

able to provide the benefits due in future, in particular if investment returns are below expectations and/or members live longer than expected in retirement.

A variation on a final salary scheme is a career average scheme where benefits are based on the average salary (usually with some form of revaluation) over the member's career with the employer, rather than salary close to retirement. This reduces the risk to employers of members' pension promises rising steeply as a result of large salary increases near retirement, but all other risks remain. This type of arrangement can have advantages for members on career paths where their salary progression is more limited or irregular; for example, part-timers or those whose earnings decline as they near retirement. A more recent variation, particularly common in the United States (Watson Wyatt, 2007b, p. 1), is the cash balance plan which is similar to a career average pension scheme but delivers a cash sum rather than a pension at retirement – thereby removing the longevity risk from the employer.

The above are all defined benefit arrangements. The alternative approach is to define the level of contributions rather than the level of benefits. These are known as defined contribution or money purchase arrangements, the terms being used interchangeably. Personal pensions taken out by members dealing directly with a provider normally have no involvement from the employer.

Stakeholder pensions are a low-cost form of personal pension that, since 2001, employers have been obliged to offer (but not necessarily contribute to) if they are not providing alternative pension provision. The main difference between defined contribution and defined benefit arrangements is that, with the former, the member bears all the risk of the contributions invested not being sufficient to provide the level of benefits anticipated, whereas with the defined benefit arrangements the employer bears the major part of the risk. Aiming to strike the right balance as to who should bear the risk is one of the themes which we will explore further in this chapter.

State pensions

In the United Kingdom, the basic state pension is a (relatively modest) flat-rate pension available to everyone who has paid national insurance contributions for the required period and is funded by the state (that is, tax payers generally) on a pay-as-you-go basis. Once in payment it is currently increased in line with price inflation, although the Pensions Act 2007 commits the government to restoring the earnings inflation link from a yet unspecified future date. There is also a second tier of state pension provision, currently called the State Second Pension, which provides a career-average form of pension (although it is possible to opt out of this tier).

The structure of state benefits differs significantly in other countries; for example, the level of benefit (which is significantly higher in France and Spain) and the extent to which benefits are means-tested (Association of British Insurers, 2004).

Changes to occupational pensions in the past few decades

To understand how the current pension revolution has evolved, it is useful to look back at how pensions have developed over the past twenty years or so of the twentieth century.

Increasing benefits

Prior to the late 1970s, there were few limitations on the form of pension provision, other than tax legislation restricting the amount of benefit that could enjoy the significant tax benefits. To a large extent, tax constraints drove the format of defined benefit provision and gave rise to the typical two-thirds final salary promise. This fitted well with an environment where job security was expected, with many individuals having an entire career with one employer. Such pensions were promises based on the best endeavours of employers to meet them rather than, as is now the case because of legislative changes, guarantees. Members of such schemes, however, might not have appreciated this.

During the late 1970s and early 1980s, there was an increasing focus on imposing minimum levels of provision and pension increases. With increasing job mobility, there was particular emphasis on providing pensions for those changing jobs. Since 1975, those leaving a pension scheme before retirement have been entitled to a pension preserved until their retirement age. Over the next few years, the minimum period of service which members needed to qualify for preserved pensions (the vesting period) was reduced (Social Security Act, 1986) and legislation was introduced to require preserved pensions to be increased (broadly in line with price inflation capped at 5 per cent per annum.). (Social Security Acts, 1985 and 1990). Until 1997 there was no requirement to increase pensions in payment – increases depended on individual scheme rules and were often discretionary. The Pensions Act 1995 introduced a statutory minimum level of pension increases (in line with price inflation capped at 5 per cent per annum) for all pensions in respect of service after April 1997.

While improving the position for members, this legislation added significantly to the cost and complexity of pension schemes. The 1980s and early 1990s, however, saw buoyant equity markets and pension fund 'surpluses' which were used to maintain, reduce, or suspend employers' contributions (the so-called 'contribution holiday') and sometimes to fund generous early retirement schemes which assisted company restructuring. As a result, our experience was that schemes were able at the time to absorb the costs which the additional legislation imposed.

Increasing security

During the 1990s, there was a major focus on increasing the security of pension arrangements, but with limited success. This was driven by the Maxwell crisis in 1991 when, following Robert Maxwell's death, it was found that significant sums of money had been diverted from the Mirror Group Pension Fund pension as unauthorised loans to his private companies. As a result of this, in 1993 the Government charged the Pensions Law Committee, headed by Professor Goode, with considering how to increase pension fund security. This led to the Pensions Act 1995 which introduced a new regulatory authority, imposed a Minimum Funding Requirement on pension schemes, and introduced statutory pension increases, but which did nothing to prevent the type of fraud as happened in the Maxwell case from recurring. In particular, the Minimum Funding Requirement was arguably a misleading term for a level of funding which fell well short of the cost of guaranteeing pension provision.

Increasing choice

A third theme emerging over this period was that of individuals' choice about their pension provision. However, this choice did not go hand in hand with greater financial education. In 1988, the ability of employers to require employees to join their occupational pension scheme was abolished (Social Security Act, 1986) and at the same time, personal pensions were introduced. These arrangements enabled members to set up their own money purchase arrangements independent of the employer. While these arrangements provided some benefit to those without an alternative pension plan, significant amounts were often charged by pension providers, penalising low earners; (this was partly addressed by the introduction of stakeholder pensions in 2001) and they were unlikely to be suitable for those whose employer contributed to their occupational pension plan but not to a personal pension. The following mis-selling scandal was in part to blame for the public's increasing mistrust of pensions. Together with other factors, such as the problems with Equitable Life (the insurance company nearly collapsed when the High Court ruled in 2000 that some of the pension promises it had made were actually guarantees, even though the company had insufficient resources to meet them), the mis-selling scandal had led to a general underinvestment in pensions. For example, research carried out by Baring Asset Management (press release in October 2007) showed some 33 per cent of UK adults are not currently making any pension provision for retirement.

Position at the end of the twentieth century

By the end of the twentieth century, the UK occupational pension scene was still dominated by defined benefit final salary arrangements, in both the private and public sectors. Indeed, as recently as 2000, a majority of larger private sector occupational pension arrangements still provided defined benefits for new joiners, while all of the major public sector schemes provided final salary defined benefits (see Figure 10.2).

Looking beyond the benefits offered to new joiners and taking into account the arrangements for existing employees, an even higher proportion of active members of occupational pension schemes were still accruing defined benefit style pensions in 2000. Some 82 per cent of active members in the private sector were building up

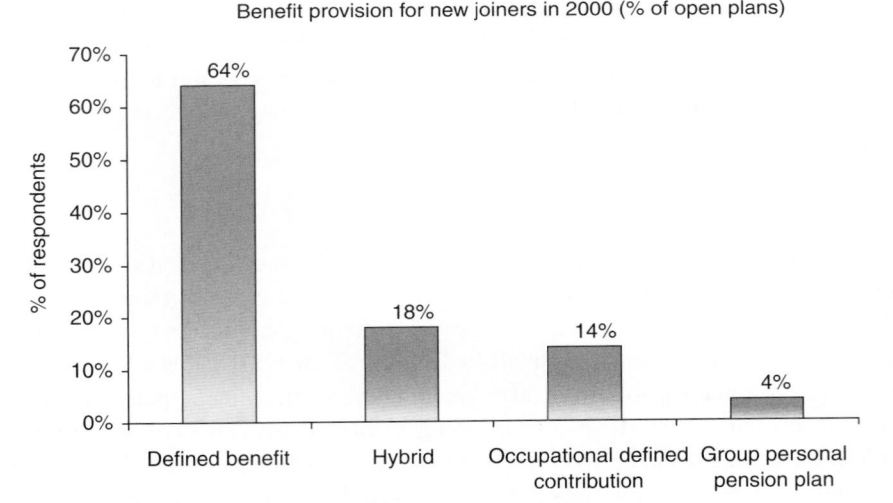

Benefit provision for new joiners in 2000 (% of open plans)

Figure 10.2 Benefit provision for new joiners in 2000

Source: Watson Wyatt Design Plan Survey, 2000.

defined benefits and, taking public sector schemes into account, the proportion was over 90 per cent (Government Actuary's Department, 2003, p. 16).

The pension revolution in the past ten years

The picture today at the time of writing in 2007 is very different. In particular, there has been a significant move away from defined benefit arrangements, especially for new joiners, and by 2006, only 33 per cent of open private sector plans in the United Kingdom provided final salary benefits to new joiners (Watson Wyatt, 2006, p. 3; See Figure 10.3 which summarises the trend from 1998–2006).

At the same time, the level of benefits provided by many of the remaining final salary plans has been reduced. For example, in many schemes, the retirement age has been increased and/or members are now required to make greater contributions themselves towards funding their benefits (Watson Wyatt, 2006, p. 4).

There is little or no evidence that employees today place a lower value on reward provided in the form of a defined benefit pension. Indeed, if anything, the experience of the authors has been that the closure of so many defined benefit arrangements has increased employee appreciation for such benefits. Also, there has not been a fundamental change in the need for private (as opposed to state provided) pension provision.

So what has led companies to change, so significantly and so rapidly, a benefit which for many individuals is the second largest element of reward after cash

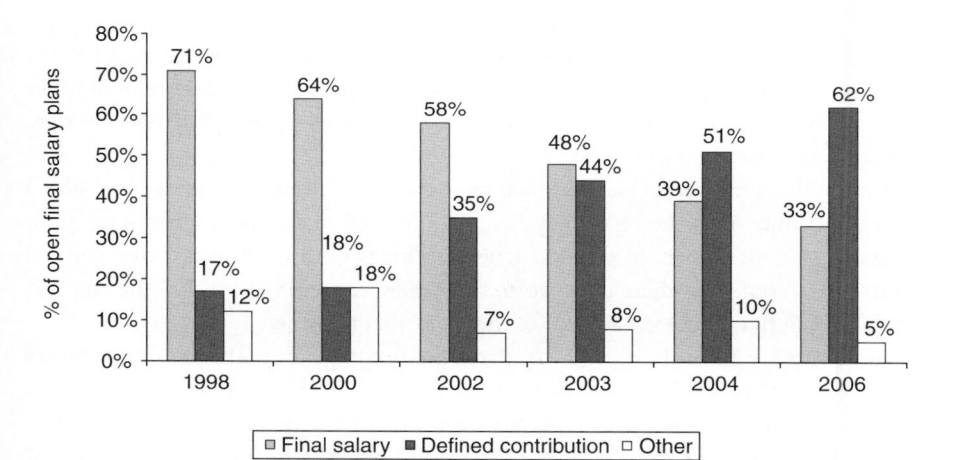

Figure 10.3 Trends in pension provision for new joiners

Source: Watson Wyatt plan design survey, 2006.

salary? What are the consequences of the resulting transfer of risk and responsibility towards individual employees?

The press is often keen to attribute the decline of the traditional defined benefit scheme to a particular event or cause. For example, there has been much press commentary in the United Kingdom regarding the impact of changes to the tax regime in 1997 which meant that pension schemes could no longer claim imputation credits on dividend income, adding substantially to their cost (see, for example, 'Did Brown's decision play a part in funding crisis?' from the *Guardian* on 3 April 2007 or 'Brown cannot take all the blame for pensions debacle' from the *Financial Times* on 2 April 2007). No doubt the changes to the tax regime have been a contributing factor to the changes seen in the UK pension's landscape, but it is a rather simplistic assessment: the changes seen in the United Kingdom have been mirrored just as rapidly, if not more so, in other developed economies such as Australia and the United States (Broadbent et al., 2006, p. 14).

The reality is that the speed and the extent of the changes in pension provision reflect a coming together of a wide range of demographic, economic, and legislative factors.

The drivers for change

Investment issues

In a traditional defined benefit pension scheme, the benefits provided to members are not linked to the performance of the assets actually held to back the liabilities. UK pension schemes have traditionally invested a significant proportion of assets in equity markets. As a result, during the 1990s, pension schemes benefited from strong equity performance, with many employers taking a 'contribution holiday'.

This all changed with the downturn in equity markets beginning in 2001. Over the five-year period from 1995 to 2000, UK equity returns averaged more than 15per cent per annum above inflation. Over the following five years, real returns were negative as shown in Figure 10.4.

Although equity markets have since recovered, the negative returns highlighted for many companies the risks they face and, indeed, have always been facing, in operating a defined benefit pension scheme. This is in direct contrast to a defined contribution scheme, where the costs to the employer are fixed and it is the employees who benefit or suffer as a result of the investment performance.

In an effort to control this risk, the investment strategy for many pension schemes was changed to reduce the weighting towards equities. However, given the low yields offered by gilt instruments and corporate bonds in recent years, as illustrated in Figure 10.5, such a change was accompanied by an increase in the expected cost of providing a defined benefit (lower expected investment returns mean that it is expected to cost more to provide the defined benefit promises).

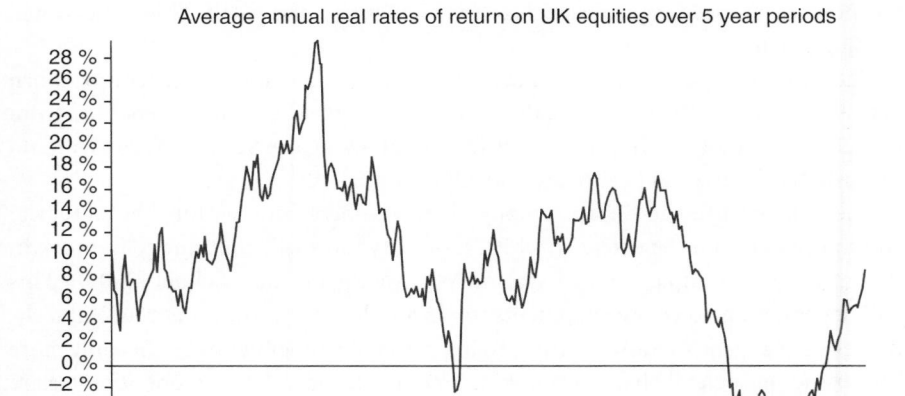

Average annual real rates of return on UK equities over 5 year periods

Figure 10.4 Average annual real rates of return on UK equities

Source: FTSE actuaries UK all share total return index.

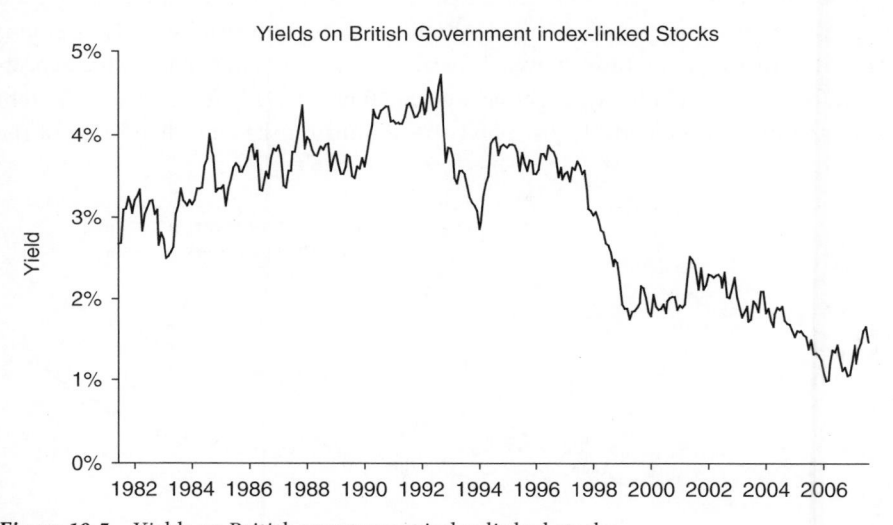

Yields on British Government index-linked Stocks

Figure 10.5 Yields on British government index-linked stocks

Source: FTSE Actuaries Government Securities Index-linked Real Yield over 5 years (5 per cent inflation) Index.

Longevity issues

At a similar time, research was released showing that not only are people living longer today than in the past, but that the rate at which mortality has improved in recent years has been much faster than was previously anticipated. This is illustrated in Figure 10.6.

The rate of improvement has been particularly rapid for the generation born between 1925 and 1945 (the so-called 'favoured' cohort) who have benefited from reductions in smoking, improvements in diet following the Second World War and the growth of universal healthcare and education.

There is significant debate among demographers and within the actuarial community around the extent to which mortality rates will continue to improve in the future (for example, refer to Watson Wyatt/Cass Business School (2005)). This will depend on medical developments (for example, on the one hand medical techniques such as gene therapy continue to improve but pandemics might become more likely) and on societal changes (smoking rates continue to fall, but obesity rates are on the rise).

As life expectancy has increased, so has the expected cost to an employer of providing defined benefit pensions. Typically, an increase in life expectancy of one year increases the value of a pension benefit to the member by between 2.5 per cent and 5 per cent. The increases in life expectancy have been accompanied by historically low bond yields and lower expectations for future returns.

Table 10.1 below illustrates the increase in the life expectation for a 65 year old over the past 30 years as based on the mortality tables published by the Continuous Mortality Investigation Bureau over the years. The results show that the life expectation for a 65 year old today might be around 60 per cent higher than was thought to be the case in the early 1970s. The two columns on the right hand side of the

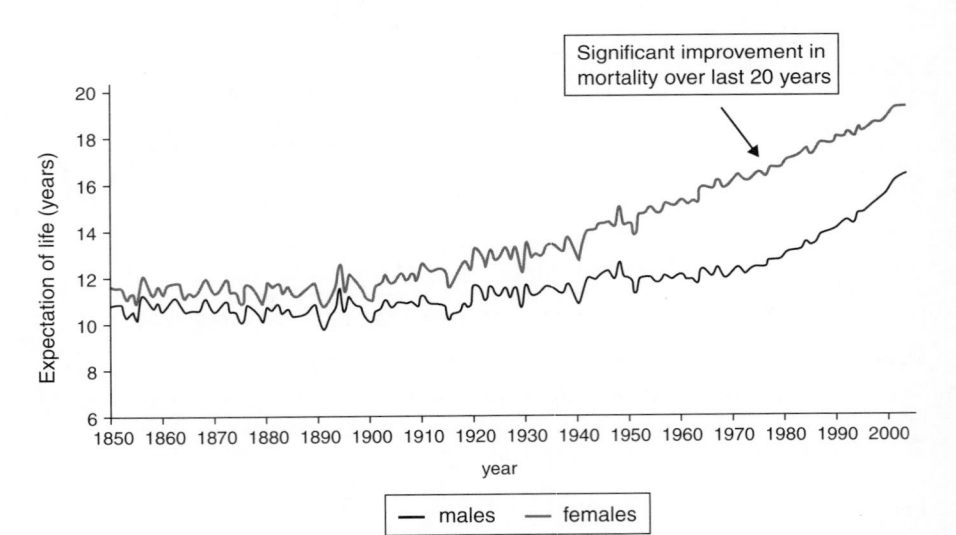

Figure 10.6 Expectation of life at age 65

Source: GAD (9/9/05) – England and Wales, period analysis.

table illustrate the impact of the increase in life expectation and lower expected investment returns on the value of an annuity of £1 per annum payable to a man from age 65.

The combination of low real returns, low inflation (which increases the real value of fixed and capped pension benefits), low gilt yields, and increasing life expectation has served both to increase the cost of providing pensions and to highlight the mortality and investment risks an employer faces through sponsoring a defined benefit pension scheme.

The increases in cost have come at the same time as many companies have found themselves under commercial pressure to cut costs and better manage risk.

Accounting changes

In recent years, the standards covering the method by which companies must account for the pension schemes they sponsor have changed. Listed UK companies are now required to report for pensions under International Accounting Standard 19, which has a strong market-related focus and provides a direct link between the financial position of the pension scheme and the sponsoring company's balance sheet. A similar standard applies for non-listed companies.

The standards now require the use of a discount rate that is based on corporate bond yields when valuing pension liabilities. Given that few schemes invest solely in corporate bonds, there is a mismatch between the value of the assets held and the value placed on the pension liabilities and this has led to additional volatility in corporate balance sheets. For example, for a pension scheme with liabilities of £1 billion (fairly typical for a FTSE 100 company), a modest change in corporate bond yields of just 0.1 per cent per annum, might lead to a change in the company's net balance sheet of around £20 million.

A consequence of the new requirements is that companies and the users of financial statements, such as investment analysts, are now placing much more emphasis on pension arrangements and the associated risks.

Table 10.1 The impact of changes in life expectation and yields on the value of a pension

Mortality table	Publication	Expectation of life (in years)	Value of £1 pa. payable to a man for life from age 65	
			4 % yield	2 % yield
PA90 male	Early 1970s	14.6	£10.40	£12.20
PMA80 projected to 2010	1988	16.9	£11.70	£13.90
PMA92 projected to 2010	1998	19.0	£12.70	£15.40
PMA92 Medium Cohort	2002	21.7	£14.00	£17.20
PMA92 Long Cohort	2002	23.4	£14.60	£18.20

Source: Watson Wyatt, 2005, p. 5.

Difficulties in integrating defined benefits with total reward and flexible working

In a defined contribution scheme, as noted above, the cost to the employer of providing the benefits is clear to all parties (it is simply the contribution paid) and can be adjusted directly by changing the rate of contributions paid. Of course, while the upfront cost is clear, the ultimate benefit to the individual is uncertain.

In the case of a defined benefit scheme, there is a greater degree of certainty about the level of benefits that will be provided. However, the actual cost to the employer of funding those entitlements depends on a wide range of factors which are not known in advance, such as lifespan, investment returns, and inflation levels. The expected cost can be calculated, but this will depend on assumptions made about the future and the method used. Whilst employers have developed approaches to address this issue, it does mean that defined contribution schemes are often seen as fitting more easily into a flexible benefits program. Also, defined contribution schemes are often simpler to integrate with flexible working patterns.

Changing regulatory framework

A number of changes have been made to the regulatory framework governing pensions in the United Kingdom since 2000, in an attempt to increase the level of security members have regarding their pension entitlements, including

- the introduction of the Pension Protection Fund (PPF) established under the Pensions Act 2004, which is intended to ensure that a minimum level of benefits is provided to members if their employer's business fails, and the associated moral hazard provisions which enable the Pensions Regulator to force an employer or a connected company to make contributions to the pension scheme in cases of 'corporate manipulation' (which can include the sale of employer assets, the payment of large dividends, or transfers of employees to a service company);
- changes to the rules regarding the winding up of a scheme where the employer remains solvent – where a scheme is wound up with a solvent employer, a debt is triggered on the employer reflecting the additional assets needed to buy out the pension liabilities with an insurer (The Occupational Pension Schemes (Winding Up and Deficiency on Winding Up etc.) (Amendment) Regulations, 2004);
- changes to the rules regarding the debt imposed on a company when it ceases to participate in a pension scheme (for example, following the sale of a business) – the debt now reflects a share of the cost to buy out the liabilities with an insurer (The Occupational Pension Schemes (Employer Debt) Regulations. 2005);
- changes to funding rules resulting from the Pensions Act 2004 which have, in many cases, granted additional powers to scheme trustees when it comes to negotiating with the company regarding funding matters.

In general, these changes provide members of private sector pension arrangements with a greater level of security regarding their pension entitlements. However, the changes have also served to increase the potential risks and cost for the employer of operating a defined benefit arrangement and have proved to be a particularly thorny issue when it comes to merger and acquisition activity.

The outcome – the pensions environment today

The factors described in the previous section have served to improve the security of members' benefits. However, associated with this there has been

- an increase in the cost of funding defined benefits;
- an increase in the focus on the risk of providing defined benefits (the risk was there before, but perhaps was not fully appreciated);
- concern among employers that defined benefit provision can potentially restrict corporate activity.

This has had a dramatic impact on company pension provision in the United Kingdom, most clearly represented in the shift from defined benefit to defined contribution schemes for new employees. At the same time, changes have been made to many of the remaining schemes to reduce benefits or increase the share of the cost met by members (Watson Wyatt, 2006, p. 4).

Participation in occupational pension schemes

The number of active members in occupational pension schemes has been declining over time, see Figure 10.7. Of particular note is the sharp decline in private sector membership, especially since 2000, although in terms of overall numbers this has been partly offset by the recent growth in the number of active members of public sector schemes.

The trend from defined benefit to defined contribution schemes

At the same time as overall membership of occupational pension schemes has been falling, there has been a very significant shift towards defined contribution arrangements for the provision of benefits for new employees. Whilst around 75 per cent of all active employee members in 2006 were still in a defined benefit arrangement (National Statistics, 2007, p. 2), only 38 per cent of schemes continued to provide final salary defined benefits for new joiners (Watson Wyatt, 2006, p. 3).

In addition, among open defined benefit schemes, there has been a shift towards risk-sharing designs such as career average and cash balance plans where the level of risk borne by the employer is less than under a traditional final salary design.

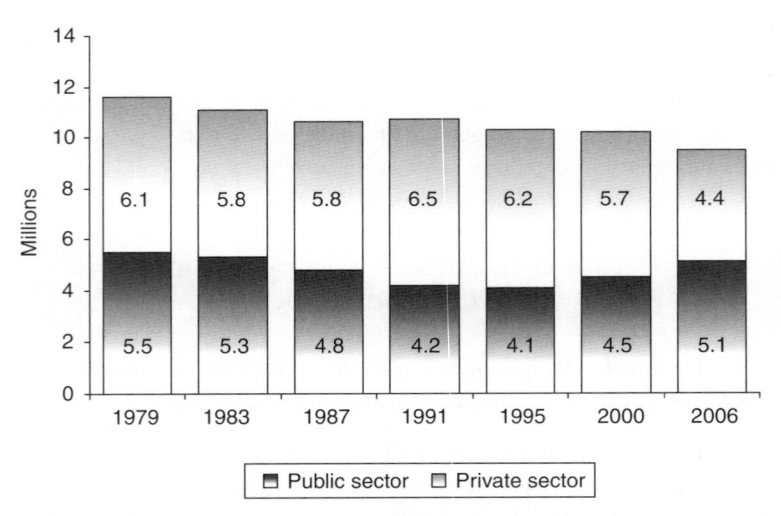

Figure 10.7 Numbers of members of occupational pension schemes

Source: Government actuary's departement, 2004, p. 34 and national statistics, 2007, p. 1.

Changes to defined benefit plans

At the same time as many defined benefit schemes have been closing, there has been a strong trend among remaining schemes towards reducing the level of benefits provided to members; examples of such changes include increases in the retirement age and increases in the level of cost that falls on the member through member contributions, see Figure 10.8.

Some consequences of the shift to defined contribution arrangements

Retention and attraction issues

There is no inherent reason why a defined contribution arrangement should be expected to provide inferior benefits compared to a defined benefit scheme. The objective in both cases is to provide the individual with retirement benefits. Fundamentally, the only difference is where the risks are borne and the level of engagement required from the individual. Further, defined contribution arrangements can offer individuals greater flexibility in the way that benefits build up, particularly in the context of increasing labour mobility, and in the manner in which benefits are ultimately paid.

On average, however, the contributions payable to the new defined contribution arrangements that have been set up by employers in the United Kingdom have been well below the cost of the defined benefit arrangements that they have replaced. For example, in 2006 employer contributions to private sector defined benefit schemes

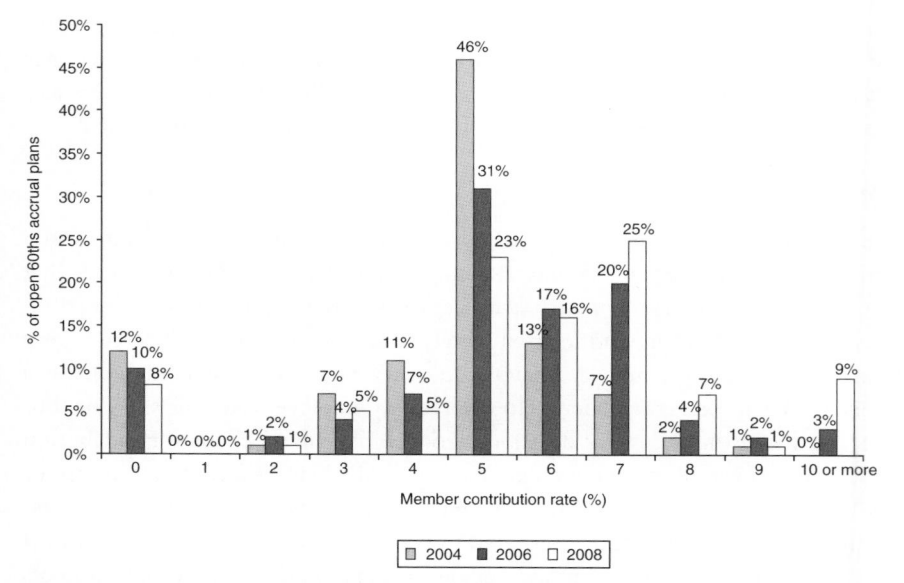

Figure 10.8 Member contribution rates (schemes providing 1/60th accrual)
Source: Watson Wyatt, 2006, p. 4.

(as a percentage of salary) were over double the contributions paid to defined contribution schemes (National Statistics, 2007, p. 7). Therefore, it would seem that along with the shift in risk, employers are reducing the element of remuneration that is provided through pension schemes.

On a related point, many companies now operate a two-tiered workforce, with employees in the exact same position within an organisation receiving different pension benefits (defined benefit or defined contribution) of potentially materially different values, depending on when they joined the company. In such cases, our experience has been that other items of remuneration are rarely adjusted to reflect the difference in the value of pension, perhaps because, as yet, this has not become a major industrial issue and may be seen as being transitory in nature.

Evidence suggests that retention rates are higher for employees with a defined benefit pension arrangement. For example, the Watson Wyatt Total Reward survey (Watson Wyatt, 2004, p. 11) found that the operation of a defined benefit pension scheme increases employee satisfaction and reduces employee turnover rates by between 15 per cent and 20 per cent.

This may partly reflect the difference in the profile of the membership of the two types of plans (defined contribution plans may be largely composed of younger, shorter serving members amongst whom higher turnover is expected). However, it is also likely to reflect the reduction in the number of open defined benefit arrangements. Members who leave a defined benefits arrangement to join a new employer are very likely to be offered a (lower cost) defined contribution rather than a defined benefit plan and so may be more reluctant to move employment. Additionally, our experience is that those employers that offer an open defined benefit arrangement use this as a selling point for potential employees (the public sector is a good example of this).

Member education

With the shift in investment and longevity risks to the individual members in a defined contribution scheme, along with the additional, and difficult, choices that must be made by members of such arrangements (covering investment, contribution levels and the timing and form of benefits), financial education becomes very important and many employers have made this a priority when introducing a defined contribution arrangement. However, many employees lack the skills or confidence to make the necessary decisions around investment choices, contribution levels, and the form of retirement benefits. This is likely to be a contributing factor to the relatively low participation rates among employees in defined contribution schemes – around 65 per cent, compared to participation rates of over 90 per cent in defined benefit schemes. Similarly, evidence suggests that substantial numbers of members are making what, on the face of it, would appear to be inappropriate investment decisions. For example, over 10 per cent of members in their thirties and forties are investing their pension in cash funds despite being 20 or more years from retirement (Watson Wyatt, 2007c, p. 3).

Innovative approaches to cost and risk management

The majority of closed final salary schemes have been replaced with defined contribution arrangements under which the entire investment and longevity risk is transferred to the employee. However, as we discuss later, some organisations are beginning to look instead at ways by which risk might be shared between the employer and employee. In the Netherlands such risk-sharing arrangements are particularly common, perhaps reflecting a more general emphasis in society on a collective approach than in the Anglo-Saxon model. Whereas employers in the United Kingdom and the United States have responded to the forces described earlier in this chapter by moving towards defined contribution arrangements, Dutch pension schemes continue to provide predominantly defined benefits, following the career average approach. In addition, rather than guaranteeing a level of indexation, increases in benefits in Holland are linked to the financial strength of the scheme. In this way, employers and members share the upside and downside risks faced by the pension scheme (Ponds and Van Riel, 2007).

Union reactions

There is a high correlation between the level of unionisation in a workplace and the existence of an employer pension scheme. For example, the 2004 Workplace

Employment Relations Survey (Kersley et al., 2006, p. 200) showed that 92 per cent of workplaces where there was any form of collective bargaining had an employer pension scheme, compared to 54 per cent of workplaces where there was no collective bargaining.

As the focus on pensions has increased, so has union expertise in the area and it is now seen as a key part of any consultation process – indeed, companies are now legally obliged to consult with employees on major changes to pension arrangements such as changes to members contributions, the rate at which benefits accrue, or in the style of benefits offered (see Section 262 of the Pensions Act 2004 which modified Section 67 of the Pensions Act 1995), see also Chapter 3. Unions have also demonstrated an understanding of the issues and drivers discussed in this chapter and, in our experience, have generally taken a fairly pragmatic approach to considering changes to benefits, particularly where they are involved from an early stage.

Indeed, the focus today among unions seems to be on negotiating least bad solutions, whereas ten years ago there was much more emphasis on negotiating benefit improvements. For example, provided that there is security around the benefits, unions have shown themselves to be open to more cost sharing by employees, particularly through increased member contributions, and, in the authors' experience, unions have not typically taken a strong line regarding the terms for new entrants.

However, moves to close final salary benefits for existing employees were a key factor in strike action taken by Royal Mail employees during 2007 and, at the time of writing, in proposed strike action by employees of Siemens. In such cases, the unions have argued that pension deficits were, in part, the fault of employers' past behaviour in that they had taken contribution holidays.

Interestingly, industrial action over pensions is not limited to the United Kingdom. French unions too have organised strikes in transport, gas, and electricity to challenge government proposed pension changes (Chrisafis, 2007).

Public sector arrangements

The existing public sector pension arrangements in the United Kingdom continue to provide members with defined benefits. (Civil servants also have the option to join a defined contribution arrangement). However, many of the drivers described above (for example, changing working patterns and increases in cost from increases in life expectancy) apply equally to the public sector as well as the private sector and, as a result, changes have recently been implemented in a number of public sector arrangements.

The key themes in these reforms include increases to normal retirement ages for new entrants, additional flexibility around lump sum retirement benefits, the introduction of tiered member contribution rates by earnings, capping employer contribution rates, introducing an element of cost sharing, and, in some cases, moving to a career average design (for example, the scheme applying to new civil service recruits from July 2007).

The public sector is likely to continue with defined pension provision for the majority of its workforce for some time to come. This could continue to be a significant factor in attracting and retaining good quality staff. The main sources of pension provision for those working in the private sector, however, will be defined contribution and there may be an increasing divide in occupational pension provision between the two sectors.

Future trends

Increasing number of pensioners; reducing amounts of pension?

The UK population is ageing. Looking forward, there is expected to be an increase in the old age dependency ratio (the number aged 65 and over to the number age 20–64 in the United Kingdom) from 27 per cent in 2003 to around 47 per cent by 2050 (Office of National Statistics, 2005, p. 7). Life expectancy is likely to continue to increase, while the numbers in occupational pension schemes may be expected to fall. There may be an increasing divide among the pensioner population, for example between those who have participated in generous defined benefit arrangements and those who were members of (lower cost) defined contribution pension plans.

The issues of an ageing population, the decline in occupational and private pension provision, and the need for a simple affordable sustainable model are not issues that affect the United Kingdom alone. For example, in Italy and Spain the old age dependency ratio is projected to exceed 70 per cent by 2050 (OECD, 2007, p. 42). Most countries are looking at ways to tackle these issues.

Pension provision must be sourced from the state, individual, or employer and getting the future right will mean striking the right balance between these three pillars of provision.

What is the government doing?

It might be reasonable to expect the state to continue to provide some form of minimum provision although whether this is for all or only the neediest remains to be seen. The government is committed to a gradual increase in State Pension Age (to age 68 by 2046), an easing of the contribution qualifications for the full state pension and increasing pensions in payment in line with earnings rather than prices. State pension provision is however still likely to be well below the levels seen in a number of other European countries such as Italy and Spain (Association of British Insurers, 2004) although it is questionable whether their higher level of provision will prove sustainable.

The government's response to the concern about the inadequacy of future saving currently in the United Kingdom has been to legislate to introduce a money purchase arrangement intended to cover all employees without alternative pension provision, but which stops short of full compulsion. The Pensions Act 2007 established a body, the Personal Accounts Delivery Authority, to assist with establishing this arrangement. The Personal Accounts scheme is intended to be a low-cost, defined contribution arrangement into which workers aged between 22 and State Pension Age earning more than a minimum threshold will be enrolled automatically, unless they are to be auto-enrolled into an alternative employer sponsored scheme meeting certain criteria. Workers may, however, choose to opt out, irrespective of whether they have any other provision. Employees will be required to contribute 3 per cent of their pay and employers 4 per cent with the government adding a further 1 per cent tax relief.

Australia provides an interesting example of the impact that compulsion can have on the way employers approach retirement savings. Since 1992, Australian employers have been required to provide employees, with very limited exceptions, with a minimum level of superannuation. This can be achieved either through providing a minimum level of contributions, currently 9 per cent of salary, or a minimum level of benefit which is intended, on certain assumptions, to have a similar cost to the contribution minimum. As a result of the compulsory system, superannuation savings have increased dramatically, quadrupling over the 10 years in 2007, although in part this has been offset by reductions in other saving. For example, Ellis Connolly and Marion Kohler estimate that around 38 cents of each dollar in superannuation contributions are offset through a reduction in other saving (Connolly and Kohler, 2004, p. 25).

Defined contribution arrangements now dominate in Australia, with 91 per cent of assets in this form. As in the United Kingdom, defined benefit provision in Australia suffered as a result of increasing compliance requirements and risk aversion on the part of employers. However, the introduction of compulsory provision also played a significant role as the system was largely designed with defined contribution benefits in mind. In addition, as the compulsory level has increased, the scope for employers to use superannuation as a differentiator has diminished. Employers most typically provide the minimum level of support, although employees are often able to sacrifice other elements of reward in return for additional contributions. There has also been a significant shift away from employer-sponsored arrangements towards large master trusts operated by financial institutions and multi-employer industry funds (APRA, 2007, p. 18).

What should individuals be doing?

If there is to be a significant take-up in savings for pensions, other than by compulsory means, then there needs to be a large-scale improvement in financial education. A survey carried out in 2006 showed that only 23 per cent of respondents knew enough about pensions to decide with confidence how to save for retirement (Department of Work and Pensions, 2007, p. 22). Without this, employees may not make adequate decisions about the future. The authors are already seeing this where defined contribution schemes have been in place for some time and employees are only just waking up to the fact that their actual retirement benefits will be or already are below their expectations.

What are employers doing?

One argument is that employers will eventually decide that pension provision is too much of a drain of company resources – both in time and money. On the other hand, what has arguably worked reasonably well for the past 100 years or so could continue, albeit with greater risk-sharing between employers and employees.

The trend towards defined contribution arrangements discussed in the previous sections may be expected to continue. Some of those employers who have already closed their defined benefit schemes to new entrants are looking to replace future defined benefit accrual for existing members with defined contribution arrangements (for example, Rentokil) or a reduced form of defined benefits (for example, British Airways). In these cases cost, or at least the ability to control cost, is generally the driver (CBI, 2007). However, we are also seeing some acknowledgement that reducing costs too far now may result in a hidden cost in decades to come as dissatisfaction with the ultimate level of benefits emerges.

There is increasing interest in some form of risk-sharing between employers and employees and recognition that, with the right communication, this can deliver benefits in terms of employee appreciation and performance. Some of the approaches include:

- *Introduction of cash balance and career average schemes.* Under a career average plan, the benefits depend on the individual's average salary over their career, rather than at the point of retirement, thereby reducing the employer's exposure to salary inflation and dealing more equally between employees with different lengths of service. A cash balance plan is more like a defined contribution arrangement, but with guarantees attached to the investment returns credited to members' accounts. This limits the investment risk faced by the member, but allows the employer to limit its exposure to longevity risks.

- *Cost sharing arrangements.* A number of final salary schemes, both in the private and public sector, have introduced some form of cost sharing whereby future changes in the cost of funding the pension benefits are to be shared between the members and the employer (for example, the government plans to introduce cost sharing for Civil Service pensions). This can be achieved through caps on the employer cost or through an explicit link between member contributions and the overall cost of benefits. Alternatively, in some cases the benefits provided by the scheme will be adjusted in pre-defined circumstances, for example by linking the retirement age to changes in life expectancy, thereby sharing the longevity risk (for example, BAE).

However, the current regulatory regime limits the extent to which risk-sharing is possible. In December 2006, the government appointed Chris Lewin and Ed Sweeny to review the regulatory framework. A number of their proposals (for example, removing the need to provide pension increases in payment) were rejected by the government in October 2007 but it is consulting on reducing the rate of revaluation of preserved pensions prior to retirement.

Legacy arrangements

Whatever happens about future pension provision, employers will have a legacy of significant defined benefit provision for many years to come. New entrants, for example, Paternoster, are coming into the pension buy-out market looking to take pension liabilities either partly or fully off employers. Some of these new players are aiming to provide enhanced security but for less than the cost of purchasing annuities from insurance companies. At the time of writing, there have been few formal contracts signed in this area but it may be an attractive proposition for employers to remove risk if the cost and security balance can be managed.

Influence of European legislation

European legislation is likely to be a further factor affecting UK pensions in the future. A particular concern is that the requirements for insurance companies incorporated in Solvency II will in due course be extended to occupational pension schemes with the result that all such schemes will need to be fully funded on an insurance company buy-out basis. This is a significantly higher funding standard than is currently required in the United Kingdom and the costs imposed, if this were introduced, would have a significant impact on the future of occupational pension schemes in the United Kingdom.

Summary and conclusion

The market is likely to continue to provide for some form of employee income in retirement, in addition to income from the state. This might be from individual savings, selling the family home and downsizing or from specific arrangements put in place by sponsoring employers.

What type of employment-related pension arrangements are going to be there in the United Kingdom in 10 to 20 years time? The public sector is likely to retain defined benefit pension provision for much of its workforce for some time to come and this will remain a significant factor in attracting and retaining good quality staff. In practice, however, defined benefit pension provision is unlikely to be the norm in the private sector. We are likely to see a wide variety of different approaches adopted and a gradual change in the working patterns of the employees as we stay healthier longer (hopefully!). We will, in many cases, have a continuing interest in gainful employment in retirement, not just for the immediate financial reward, although this will be obviously of key importance in funding overall pension provision, but also from the more general benefits of social interaction with the wider society.

By their very nature, pension changes are long term and the effect of changes can often not be apparent for many decades after the initial catalyst for change. For example, it may be many years before the emergence of the practical consequences of the inadequacy of some defined contribution pension arrangements.

Ultimately, there can be no pension guarantees. Pensions for future retirees, whether from the state or from the private sector, are financed by employees still working. Each month a pensioner draws his or her pension and spends it on goods and services, those goods and services are being provided by the then current workforce. (This is strictly true for the global economy as a whole; for the UK economy considered in isolation the net effect of overseas investment needs to be included.)

In effect, what all pension schemes do is give employees a 'voucher' which they can redeem for goods and services at some future date. Defined benefit pension schemes link the value of these 'vouchers' to salary near to retirement and often allow these 'vouchers' to increase (in fact, legislation requires it) in line with prices (albeit subject to a cap). Defined contribution pension schemes in effect provide 'vouchers' which increase in line with the investments chosen by either the employer or the employee or both. What effect does this 'voucher' system have on the overall economy? Does it actually encourage the growth needed to provide the goods and services being promised? There is not a clear answer to this question.

Should pension schemes be designed with a view to encouraging wider economic growth? In some countries, pension schemes are used as a means of fostering social change or developing a nation's infrastructure and the pension aspects are almost a by-product – for example, provident funds in developing countries such as Malaysia or Singapore where there is centralised investment management (Issue 42, June 2002, of id21 insights). In the developed world, however, pension structures have a less clear role in terms of economic growth.

In conclusion, therefore, is the pensions revolution really a revolution? Perhaps surprisingly, we would suggest not. There have been significant changes but the process remains one of evolution rather than revolution. The fundamental underlying principles remain the same and the pension reward structure is evolving and developing in a way that matches the changes in the society in which the pension arrangements are based. In many ways, the design structure of pension schemes reflects the beliefs and values of the society in which they are embedded – including the balance between individual responsibility and collective provision and protection.

The content of this chapter is for information purposes only and does not constitute professional advice.

References

APRA (2007) *Insight Issue 2 2007: Celebrating 10 Years of Superannuation Data Collection 1996–2006*, Australian Prudential Regulation Authority.

Association of British Insurers (2004) *European Pension Reform and Private Pensions, An Analysis of the EU's Six Largest Countries*, London: Association of British Insurers.

Broadbent, J., Palumbo, M., and Woodman, E. (2006) The Shift From Defined Benefit to Defined Contribution Pension Plans – Implications for Asset Allocation and Risk Management, Working Group on Institutional Investors, Global Savings and Asset Allocation established by the Committee on the Global Financial System.

CBI (2007) A View from the Top 2007, A Survey of Business Leaders Views on The Pension Provision , London: CBI.

Chrisafis, A. (2007) 'From Opera to Power Stations: Stoppages over Pension Changes Divide Country', *Guardian*, 15 November, 25.

Connolly, E. and Kohler, M. (2004) Research Discussion Paper 2004–01 – The Impact of Superannuation on Household Saving, Economic Research Department, Reserve Bank of Australia.

Department of Work and Pensions (2007) *Attitudes to Pensions: The 2006 Survey* , London: Department for Works and Pensions.

The Financial Times article, http://www.ft.com/cms/s/0/48971956-e0b6-11db-8b48-000b5df10621.html (the author is Nicholas Timmins) (accessed 24 June 2008)

Government Actuary's Department (2003) *Occupational Pension Schemes 2000 – Eleventh Survey by the Government Actuary – April 2003*, London: The Government Actuary's Department.

Government Actuary's Department (2005) *Occupational Pension Schemes 2004 – Twelfth Survey by the Government Actuary – June 2005*, London: The Government Actuary's Department.

The Guardian article, http://www.guardian.co.uk/politics/2007/apr/03/uk.money (accessed 24 June 2008)

Issue 42, June 2002, of id21 insights, enabled by DfID and hosted by IDS at the University of Sussex. Web site: www.id21.org/insights.

Kersley, B., Alpin, C., Forth, J., Bryson, A., Bewley, H., Dix, G., and Oxenbridge, S. (2006) *Inside the Workplace: Findings from the 2004 Workplace Employment Relations Survey*, Abingdon: Routledge.

National Statistics (2005) *Pension Trends 2005 Edition*, London: National Statistics.

National Statistics (2007) *Occupational Pension Schemes Survey 2006*, London: National Statistics.

OECD (2007) *Society at a Glance: OECD Social Indicators – 2006 Edition*, Paris: OECD.

Ponds, E. H. M. and Van Riel, B. (2007) Sharing Risk: The Netherlands' New Approach to Pensions, Center for Retirement Research at Boston College.

Watson Wyatt (2004) *Total Reward Survey 2004*, Reigate: Watson Wyatt Limited.

Watson Wyatt (2005) Occupational Pensions Research Report on Initial Scoping Research on the Occupational Pensions Environment to Inform the Full Comparative Valuation (Prepared for the Office of Manpower Economics by Watson Wyatt Limited).

Watson Wyatt (2006) *Pension Plan Design Survey 2006*, London: Watson Wyatt Limited.

Watson Wyatt (2007a) *Report on the Review of the Parliamentary Pension Fund*, London: Watson Wyatt Limited.

Watson Wyatt (2007b) *2006 Survey of Actuarial Assumptions and Funding*, USA: Watson Wyatt Worldwide.

Watson Wyatt (2007c) *DC Governance Survey 2007*, London: Watson Wyatt Limited.

Watson Wyatt/Cass Business School (2005) *The Uncertain Future of Longevity*, Reigate: Watson Wyatt LLP.

11

Flexible benefits: shaping the way ahead?

Angela Wright

Allowing individuals a choice in structuring their benefits has been made much more feasible by changes in information technology (IT) (Incomes Data Services, 2005). But is such flexibility really presaging the future shape of benefits – and reward – practice or are there organisational or other factors which limit the growth of such schemes? Are flexible benefits yet another, over-hyped initiative, promoted by management consultants and consumed by 'changeholic' managers keen to make their mark? Or are the organisations which have gone down the flexible route just the first of many?

This chapter is divided into four sections. In the first section the chapter reviews evidence on the growth and prevalence of flexible benefits, the types of schemes adopted, and the elements included. Drawing on an analytical framework from various theoretical perspectives, the chapter then considers in the second section whether flexible benefits give organisations value for money and how organisations might evaluate 'value'. In the third section, the author reports the findings of her research into organisations which have 'flexben' arrangements. The chapter concludes by discussing the important factors, which might be affecting or limiting the growth of schemes such as the potentially higher transaction costs of setting up and running schemes.

The position

Growth of flexible benefits in the United Kingdom

Cafeteria, menu-based or flexible benefits are certainly not new. They have their origins in the United States of America (USA) where many company schemes have been established, particularly in the 1980s. In the USA such arrangements grew from only a handful of companies offering flexible benefits in the early 1970s to an estimated 70 per cent of the Fortune 1,000 list of the USA's largest companies having plans in place (Barringer and Milkovich, 1998; Heneman et al., 2000). Flexible benefit plans grew in popularity in the USA, in part because of the favourable tax treatment given to companies' insurance-based benefit plans.

In the United Kingdom (UK) both fiscal policy (taxing benefits at something like their true value) and the absence of the need for employers to fund health care, as in the USA, seem to have limited the growth of flexible benefits. Nevertheless, they have been in evidence in the UK certainly since the 1970s expansion of benefits during the government incomes policies. Their expansion beyond small-scale schemes mainly for executives seemed to be limited by administrative costs, but the development of IT systems has facilitated the administration of setting up and running such schemes. This prompts the question: are they due for their long-promised expansion?

Certainly, the development of schemes in the UK seems to fit the context of increased individualisation of pay determination (Brown et al., 1998), in the wake of the decline in collective bargaining. Such schemes potentially offer a more employee-centred approach to at least one aspect of reward practice, since instead of a standardised package they offer employees a real choice over the benefits that suit them as individuals. Arguments that employers should adopt a broader definition of reward, possibly using the 'total reward model' (WorldatWork, 2007) suggest that choice over benefits may indeed be the beginning of a more employee focused and wider span of the traditional pay and benefits area. See also Chapter 13.

Most UK employers, however, have continued to adopt a standardised, non-flexible, approach. The UK benefits tradition has tended to have been characterised as ' paternalistic' with company-provided occupational welfare benefits policies (Russell, 1991), while the trend in recent years has been towards harmonisation or standardisation of benefits provision across different employee groups, breaking down traditional demarcations. In some ways flexible benefits, which emphasise individuality, seem to run counter to this harmonisation trend. Nevertheless, certain companies – as reported by the Industrial Society (2000) for example – use flexible benefits as a way of harmonising different sets of benefits for different employee groups.

Indeed, the trends in scheme development have been very different in the UK to those in the USA. Overall the pace of growth of flexible benefits schemes has been modest (CIPD, 2005, 2006, 2007; Employee Benefits 2003[1]) The latest estimate is that about 8 per cent of organisations have schemes and only a small degree of future growth is anticipated by employers. The CIPD found that 16 per cent of respondents to their annual reward survey said that they were considering their introduction (CIPD, 2007).

Types of scheme

Incomes Data Services (IDS, 2005) reports that it is becoming difficult to generalise about flexible benefits schemes. IRS (2005) distinguishes between 'voluntary benefits' schemes – where the employer offers group discounts and vouchers – and more substantial well-funded employer provided schemes. The former are more common than the latter. IDS distinguishes between schemes where the cost of benefits is borne by the employer and 'salary sacrifice' schemes where the cost to the employer is minimal. In these latter schemes, it is the employee who pays, while employer and employee may gain some tax advantages.

Flexible benefit schemes are more common among larger, private service sector employers with young workforces than in the public or voluntary sectors. Voluntary benefits are provided by 24 per cent of the CIPD's sample, again more often in larger private sector firms than in the public sector. The latest data are in tune with earlier surveys (CIPD, 2005, 2006) and seem to suggest that low or nil cost voluntary benefits are now much more popular than flexible benefits schemes.

Which benefits can be flexed?

In essence there are two types of scheme:

- Core plus' schemes in which there are a standard set of core benefits, with flexibility available over a menu of other benefits.
- inimal mandatory benefits with wider range of choice.

Schemes give a flexible 'fund' (expressed in terms of either cash or points) to employees to 'spend' on their benefit selections, typically asking employees to make choices once a year to minimise administration. According to IDS (2005) the most common flexible benefits provided are childcare vouchers, critical illness insurance, dental insurance, health screening, buying and selling holiday entitlement, income protection plans, life assurance, private medical insurance options, retail vouchers.

Take-up

Looking at the take-up rates for different benefits, as reported by IDS (2005), buying and selling holiday, especially buying holiday, is seen as the benefit which is most popular. This echoes the findings of Hillebrink et al. (2003) whose analysis shows that buying holiday entitlement is a very popular benefit selection; but it is not universally popular, as employees with high intrinsic motivation tend to prefer to trade time off for money. As Table 11.1 shows, various insured schemes concerning health also feature strongly in take-up by employees in major companies with flex schemes.

Table 11.1 Take-up rates of flexed benefits: in five companies with flexible schemes

Organisation	Overall take-up	Three most popular flexed benefits
LogicaCMG	42 % (first year)	Buying holidays Dental insurance Critical illness cover
Ofcom	88 % (proportion of employees who exercised a choice)	Pensions Holiday (buy or sell) Critical illness cover
Emap	56 %	Share incentive scheme Holiday buy or sell Dental cover
Lloyds TSB	60 %	Holiday (trading up/down) Critical illness cover Life assurance
Greene King- managers	100 %	Private medical insurance Pension Company car

Source: IDS (2005).

Legal aspects

A variety of regulatory conditions applies to flexible benefits. Some of the key aspects are:

- *Working Time Regulations and holiday trading.* Employees who want to 'sell' holiday entitlement under a flexible scheme may not do so in such way as to take their paid holidays below the statutory minimum holiday entitlement, increased to 24 days a year from 1 October 2007 and increasing further to 28 days if you work a five-day week from 1 April 2009 (inclusive of bank holidays)
- *Contractual issues.* If the contractual commitments are very specific in relation to particular benefits – for example, an insured scheme with a particular provider – then changing the detail can require the usual process for a change of contractual terms.
- *Age discrimination.* This aspect of law is likely to be most relevant when service-related benefits (for service above five years) are offered. See Chapter 8.
- *Salary sacrifice.* When the scheme includes a range of salary sacrifice options, the requirements of HM Revenue & Customs must be observed. There are National Insurance (NI) and tax breaks for certain benefits – pensions contributions and bicycles for work are tax and NI free; and the first £50 a week of childcare vouchers is tax and NI free.

Value for money

Previous research

Most companies with flex schemes monitor take-up of benefits but how do they assess whether such schemes give value for money? There are perhaps two opposing views on flexible benefits in terms of their value to the organisation. On the one hand, it may be argued that flexible benefits are too administratively costly carrying high transaction costs for the small amount of organisational benefit. On the other hand, positive business advantages are asserted for flexible benefits schemes by some commentators and consultants.

Wreford (2005), for instance, suggests that organisations introducing such schemes have a wide array of (seemingly ambitious) objectives. A survey by Employee Benefits (2003) indicates self-reported positive outcomes[2] from organisations with schemes. These include showing employees the value of their benefits; aiding recruitment; improving retention; harmonising benefits; reinforcing company culture; improving/maintaining staff motivation; aiding 'employer of choice' status; reducing/removing status symbols; and reducing/containing the cost of reward.

However, there is little systematic research in this area. One study, which has been published, Barber et al. (1992), indicated that flexible benefits may increase employee satisfaction with benefits, while helping employers to reduce benefit costs. The generalised nature of its findings, however, is open to question since although Barber et al. report a statistically significant increase in employee satisfaction with benefits following the introduction of a flexible scheme within a US financial services company, they recognise the need for more research into the processes through which flexible benefits might have an impact on employee reactions or perceptions.

There are some useful studies (Baughman et al., 2003; Dale-Olsen, 2005; Hong et al., 1995; Tsai and Wang, 2005) which have used quantitative techniques to establish associations between benefits more generally and certain positive organisational outcomes. All these studies indicate that benefits programmes are associated with positive effects, in relation to either productivity, and/or motivation and/or employee retention. Moreover, the studies by Baughman et al. and Dale-Olsen find that benefits, which are related to childcare or other 'family friendly' terms, can raise productivity or result in better employee retention. These findings seem to be in step with more emphasis on employment policies which recognise the diversity of lifestyles and interests of the workforce (Sparrow, 1998). It must be emphasised, however, that these studies were looking at benefits generally, rather than the impact of flexible schemes versus the impact of non-flexible schemes, so what potential benefits can be realised by employers who use a flexible benefits scheme?

Theoretical perspectives

Before turning to how such an evaluation might be conducted, it is necessary to examine the theoretical underpinning for it, and theory from three disciplines is potentially relevant to an evaluation of flexible benefits. From the psychological perspective motivation theory including expectancy theory, organisational justice theory and the concepts of the psychological contract seem to offer most potential. From economics, institutional theory, resource dependence theory, and agency theory are considered. In addition, from marketing, relevant concepts relating to market segmentation are discussed.

Psychological perspectives

Under expectancy theory, the element of choice in flexible benefits could itself be argued to lead to greater employee satisfaction with the benefits package provided, when employees are 'empowered' to select those benefits which have a particular value to them. A key problem for employers, as mentioned by – for example – Wreford (2005), is that employees tend to undervalue the often quite substantial spend of their employers on benefits. He argues that flexible systems maximise employee perceptions of the value of benefits. This theory has not directly been tested through systematic research.

Under organisational justice theory, the concepts of both procedural justice and distributive justice are relevant. There is accumulating research on the importance of procedural justice in the reward field (Newman and Milkovich, 1990); and Cole and Flint (2004) more directly use organisational justice theory in a study that compares the aspects of traditional benefits programmes compared with flexible benefits. They conclude that employers who offer a flexible plan may be able to increase employee perceptions of procedural justice without any reduction in perceptions of distributive justice. (Some diminution of distributive justice perceptions might have been expected under a flexible scheme in which people choose certain benefits and do not choose others. While in some cases the choice for individuals may be clear-cut, for others choices may be evenly balanced and they may perceive that they are losing out on some benefits.)

The growing literature on the psychological contract is also relevant to a study of flexible benefits because of the elements of choice and selection. Rousseau and Ho (2000) use a categorisation of types of psychological contract and argue that flexible benefits are characteristic of a 'balanced' psychological contract, in which the relationship of employee with employer is perceived as long-term and pay is related to 'contribution'. As such, the relationship is different to that in both short-term 'transactional' contracts and in traditional long-term 'relational' contracts. Their propositions are largely untested by empirical research in relation to flexible benefits.

Issues concerning the relationship between intrinsic and extrinsic motivation are discussed by Hillebrink et al. (2003) who suggest that flexible benefits can raise the intrinsic motivation of employees, when the scheme is perceived by employees as a supportive, as opposed to a controlling, intervention. However, individuals who are highly absorbed (have high 'flow') in their jobs may have different preferences to those who are not so highly absorbed.

Linked to the above and potentially of relevance to flexible benefits is the new research area of employee engagement. It overlaps with more established areas of employee commitment and organisational citizenship behaviour and the study by Robinson et al. (2004) shows that the management of pay and benefits feature in the spectrum of factors affecting employee engagement, but it does not disentangle reward from the other aspects of HR practice and management.

Economic perspectives

Barringer and Milkovich (1998) raise theoretical perspectives from the discipline of economics, which can be of value in understanding the development of flexible benefits, particularly from the employer viewpoint. Under institutional theory, organisations may adopt an initiative like flexible benefits, even if it is 'technically' inefficient for them to do so, to gain legitimacy or to conform to accepted standards of 'best practice'. By adopting flexibility managers feel that they or their organisations will be seen as 'modern' or 'professional'.

Barringer and Milkovich (1998) suggest that the institutional model could be more convincing when integrated with other theories, such as resource dependence theory. Resource dependence theory assumes that organisations are dependent on their various stakeholders. It therefore focuses on those that are perceived as critical for the business. Hence, if employees are seen as the most important resource, then employers will use resources to ensure that they recruit and retain those critical to the business. Resource dependence theory sees organisations responding more strategically to external pressures than institutional theory. Barringer and Milkovich quote some studies using this theory, which found that resistance to pressures to adopt family friendly policies varied with the percentage of women in the organisation's workforce.

Although usually used in the context of incentive schemes, not benefits, agency theory could possibly be extended to benefits. Agency theory implies that reward packages should be designed to motivate employees to act in the best interests of the principal (company owners). It has not been used in empirical studies of flexible benefits.

Finally, it can be questioned whether the nature of flexible benefits, which offer people choice, might be encouraging employees to see themselves as customers. Although exclusively focused on pensions, not benefits in general, Hales and

Gough (2003) raise the idea of employees as consumers of their employers' HR policies.

Using marketing techniques

If employees are customers, it might then follow that the concepts of marketing, particularly market segmentation, may be relevant. The review of the literature on market segmentation by Tynan and Drayton (1987) gives some useful pointers to how a differentiated response to benefits might be analysed, particularly in relation to the definition of segments. One could argue that several of the bases marketers use for segmentation could be useful, viz:

- Demographic factors – age, gender, socio-economic group, family size, life cycle, income, occupation, education.
- Psychological factors such as attitudes and motivation.
- Psychographic factors such as lifestyle, activities, interests, values.
- Behaviour – including take-up rate and preferences

Speaking at the 2006 *CIPD Annual reward at work conference*, Pete Harris, manager responsible for flexible benefits at insurance company, Friends Provident, described how the company had borrowed some of the lifestyle and demographic groupings used by its marketing department to analyse responses to company benefits. This analysis revealed not only some differences but also some similarities across the groupings used. For example, part-time and women employees placed more value on the childcare benefits, but all groups highly valued flexible working. Interestingly this example contrasts with Barber et al.'s 1992 study, which found no significant differences in benefit satisfaction between employees based on demographic categories.

Aside from anecdotal examples, there is as yet no evidence of the validity of these marketing concepts in analysing flexible benefits.

Evaluating effectiveness

A number of the above conceptual frameworks could be valuable in understanding the effectiveness of flexible benefits. Table 11.2 proposes a model for evaluating flexible benefits schemes in relation to potential organisational outcomes, drawing on several theories and proposes the use of employee surveys and other instruments to gauge the impact of the scheme.

It seems critical that an evaluation of the value of flexible benefits considers intervening variables (Guest, 2002) and processes, because purely quantitative methods might only show an association rather than the direction of causality.

Table 11.2 Flexible benefits – how might potential organisational outcomes be assessed?

Potential organisational outcome	Relevant theory	Contextual factors	How evaluate – research method(s)
Integration of benefits policy with business strategy	Agency theory, institutional theory, resource dependence theory	Extent to which benefits policy and practice integrated into HR strategy, vertically	In-depth interviews with senior management of the business
Higher perceived value: - the benefits package is of value - the flex package seen as better than a standard package would be	Expectancy theory; psychological contract	Individual perceptions of the value of the package in relation to lifestyle and demographic factors	Attitude survey of employees covered by scheme
Does the flex package attract people to the organisation?	Institutional theory, resource dependence theory; labour market dynamics	External and internal labour market conditions	Monitoring of job applicants; attitude survey of applicants/ potential applicants and of recruiters/employing line managers
Benefits provided seen as fair; the choice of benefits relevant to individual and the right balance of benefits is provided	Organisational justice theory – distributive and procedural justice	Job and organisational factors and perceptions of fairness of employer actions generally	Interviews and focus groups with representative sample from different levels/jobs in the organisation; demographic and lifestyle segmented structured sample
Improved job satisfaction Career satisfaction	Intrinsic and extrinsic motivation; degree of 'flow'	The individual's perception of and interest in their job and career plans	Attitude survey, taking account of individuals' degree of self-reported 'flow'; with measures to counter non-responses
Improved employee retention	Organisational justice theory; psychological contract	Recognise that intention to quit a multifaceted phenomenon, strongly leavers and current employees to	In-depth qualitative study of both

		affected by nature of job preview, relationship with line manager, perceived career expectations	assess the role of benefits provision within the factors that could influence intention to quit
Responsiveness to diverse workforce needs	Market segmentation concepts; labour market diversity	Employee may have preferences that although a certain service or benefit is needed they may not want it provided by employer; multiple layers or segments	Analysis of attitudes to individual benefits by demographic, family formation, and lifestyle factors
Communication with workforce	Employee voice concepts	Communication issues – remote system/call centre communication – employee preference for f2f communication – general perceptions of employer communication	Employee surveys and focus groups
Employee engagement	Employee commitment theories; unitarism and pluralism	Employee engagement – trust in employer – commitment – longer-term, short-term – willingness to exert effort on behalf of the organisation – intention to stay with the organisation – acceptance of the goals of the organisation – loyalty to employer belief that employer values them	Qualitative research and employee surveys

The author's research

Turning from the theoretical to the empirical, three separate but linked pieces of research by the author are summarised below:

- A study of 30 organisations with flexible benefits schemes.
- Examination of a detailed in-company survey assessing responses from employees covered by a flexible benefits scheme in a financial services company.
- The preliminary results of an employee survey and interviews within a housing sector organisation which has a combined flexible working and a flexible benefits scheme.

The study of 30 organisations

This study comprised interviews with employers (in each case the manager or HR specialist responsible for running the scheme). All these employers had had flexible benefits schemes in place for at least three years according to a survey by the Industrial Society (2000). The aim of the research was to establish if the organisations had evaluated their schemes and, if so, to examine how this had been achieved.

The research found that while employers might have benign or positive views on their schemes in practice, they had little evidence to support their views. No employers were evaluating the effectiveness of their flexible benefits schemes in any detailed way. Most managers were not even fully aware of the full costings of their scheme.

One organisation, which had done some work collecting and analysing HR data, believed they showed some association between the flexible benefits uptake and positive results in terms of organisational indicators such as turnover and absence, but no evidence of causal links was available and no work had been done to disentangle the effects of the flexible benefits scheme from other HR initiatives taking place at the same time.

Such findings are in keeping with those of the CIPD (2007) which found that the metrics used by employers to evaluate the effectiveness of their reward strategies are benchmarking data – as in the example quoted above – but there is also increasing use of employee surveys (used in 42 per cent of workplaces) in line with the findings of the WERS 2004 survey (Kersley et al., 2006). Strangely, in view of their lack of robustness as a research or managerial method (as shown, for example, in Steel et al., 2002) the CIPD's sample shows that 73 per cent of organisations deploy exit interviews to gauge reward effectiveness. One could certainly question whether an accurate picture is being given by the use of this method.

The financial services company

After this, the author studied flexible benefits in a large UK financial sector company. First, a company-conducted survey, covering both those who had chosen to take part and those who, although eligible, had opted not to take part in the scheme, was analysed. The scheme offers a substantial range of benefits including a facility to buy and sell holiday entitlement and child-care options, but also includes some 'salary sacrifice options'.

The analysis showed that take-up of the scheme was very variable across the six distinct divisions of the company, and varied significantly in relation to occupation and grade. Although the scheme was available to all staff the main users of the scheme were in the middle grades. Neither those in the highest grades nor those in the lowest grades (particularly those geographically remote from head office) seemed interested.

Data were collected via open-ended survey questions on employees' reasons for not taking part. These responses were categorised as follows:

- No interest in the options available (there was no distinction by grade).
- Price of benefits options too high (included those who preferred cash to benefits).
- Procedural issues/too busy.
- Technical problems with the selection of benefits (for example, passwords).

As Figure 11.1 shows, 'no interest' was the main reason given by respondents for not participating in the flex-ben scheme. This research also seemed to lend some support first to the idea that employees seem to view the 'purchase' of benefit options in a consumer mode; second, there seemed to be differences in take-up by occupational/seniority level, with employees who were considered most engaged in their work not taking part; third, lifestyle differences and lifecycle issues seemed to have some influence, although more flexible working and time were asked for by a range of different occupational levels and age ranges; fourth, procedural issues and ease of use of the system and effectiveness of communication on it were highlighted by some respondents.

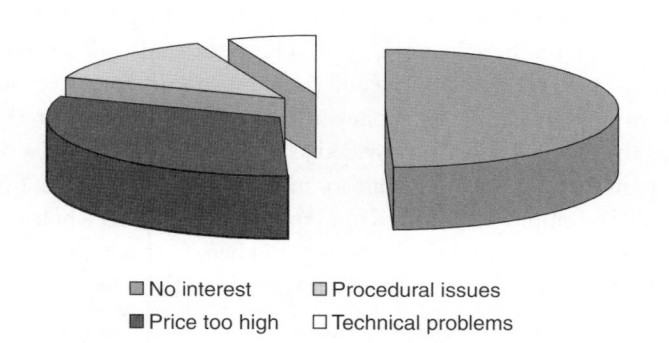

■ No interest   □ Procedural issues
■ Price too high   □ Technical problems

Figure 11.1   Reasons employees gave for not participating the flex-ben scheme

The housing sector organisation

The third element of the author's research was a housing sector organisation which has housing estate based staff as well as office-based staff, and had introduced a scheme to harmonise terms and conditions in a merged company. This scheme combines both flexible working options (the 'benefit' employees said they most wanted in the first company) and a range of benefits including buying/selling holiday entitlement and salary sacrifice options such as childcare vouchers and various insured options – dental, travel, and so on.

Two surveys were conducted: a survey of employees covered by the new scheme, and a survey of those who were not covered (either because their part of the business had yet to introduce it or because they opted to stay on their previous terms and conditions – some of which included more generous sick pay terms than the new scheme). These two surveys were followed by interviews of key managers and employees in different parts of the business.

Preliminary results of this research show that the majority of employees covered by the new arrangements were very positive about the scheme. It was particularly popular with full-time office-based staff. However, even those who were the most positive had complaints. Some typical responses were:

> I think that the scheme is good but.... The new yoga classes are a very good idea but for some staff perhaps not cheap.... The web site is difficult to use because you have to remember yet another password and then some of the sub sections have passwords. For that reason I don't use it.... The security is a nuisance and needs rethinking. (Full-time, male with 1–3 years' service, Head Office)

> I would like to see further additional days of holiday trading. (Male, full-time, aged 40–55, more than 10 years' service)

> Benefit scheme is NO substitute for paying a competitive salary!!!!!!!!!! (Full-time male, aged 40–55, 4–6 years' service)

> Would like to see improved website. How about gym membership packages. (Female, aged 16–24, less than one year's service).

Nevertheless, the majority of respondents (70 per cent) thought the scheme of value to them. Furthermore, the scheme seemed to be associated with a positive view of the company: 87 per cent thought it a good company to work for. Nevertheless, there were problems in seeing value for money in the scheme. Just under a third (29 per cent) viewed the range of benefits provided as not good for them and a similar proportion thought they did not offer value for money. However, much of this response seemed affected by employees taking a total reward view of their whole reward package. Only a half (55 per cent) thought the pay and benefits package competitive.

Typical views of those who were most negative about the scheme were:

> What a waste of my time, and company money I like... to get on with my job, and give my time to the residents who need it, in the Sheltered Housing Scheme where I work.... there

just is not enough time in the day. (Female, full-time aged 40–55, more than 10 years' service)

None ... were of ... interest to me, as my current annual travel insurance is cheaper and more comprehensive, already .... have life/critical insurance cover elsewhere. (Female, full-time, 1–3 years' service).

Unable to take up ... because they said I was below the minimum wage for tax purposes and would not allow me to do them. I am very disappointed that I have not been given the same opportunity as other employees. (Female, full-time, aged over 56, 4–6 years' service)

a line manager can, seemingly at whim, decide that they are the only member of staff within the Department who can work compressed hours, is unfair and somewhat ridiculous .... My understanding is that provided the demands of the office are covered, requests to work either compressed or flexi time should be considered; however that does not happen in this section. (Female, full-time, aged 40–55, 1-years' service.

Recruitment and retention effects

A large majority (88 per cent) of employees said they were attracted to work for an organisation which offered good benefits, and 70 per cent thought the scheme was of value to them, but only 7.5 per cent of recent joiners said the scheme specifically attracted them to work for that organisation. Such results seem contradictory, but again the overall perceived competitiveness of the package seemed to be a crucial issue.

One manager who recruited staff said: 'Most people look at the cash and need to get the money right first. After that the flexitime and compressed hours are attractions, but only if the money is right.'

A retention effect was not clear. While 79 per cent of respondents to the survey said they intended to stay with the organisation for the foreseeable future (and there was no significant difference in response to this question in relation to positive or negative views of the flexible benefits scheme) the capacity of the scheme to positively retain people who are bent on leaving is in doubt. A manager within HR said: 'It is not the same as a final salary pension, which might retain people; it is not enough to hold people who are unhappy and want to leave.'

Levels of understanding and awareness of benefits

The scheme was not well understood: 36 per cent said they did not fully understand it. Respondents who felt strongly negative about understanding tended also to have the most negative views on the scheme generally. The capacity of what is read 'between the lines' by employees in company communications may also be as important as what is actually said. For example, although respondents liked the flexible working aspects of the scheme and many liked some of the other benefits, there was less convincing evidence that the scheme seemed employee-centred to the employees themselves. One typical comment was:

> *The additional benefits ... feel like an 'off the shelf' benefits package put in place more to pad the existing benefits rather than to offer any incentive to staff as most organisations of a certain size and above offer a largely identical package.* (Male, aged 25–39, 4–6 years' service)

Communications issues

The HR managers believed the scheme was not communicated well; and the majority of respondents rated the various forms of communication on the scheme as 'average' or 'poor'. In contrast, 69 per cent said that they thought in general the company communicated well with its employees. A particular problem was with the on-line system (mirroring the experience of the financial services company). The problems experienced with passwords and other security measures seemed to be a real barrier to people taking part in the scheme.

The scheme's planners seemed to assume that people would invest time in seeing the potential of the scheme for themselves, but this was not borne out in practice. Indeed, this factor seemed to influence many of the negative views, coupled with the inevitable complexities of benefit choices. Even quite straightforward aspects of the scheme were difficult for some, as in the following example:

> *Remember hearing about the holiday trading but seemed very complicated.* (Full-time, female, aged more than 56)

Conclusion

Communication is central to the success of flexible benefits and it cannot be assumed that people will be willing to invest time in a complex and intricate system. It is notable that face-to-face communications seemed to be preferred by employees. In both of the organisations, studied on-line and call centre systems for dealing with choices and queries were rated poor by employees. This finding is echoed in the experience of Lloyds TSB (IDS, 2005), which also found that face-to-face communication on flexible benefits was requested by staff.

This can obviously be a problem for employers who have worked out the costs of their scheme on the basis of a less labour intensive approach. To communicate well can clearly present substantial transaction costs, which the organisation might not be able to justify in terms of the positive outcomes of the scheme. Moreover, because employees' awareness of the detail of their benefits has a strong link to the impact benefits can have in the organisation (Hennessey et al., 1992), the success or otherwise of a scheme in achieving positive organisational outcomes may hinge on the quality of communication.

The recruitment and retention effects of flexible benefits seem weak. However, organisational context is crucial. In specific circumstances benefits in general, as distinct from flexible benefits, could act to retain people – but whether they always retain the people that are the highest performers is another question.

The research seems to offer little evidence of resource dependence theory at work, since organisations did not seem that keen to investigate the recruitment and retention effects in practice, although these may have been quoted (IDS, 2005) as one of the initial reasons for the scheme.

Indeed, companies may consider that their main purpose is to be seen to be a forward-looking employer by merely offering the scheme, regardless of its cost effectiveness. Furthermore, they may see evaluation as unnecessary and complex. More broadly, one assumption underlying the demand to evaluate schemes seems an implied rationalist approach, which has its critics (Corby et al., 2005).

Time does seem to have value to employees as evidenced by the popularity of holiday trading within flexible benefits and the demand for flexible working. However, this does not necessarily imply that employees want a scheme that combines the two.

Benefits seem to have a variable value to individuals and flexible benefits could be a valid response from employers with an individualistic and unitarist frame of reference. However, deploying standardised approaches to the communication aspects could mean employers fail to persuade people that they are being treated as individuals and therefore potential positive outcomes may be limited. Perhaps those considering introducing flexible benefits or embarking on evaluation of an extant scheme could usefully re-read the Hawthorn experiments!

Overall the prospects for a further growth of flexible benefits schemes do not seem likely in view of the potentially high transaction costs needed to make a scheme succeed both in terms of communicating as well as other administrative requirements. Such costs might be justifiable if there were significant recruitment, retention, and motivation gains to be had. However, the evidence of this is as yet unclear.

Notes

1. Estimates and survey samples vary and there is no systematic source of data.
2. The question asked was 'Do you believe your flexible benefits plan has been effective in any of the following?'.

References

Barber, R., Dunham, B., and Formisano, R. (1992) 'The Impact of Employee Benefits on Employee Satisfaction: A Field Study', *Personnel Psychology*, 45, 55–75.

Barringer, M. and Milkovich, G. (1998) 'A Theoretical Exploration of the Adoption and Design of Flexible Benefit Plans: A Case of Human Resource Innovation', *Academy of Management Review*, 23, 2, April, 305–324.

Baughman, R., DiNardi, D., and Holtz-Eakin, D. (2003) 'Productivity and Wage Effects of "Family-Friendly" Fringe Benefits', *International Journal of Manpower*, 24, 3, 247–259.

Brown, W., Deakin, S., Hudson, M., Pratten, C., and Ryan, P. (1998) *The Individualisation of Employment Contracts in Britain*, Research Paper for the Department of Trade and Industry, Centre for Business Research Department of Applied Economics, University of Cambridge.

CIPD (2005) *Reward Management Survey 2005*, London: Chartered Institute of Personnel and Development.

CIPD (2006) *Reward Management Survey 2006*, London: Chartered Institute of Personnel and Development.

CIPD (2007) *Reward Management Survey 2007*, London: Chartered Institute of Personnel and Development.

Cole, N. and Flint, D. (2004) 'Perceptions of Distributive and Procedural Justice in Employee Benefits: Flexible Versus Traditional Plans', *Journal of Managerial Psychology*, 19, 1, 19–40.

Corby, S., White, G., and Stanworth, C. (2005) 'No News Is Good News? Evaluating New Pay Systems', *Human Resource Management Journal*, 15, 1, 4–24.

Dale-Olsen, H. (2005) *Using Linked Employer-Employee Data to Analyze Fringe Benefits Policies. Norwegian Experiences*, Institute for Social Research, Norway, Paper presented at Policy Studies Institute Seminar, July 2005.

Employee Benefits/MX Financial Solutions (2003) Flexible benefits research 2003, *Employee Benefits*, April, 4–9.

Guest, D. (2002) 'Human Resource Management, Corporate Performance and Employee Wellbeing: Building the Worker into HRM', *The Journal of Industrial Relations*, 44, 3, 335–358.

Hales, C. and Gough, O. (2003) 'Employee Valuations of Company Occupational Pensions: HR Implications', *Personnel Review*, 32, 3, 319–340.

Heneman, R., Ledford, G., and Gresham, M. (2000) 'The Changing Nature of Work and Its Effects on Compensation Design and Delivery', in Rynes, S. L. and Gerhart, B. (eds) *Compensation in Organizations: Current Research and Practice*, San Francisco, CA: Jossey-Bass, 2000, 195–240.

Hennessey, H., Perrewe, P., and Hochwater, W. (1992) 'Impact of Benefit Awareness on Employee and Organizational Outcomes: A Longitudinal Field Examination', *Benefits Quarterly*, 8, 2, 90–96.

Hillebrink, C., Schippers, J., Peters, P., and van Doone-Huizkes, A. (2003) 'Choosing Time or Money: A Study into Employees' Decision-Making Regarding Flexible Benefits', Paper Presented at the HRM Network Conference, Twente: Netherlands, November 2003.

Hong, J., Yang, S., Wang, L., Chiou, E., Sun, F., and Huang, T. (1995) 'Impact of Employee Benefits on Work Motivation and Productivity', *International Journal of Career Management*, 7, 6, 10–14.

Incomes Data Services (2005) Flexible Benefits, *IDS HR Study Plus*, 811, December.

Industrial Society (2000) Flexible Benefits, *Managing Best Practice* 75, September.

Kersley, B., Alpin, C., Forth, J., Bryson, A., Bewley, H., Dix, G., and Oxenbridge, S. (2006) *Inside the Workplace: First Findings from the 2004 Workplace Employment Relations*, London: Department of Trade and Industry.

Newman, J. and Milkovich, G. (1990) 'Procedural Justice Challenges in Compensation: Eliminating the Fairness Gap', *Labor Law Journal*, August, 575–580.

Robinson, D., Perryman, S., and Hayday, S. (2004) 'The Drivers of Employee Engagement', *IES Report* 408, Brighton: Institute of Employment Studies.

Rousseau, D. and Ho, V. (2000) 'Psychological Contract Issues in Compensation' in Rynes, S. and Gerhart, B. (eds) *Compensation in Organizations: Current Research and Practice*, San Francisco, CA: Jossey-Bass.

Russell, A. (1991) *The Growth of Occupational Welfare in Britain: Evolution and Harmonisation*, Epping: Gower Publishing.

Sparrow, P. (1998) 'Can the Psychological Contract Be Managed? Implications for the Field of Rewards Management', in Perkins, S. and Sandringham, S. (eds) *Trust, Motivation and Commitment: A Reader*, Farringdon: Strategic Remuneration Research Centre.

Steel, R., Griffith, R., and Hom, P. (2002) 'Practical Retention Policy for the Practical Manager', *Academy of Management Executive*, 16, 2, 149–162.

Tsai, K. and Wang, J. (2005) 'Benefits Offer No Advantage on Firm Productivity?', *Personnel Review*, 34, 4, 2005, 393–405.

Tynan, C. and Drayton, J. (1987) 'Market Segmentation', *Journal of Marketing Management*, 12, 3, 301–335.

WorldatWork (2007) *Handbook of Compensation and Benefits*, Hoboken, USA: John Wiley & Sons.

Wreford, D. (2005) *Ensuring the Benefits Package Adds Value: Objectives and Success Measures of Benefit Flexibility*, Posted on e-reward.co.uk (accessed 23 March 2005).

12

Employee share ownership in Europe

Andrew Pendleton

Introduction

Employee share ownership is a hot topic in Europe. Many large European companies have developed employee share ownership plans so that employees can acquire shares in the company. They have been encouraged to do this by governments, some of which have passed legislation to promote these plans. At European Union (EU) level, there have been several initiatives to encourage employee share owner-ship and other forms of financial participation, such as profit sharing. The rationale has been that employee financial participation can enhance productivity, competi-tiveness, and profitability of enterprises whilst encouraging worker involvement, better quality of work, and greater social cohesion (Commission of the European Communities, 2002).

Employee share ownership means that employees become owners as well as work-ers. It has been claimed that share ownership plans will align the interests of employ-ees with those of owners and managers, and will encourage employees to move away from a 'them and us' perspective on the employment relationship. This transforma-tion of employee attitudes is said to bring about changes in the way that employees work. They will work 'harder and smarter'. By so doing, company performance will improve in due course. Other perspectives on employee share ownership emphasise social justice and employee rights – providing employees with shares gives them a share of the profits of their labour. It will also deepen their involvement in the company.

It is apparent, however, that these are highly contentious claims. Employee share ownership raises fundamental issues about economic organisation and the nature of employment. Should workers also be owners, given that a fundamental characteristic of capitalism is the separation of labour from capital? Should employee share-owners be involved in the management and governance of the companies employing them? Is it fair or efficient to expose employees to the risks of concentrating their capital (human and financial) in one investment? What are the implications of employee share ownership for industrial relations, collective bargaining, and employee representation? There are no easy answers to these questions, and governments, employers, and employee organisations have divergent views on these issues.

In this chapter, we consider these actors' policies and views of employee share ownership. We evaluate the extent to which these views are well-founded by discussing the evidence on the effects of employee share ownership, especially as they relate to pay determination and collective bargaining. It will become apparent that there are differences in views between and within each group of actors. Policy objectives for employee share ownership vary between countries in Europe, and there are wide differences in the degree of governmental support for it. This is reflected in substantial variation between countries in the incidence of share ownership plans. Employer objectives tend to be more homogeneous, though once again there are national variations in the extent of support for employee share ownership. By contrast, there are substantial differences between unions in their views about employee share ownership, both between and within countries.

The chapter opens by outlining the various types of employee share ownership plans. It then provides some illustrative examples from the United Kingdom and France, before presenting information on the incidence of share plans in European countries. The chapter then discusses the policy rationales for share ownership identified by the European Commission before going on to consider variations in policy priorities between governments. Employer and union perspectives on share ownership are then reviewed, and the chapter closes with a discussion of the relationship between employee share ownership and employee representation.

Employee share ownership plans

This section examines the main characteristics of employee share ownership plans. Illustrative examples are provided from the United Kingdom and France.

Characteristics

Share ownership plans can take a number of different forms, or combinations of them. The first, and simplest, is the award of free shares to employees by companies. These might be linked to a profit sharing scheme whereby a portion of profits is used to acquire shares for employees. Governments might encourage this form of share distribution by allowing some or all of these awards to be exempted from income tax.

Alternatively, firms might establish arrangements for employees to purchase shares in the company, possibly at a discount on the prevailing market price. The acquisition of shares would typically be free of direct transaction costs unlike shares acquired via a broker. There may be tax concessions on the discount on the market price. It is also possible that companies will increase the appeal of acquiring shares by offering bonus or matching shares – for example, 'buy one, get one free'.

Another form of employee share ownership is the share option plan. Here, employees are granted an option to purchase shares at some point in the future, typically between three and ten years. This type of scheme might not lead to actual share ownership because employees might simultaneously exercise the option and sell the resulting shares.

The financial benefits that employees may expect to receive from share ownership plans are regular profit-related dividends and growth in the value of the shares, though schemes do not necessarily deliver both of these. There are varieties of additional design characteristics of share plans in addition to the core forms identified above. One consideration is whether ownership is individual or collective. Shares might be owned by individuals or might instead be collectively owned by a collective entity, such as an employee benefits trust, with a duty to act in employees' interests. In this latter case, employees might receive profit share payments derived from the dividend payments accruing to the trust-owned shares but would not be able to treat the shares as their own and would not be able to sell them. A good example of this is the John Lewis Partnership in the United Kingdom. Since 1950, this company has been owned by a trust with a duty to act for the benefit of current and future employees. Each year John Lewis employees receive a profit share based on their collective ownership of the business (see Oakeshott, 2000).

A second consideration is whether ownership is immediate or deferred. Plainly, in share option plans, ownership cannot occur until employees exercise their options. In other types of plans, it is common for full ownership to be deferred for a time. Whilst employees may receive some financial benefits (dividends, for example) on becoming beneficial owners, they may be prevented from selling the shares for a specified period (usually between three and five years). This might be achieved by initially allocating the shares to a trust. The reasons for doing this include a concern to discourage the use of share plans as a disguised form of tax-beneficial remuneration. If employees could sell shares immediately, and they receive tax benefits on the shares, employees and companies might use share plans instead of cash salary as a form of tax evasion.

A third design issue concerns the ways employees acquire shares. Do employees have to provide an up-front payment or can they contribute in instalments? In share option plans, employees make a single payment for the shares at the point of exercise. Employees typically either do a 'cashless exercise', whereby the purchase price of the shares is met by a simultaneous sale of the exercised shares (see Carpenter, 1998), or else participate in a savings scheme to accrue the funds for the option exercise. As for share purchase schemes, employees may purchase shares on a regular basis or might instead contribute to a savings plan which periodically acquires shares for the employee. In many European countries, the savings plan is the central instrument, and the savings may be used to acquire a variety of asset classes (including capital goods in some cases), of which the employer's shares are just one (see Poutsma, 2001).

A fourth issue is the taxation arrangements. Clearly, any benefit gained from share ownership, over and above any benefit from acquiring the same shares by other means, is a benefit from employment, and should therefore be subject to income tax. In practice, it is common for employees to be exempted from income tax on benefits arising from the acquisition and the sale of the shares. Instead, capital gains tax might be due on the difference between the market value price at acquisition and at sale. If there are annual capital gains tax allowances to be offset against tax, it is possible that employees will not pay any tax on the sale of their shares. Where tax might be due, it makes sense to manage the timing of share sales across more than one tax year. Although these core principles are quite widespread there are variations between countries arising from broader differences in taxation principles and arrangements. This is particularly evident in the case of stock options.

Some countries make a tax charge at the point when options are granted (for instance, Belgium); others on the difference between the market value at exercise and that when the option was granted (for instance, Germany); whilst in others tax is due at the eventual sale of the shares (most countries except Belgium and Netherlands). In some cases, tax may be due at more than one of these, or there may be some choice as to the timing of taxation (for instance, the Netherlands) (see PricewaterhouseCoopers, 2002).

There is also the issue of tax benefits accruing to the employer. The most obvious one is whether the costs of operating a scheme can be offset against company taxes. This might include the administration costs, and any transaction costs arising from purchasing shares in the open market to make available to employees. Where shares are granted free of charge to employees, employers may receive tax relief on the cost of providing these shares. The notion of the cost of shares has been a contentious one in recent years because of new accounting standards. In the case of stock options, it has been argued that there is an economic cost to the company relating to the difference between the option price and the value of the option when it is exercised into shares. International Financial Reporting Standard 2 on Share-based Payments (IFRS2) (introduced in 2005) requires that companies include a measure of this cost into their balance sheets. This is typically done by using an option pricing methodology (commonly Black-Scholes) and spreading the derived costs over the life of the option. A further possible tax relief can arise in privately owned firms where an owner might receive tax relief on the proceeds of selling their shares to their employees. Finally, employers may receive relief from employer social security contributions on the benefits employees receive from acquiring shares.

Examples of share ownership plans

To illustrate the range of design features of employee share ownership, details are now provided on two all-employee plans in the United Kingdom and the current system of employee share ownership in France.

United Kingdom: save as you earn

Save As You Earn (SAYE), often commonly referred to as 'Sharesave', is a long-established share option and savings plan scheme in the United Kingdom. Employees in companies with SAYE are typically invited to subscribe to options to be exercised in three or five years' time (extendable to seven years). These options can be granted at up to a 20 per cent discount on prevailing market prices: most participating firms offer the full discount. This discount is free of income tax. Meanwhile, the participant takes out a SAYE savings contract of up to £250 per month, usually operated by a building society. At the end of the savings period, the employee receives a tax-free bonus, and can either exercise the options or take the money. If options are exercised the shares might be sold (possibly simultaneously with exercise) or retained. When the shares are sold, the employee may be liable to capital gains tax on the growth in value. However, any liability will be offset by the annual capital gains tax allowance. In most cases, the gain will be within the annual allowance so no tax is paid.

United Kingdom: Share Incentive Plan (SIP)

Introduced in 2000, the SIP provides for share acquisition by employees in a number of ways. Employers may award employees up to £3,000 Free Shares per annum (replacing similar arrangements in the Approved Profit Sharing scheme). These can be linked to company, group, or individual performance, though most firms operating Free Shares appear not to do so. Employees can subscribe to Partnership Shares (up to £1,500 each year) by deductions from pre-tax salary. Employers may provide Matching Shares at up to double the rate of employee subscriptions. Finally, income from dividends may be subscribed to Dividend Shares. Employers can select which 'modules' of SIP they want to operate, with relatively few providing Free Shares, and most offering Partnership and Matching Shares. Shares are held in the plan for a minimum of three years: they must be held for five years for the full tax concessions to be available (Incomes Data Services, 2007).

Share ownership plans in France

In France, employee share ownership has been strongly linked with profit sharing and company savings plans. Profit sharing is mandatory in companies with 50 or more employees (*Participation*) and the proceeds of this may be passed into a company savings plan (along with performance related bonuses and voluntary employee contributions), known as the Plan d'Epargne d'Entreprise (PEE). Up to a quarter of annual salary can be invested in the PEE. Employer contributions can match voluntary employee contributions. Funds from the PEE are mainly invested in company investment funds known as Fonds Communs de Placement d'Entreprise (FCPE). These investment funds may invest in a range of financial assets, including employer shares (no more than 30 per cent of the fund), or may invest mainly in employer shares. It is a legal requirement that a PEE should offer at least one diversified fund as well as a company fund. Approximately a quarter of employee savings are invested in employer shares. Companies can offer a discount of up to 20 per cent on the stock price. Employee contributions to the PEE, including any derived from bonus payments, are exempt from taxes, whilst employer contributions can be offset against corporation tax and social security charges are not levied. Employee savings must be held in the plan for a minimum of five years (see Degeorge et al., 2004; Poutsma, 2001).

In 2001, the Fabius Law enabled small and medium-sized enterprises (SMEs) to collaborate to provide a joint PEE. In 2003, a new savings plan – Plan d'Epargne Retraite Colectif (PERCO) – was launched in which savings are frozen until retirement: these are prevented from investing more than 5 per cent of fund assets in company shares. Since 2005 it has been possible for firms to offer free shares to employees, with a vesting period of two years followed by a holding period of two years (or a vesting period of four years), and these can be paid to the FCPE. France also has provision for share option plans. Although traditionally these have been used primarily for executive remuneration, a growing number of large French firms are offering stock options to a wider group of employees. A notable feature of employee share ownership in France is that employees have the right to representation on the company board when their shareholdings exceed 3 per cent of a company's equity (see Pernot, 2004)

Incidence of employee share ownership

The use of share ownership plans is growing in many countries of the European Union. Several European countries, including Belgium, France, Germany, Netherlands, and the United Kingdom, have passed legislation in the past ten years to encourage share ownership (see Pendleton and Poutsma, 2004). Unfortunately, it is difficult to determine precisely the incidence of share plans in most countries, either because relevant statistical information is not collected or because share plans do not have a clear legal identity and hence cannot be readily recorded in official statistics. We therefore have to rely on survey data to compare the incidence of share ownership plans between countries.

A study conducted for the European Foundation in 2001 shows the incidence of employee share ownership plans in the (then) EU14. Whilst these results should be treated with a degree of caution because not all constituent surveys were fully representative, the table gives a good approximation of share plan incidence.

As Table 12.1 indicates, France and the United Kingdom have the highest incidence, followed by the Netherlands. There is then a middle group of countries, comprising the Scandinavian countries, Belgium, and Germany. The Mediterranean countries – Italy, Portugal, Spain – have very low incidence. Although not shown in the Table, an important difference between the United Kingdom and France is that around three-quarters of share ownership firms in the latter also have profit sharing, compared with around 40 per cent of UK firms. More recent entrants to the EU in eastern and central Europe (not shown in the Table) also have very low incidence of share ownership plans. In some of these countries, employee share ownership was briefly widespread because of ownership transfers at the demise of communism but this has now been dissipated. A recent study finds that there is little legislative support for employee share ownership in these countries, and few firms operate share ownership plans (Lowitzsch, 2006).

It is clear that the presence of supportive legislation and the availability of tax concessions have a strong influence on the incidence of share ownership plans. In Table 12.1, those countries with the highest incidence of share plans are those with the most long-standing and extensive frameworks for employee share ownership. This is confirmed

Table 12.1 The incidence of broad-based employee share ownership by country

Country	Percentage
Austria	4
Belgium	11
Denmark	15
Finland	15
France	23
Germany	10
Greece	7
Ireland	16
Italy	2
Netherlands	21
Portugal	2
Spain	5
Sweden	12
United Kingdom	30
Average – EU 14	16

Note: Percentage of business units with 200 or more employees with broad-based share ownership plans in 1999
Source: Pendleton et al. (2001).

by further statistical analysis: if measures for tax supports are included in a multi-variate cross-national model of the determinants of share plan presence, they have a very sizeable and significant effect on the likelihood of operating a broad-based share ownership plan (see Pendleton et al., 2003, p. 161). A further relevant factor, though by no means as important as legislation, is the size of national stock markets.

Within countries, the most important determinants of employee share ownership plans are the size and type of firm. Nearly every study of share ownership has shown that plans are most common in the largest firms, and very uncommon in small firms (Kruse, 1996; Pendleton et al., 2001). Stock market listing is also a very important influence. This is unsurprising: the use of publicly tradable shares clearly assists firms in operating schemes and provides a ready market for employees to sell their shares. The implication of this is that the extent of share ownership plans will be influenced by the extent of stock market listing in a country. On this basis, it is no surprise that the United Kingdom, with the largest number of listed firms in Europe, has the highest incidence of share ownership plans. The 2004 Workplace Employment Relations Survey found that 30 per cent of British workplaces with 25 or more employees operate an employee share ownership plan (Pendleton, 2007)

As for business sectors, European evidence indicates that share ownership plans tend to be most common in the finance sector, and less common in manufacturing and some service industries such as hospitality (Pendleton et al., 2001). There is a certain amount of evidence that workforce composition is associated with use of plans: American organisations with highly qualified workforces or high capital intensity have a higher probability of operating a share ownership plan (Kruse, 1996). Much of the literature draws attention to a potential complementarity between share ownership plans and other forms of employee participation (Conyon and Freeman, 2004; Pérotin and Robinson, 2003). However, the evidence is not clear-cut. Some studies indicate that share ownership tends to be found in more participative workplaces (ibid.) whilst others suggest that share ownership might substitute for other forms of employee involvement and participation (Pendleton, 2006a).

A key issue concerning share ownership plans is the level of participation in them by employees. Certain types of plan are likely to have higher participation rates than others. Plans where shares are given to employees are likely to have very high participation rates. By contrast, where shares have to be purchased by employees the participation rate is likely to be lower. An obvious issue is affordability – can employees afford to divert some of their income into share subscriptions? There is also the issue of risk – plans that are seen to be lower risk seem likely to have higher participation rates than those that are more risky. For instance, the UK SAYE plan, which has no downside risk for the duration of the plan, tends to have higher participation rates than the Share Incentive Plan, where employees are more exposed to movements in share prices[1].

There is little or no information on participation rates within contributory share ownership plans in most European countries, though case-study information on individual companies shows wide variations in participation. The factors that influence participation are likely to be both intrinsic to the company and intrinsic to the individual. Relevant company factors are recent movements in the share price and the quality of company communications about the share plan. Regarding the former, it is not known definitively how share prices affect participation but research on acquisitions of company stock in 401 (k) pension plans in the United States indicate that employees tend to extrapolate from share price movements in the recent past and assume that this movement will continue (Benartzi, 2001). As for individual factors, the most important influence appears to be income: the probability of participating, and the size of contributions, rises steadily with income (see DeGeorge et al., 2004). Life cycle factors appear to be important too. Participation and contribution rates rise with age but tend to fall away again as retirement approaches. As for sex, the evidence is complex. Women are more likely to participate in these plans (Huberman et al., 2003) but are less likely to subscribe to shares (Agnew et al., 2003). French evidence indicates that women are more likely to participate in a share purchase plan but to contribute less than men (Degeorge et al., 2004).

In the United Kingdom, 560,000 employees took out options under the SAYE arrangements in 2005–2006 (approximately 2 per cent of the employed workforce). Unfortunately, it is not known how many employees in total hold options from successive option grants. However, household-level information from the Family Resources Survey shows that 4 per cent of households have at least one member participating in a share scheme or profit sharing. Participation is higher (7 per cent) when the head of household is in the 35–44 age group. The household participation rate rises to 14 per cent when the combined household income is more than £1,000 per week (Department of Work and Pensions, 2006).

Government policies towards employee share ownership

Governments have a variety of objectives for promoting employee share ownership, and in Europe the balance of these tends to vary between countries. The range of rationales have been summarised recently by the European Commission (Commission of the European Communities, 2002). The overarching rationale for employee share ownership from the EU's perspective is their potential to contribute to the achievement of the policy goals of the Lisbon summit in 2000. At Lisbon, the EU set itself the target of becoming 'the most competitive and dynamic knowledge-based economy in the world, capable of sustainable economic growth with more and better jobs and greater social cohesion' (ibid., 2002, p. 3). Possibly the most important way share plans might contribute to this policy goal is by aligning employee interests with those of their company and creating a sense of shared goals and belonging. In so doing, share plans might enhance employee loyalty and commitment. As a result, share plans might contribute to increased productivity, competitiveness, and profitability. They might also bring about these outcomes by encouraging employee retention (the deferral arrangements in share plans tend to 'lock-in' employees), thereby facilitating high levels of training and skill/knowledge acquisition.

Other policy goals associated with share plans by the European Commission include wealth creation by employees, and provision of finance (for instance, by employee subscriptions to shares) for small firms. A further potential benefit of employee share ownership plans is that they may encourage greater financial transparency by companies, thereby contributing to improved corporate governance (European Economic and Social Committee, 2003, p. 31). Employee shareholders might also contribute to the monitoring of company managements.

In its recent communication, the Commission suggested that certain key principles should govern the operation of employee share ownership schemes and other forms of financial participation (Commission of the European Communities, 2002). These are that participation should be voluntary, that the schemes should be open to all employees, and that they should be established and managed in a clear and transparent way. The Commission suggests that it is especially important that employees or their representatives are informed and consulted about the details of schemes. Schemes should be based on pre-defined formulae, and should be operated regularly. Employees should not be exposed to unreasonable risks. Wages and salaries should be kept separate from plans, so that the latter cannot substitute for the former. Finally, share plans should be designed so that they do not provide rigid constraints on worker mobility (which would be incompatible with the flexibility and adaptability central to the Lisbon agenda). An important element of the Commission's perspective is that share plans (and other forms of financial participation) work best when embedded in a context of participatory management.

European governments attach varying importance to the different policy objectives and principles identified by the European Commission. In the United Kingdom, the overriding objective for share plans over the past 25 years has been to improve company productivity and performance. It is believed that making employees owners in their companies can have favourable effects on employee attitudes and views about the company. Employees will come to be more committed to the company, and will work more effectively as a result (Pendleton, 2001). In the past, a further aim of share plans has been to create an 'enterprise culture' and a 'share-owning democracy' whereby employees discard traditional 'them and us' views in favour of more entrepreneurial orientations (Baddon et al., 1989). Although UK governments have emphasised the desirability of communications with employees, they have refrained (unlike some other European governments) from any mandatory requirements on firms to secure the consent of employees or their representatives before introducing plans (Pendleton and Poutsma, 2004; Poutsma et al., 1999). By contrast, recent legislation in Belgium requires that plans to introduce share schemes be subject to collective agreement with unions, whilst in France the operation of financial participation arrangements requires the support of an employee ballot, union representatives, or the works councils (ibid.).

Rather different perspectives on the merits of employee share ownership can be discerned in other European countries. Not all governments have been convinced that employee share ownership is an effective way of improving company performance, having noted that the academic evidence on performance effects is not conclusive (Pendleton and Poutsma, 2004). Instead, share ownership has been portrayed by some as a means of enhancing flexibility in wages and wage determination. In others, share ownership is seen as a way of giving employees their legitimate stake in company success. In some countries, such as Germany, share ownership plans have to be understood in a context of a concern for income and wealth redistribution, and protection of lower earners against risk (see Poutsma et al., 1999). In the current debate on employee share ownership in Germany, the Social Democrats are arguing that share ownership should be indirect to protect employees from corporate bankruptcy. Employee contributions would be invested in a national 'Germany Fund' which in turn would acquire equity in companies in which contributors are employed.

In France and the Netherlands, financial participation generally has to be understood in the context of a concern to promote medium-term and long-term employee savings. Equally, in France, the genesis of the compulsory profit sharing scheme – 'Participation' – was rooted in a Gaullist concern to find a middle way between capital and labour (Rojot, 2002). In Southern European countries, with a history of ideological conflict between capital and organised labour, share ownership is often portrayed as a way of reducing these traditional conflicts. Yet for this reason, employee share ownership is regarded with great suspicion in some quarters, and as a result governments have not been able to progress legislation in this area (see Biagi and Tiraboschi, 2002; Pendleton and Poutsma, 2004; Tiraboschi, 2002).

Company objectives are often subtly different from the stated aims of government policies. When asked about the objectives of their share plans, company respondents often give most emphasis to a concern to create a sense of common interests amongst employees. Rather less emphasis tends to be given to harder-edged concerns to provide direct incentives to employees to be more productive or work harder (see Poole, 1989). There seems to be a widespread recognition that share plans are not well-suited to the latter because of the 'free-rider' problem (why should any single employee work harder when the benefits are shared with all?). Other important reasons for operating share plans include reduction in employee turnover and attraction of suitable recruits. In principle, share plans might be used to inhibit takeovers – employees are likely to side with incumbent owners but may vote for the takeover premium – although in practice the employee stake is usually too small to make a decisive impact on the outcome (Pendleton, 1997b). The picture is somewhat different in the United States where state-level takeover legislation often means that the combined votes of managerial and employee owners can block takeovers (Useem and Gager, 1996).

Employers also highlight other benefits of employee share ownership (and financial participation more generally). Some European employers' associations (for instance, MEDEF in France and the BDA in Germany) have emphasised the role of financial participation in encouraging employee savings. Others have suggested that employee share ownership has a role in promoting flexible remuneration systems. In some countries (for example, Belgium), employee share ownership has been viewed as a way of creating flexibility within the confines of national incomes policies, whilst in others (for example, Italy) it has been seen as contributing to decentralisation of collective bargaining and pay determination. The potential contribution of share ownership to greater flexibility has been highlighted by the European employers' organisation, UNICE (2002)

One concern that is widespread amongst employers and their associations is that employee share ownership might be linked to a greater role of employees in corporate governance and participation in company decision-making (see Pendleton and Poutsma, 2004). For this reason, it has been widely suggested that employee share ownership should be kept separate from other forms of employee participation and representation. In the Netherlands, it has been argued that employees already have extensive rights via the works council system, and that employee share ownership should not be used to expand this further. In Sweden, the possibility that share ownership might dilute the control of existing owners has been a salient issue.

The relationship between the introduction and operation of share schemes and industrial relations institutions is a significant concern in many countries. It is argued that the potential for building trust and commitment could be compromised if share plans are subject to conflictual industrial relations arrangements. The German BDA, for example, has argued that employee share ownership, and financial participation more generally, should not be incorporated into sectoral labour agreements (see Allen et al., 2007; Pendleton and Poutsma, 2004). Furthermore, it is suggested that whilst employee share ownership might be aimed at the entire workforce, unions often represent only a minority of employees. This latter argument has been strongly expressed by the French employers' association MEDEF, and reflects low levels of union membership in French private sector organisations. Union representatives might also lack the expertise to evaluate employee share ownership plans.

Trade union perspectives on employee share ownership

In the past, trade unions have tended to be suspicious of employee share ownership, though recently some unions have become more favourably inclined towards it. The unions that tend to be most hostile to employee share ownership are those espousing communist principles (for instance, communist trade union federations in southern European countries such as Italy and Portugal). Unions are also wary of share ownership in those contexts where employers link share plans to industrial relations reform (Pendleton and Poutsma, 2004). In Sweden and Italy, for instance, employer advocacy of share plans to decentralise bargaining has meant that some of the main union confederations have been wary of employee share ownership. Elsewhere, union views are becoming more sympathetic to share ownership (for example, the German Trade Union Confederation – DGB) whilst some unions that have traditionally been hostile have pragmatically accepted some involvement in the operation of share ownership plans (for instance, the CGT in France). The reasons for greater union acceptance of share ownership plans include a growing demand for share ownership from some sectors of the workforce, and a belief that share ownership might give workers and unions a stronger voice in corporate governance (Buschak, 2002).

There are several important reasons why unions have traditionally opposed employee share ownership. One reason is that employees who become owners dilute their identity as workers, and thus may lose their sense of opposition to management. One specific outcome of this may be reduction in employee attachment to trade unions. Thus, there is an anxiety that employee share ownership will have an adverse effect on union membership. This has been an especially salient issue in countries where unions have been organised on political and ideological lines, and where traditionally there has been a strong sense of an ideological conflict between capital and labour. The CGT in France and CGIL in Italy (both allied to the Communist Party) have traditionally opposed employee share ownership and other forms of financial participation for these reasons (see Pendleton and Poutsma, 2004).

A second reason is that, where workers become part-owners, trade unions can be placed in the invidious position of representing capital as well as labour (see Pendleton et al., 1995). This too has been an issue for politically based unions. The CGIL in Italy, for instance, has argued that employee shareholders should be represented by shareholder associations separately from union representation of workers.

Third, there has been widespread concern amongst unions in countries with centralised collective bargaining and pay determination that share ownership might be used to weaken the role of collective bargaining generally and to decentralise pay determination to company level specifically. (This is also discussed in Chapter 6.) Employee share schemes rarely come within the ambit of collective bargaining, though in a small number of countries (for instance, Belgium) the use of employee share ownership is contingent on a collective agreement. Further, employee share plans necessarily function at company level. Where pay determination occurs wholly or primarily above company level (for example, nationally, regionally, or sectorally), the operation of a company-level remuneration scheme will inevitably decentralise pay determination to some degree.

A fourth reason is pay substitution. There is some anxiety that company shares might be used to substitute for cash wages because it can be financially advantageous for companies to do so (share issues might be viewed as cheaper than cash); and because the linkage to performance means that firms might economise on rewards when times are hard. These economies might take the form of smaller share distributions to employees or smaller dividends to employee shareholders. Clearly, this issue relates primarily to share ownership plans where the company distributes shares free of charge to employees.

In addition, unions have been concerned that employee share ownership plans will expose employees to unwarranted risk. Clearly, employees are subject to the risk that their employer will go bankrupt and that they will lose their jobs. If they hold employer shares, bankruptcy threatens their wealth and savings as well. A classic case here is that of Enron. Many Enron employees had substantial holdings of Enron shares through their pension plans, and they lost their pension savings as well as their livelihoods when Enron collapsed. A related problem is that employees may concentrate their savings in employer shares if they are given the opportunity to do so.

American research (Liang and Weisbenner, 2002) has suggested that provision of employer shares functions as 'implicit investment advice': employees assume that the share ownership plan must be a good bet, otherwise the employer would not make shares available. Other factors include 'inertia': employees build up employer stock through repeated participation in share offers but fail to monitor and diversify their savings portfolios (Madrian and Shea, 2001). The UK research (Pendleton, 2006b) indicates that a sizeable minority of employees in share ownership plans hold half or more of their savings in employer shares. United States research (Muelbroek, 2002) indicates that employees will nearly always get better long-run returns from holding a diversified portfolio of savings. However, the availability of very favourable tax benefits, the size of which actually depends on the performance of the stock, distorts employee decision-making.

Furthermore, unions have been anxious about employee share-owners status as minority investors. A general issue is the involvement of employee shareholders in corporate governance, and some unions have been worried that employees receive an insufficient role and influence in corporate governance. As mentioned above, in most cases, employees as a whole will own just a small fraction of company stock. Although they bear greater risk than institutional investors, they have lower control rights in practice. In some cases, employee shares may be non-voting or may have smaller voting values than those of majority owners. Much may also depend on the overall level of minority investor protection.

In many European countries, ownership is concentrated in a small number of owners, often obscured by ownership pyramids, and small owners, such as employee shareholders, may have little legal protection against appropriation by large shareholders. But even where they have full voting shares, and where minority investor protection is generally strong (as in the United Kingdom), employees may be too fragmented to exert much influence (Pendleton, 1997b). A partial solution to this may be the formation of employee shareholder associations, as is found in some companies in France, but the division of responsibilities and powers between these associations and unions can be threatening to unions. Alternatively, unions may seek to represent employee shareholder interests, though this risks unions' primary role as representatives of the labour interest becoming blurred.

Finally, unions have generally been sceptical of the benefits that are said to emanate from employee share ownership plans. Along with some other observers, they have not been convinced that these plans will enhance company productivity and have been critical of what is seen as a one-sided emphasis on company productivity as a policy rationale for share ownership. However, they have strongly argued that share ownership is more likely to succeed when 'it is part and parcel of a comprehensive system of measures to promote employee involvement, where employees and their representatives are informed and consulted, and where employees are capable of influencing corporate level decisions' (Buschak, 2002, p. 81).

Trade unions and share ownership: the evidence

It is opportune at this juncture to briefly review some of the evidence on the relationship between union presence and employee share ownership. There is very little evidence on employee attitudes to unions and employee share ownership in Europe. Much of what we know derives from US (or US-inspired) research into 'dual commitment', which mainly shows that employees can be committed to both union and employer (see Angle and Perry, 1986). In the United Kingdom, research from employee-owned bus companies in the 1990s indicates that even substantial employee share ownership does not automatically lead to a weakening of attachment to unions (Pendleton et al. 1995). There is also very little conclusive evidence that share ownership plans are associated with union absence or union removal.

The WERS series in Britain finds that private sector workplaces with share ownership plans are also likely to be unionised, possibly because both are associated with size (Pendleton, 1997a). Similarly, the European Foundation study of share ownership in Europe found that there was no clear relationship between presence of employee share plans and union density levels amongst European countries (significant negative relationships are observed in Germany and Spain and significant positive in the United Kingdom, all other country results being insignificant) (Pendleton et al., 2001). The overall relationship for the European countries as a whole is a positive one between union density and use of share plans, but it is not statistically significant. Of course, cross-sectional data is at best inconclusive when referring to dynamic events. It is worth noting, however, that the use of narrow-based share plans (for executives) is negatively related to union density. We might conclude that when unions are present, firms intending to make use of some share-based compensation tend to extend it to all employees, at least in most countries. However, recent research by Kalmi et al. (2006) finds that the probability of a share ownership plan being present in large, listed firms is significantly lower when there is some form of indirect representation, be it unions or works councils.

Although evidence from the United Kingdom indicates that union presence and share ownership plans tend to coexist (see Poole, 1988), in practice union activity and the introduction and operation of share ownership plans tend to be entirely separate. Unions tend to have very little role in the design, implementation, and administration of share ownership plans. Partly this is because most unions have neither the interest nor expertise to become involved, and partly because many companies do not want share schemes to be linked to pay determination and collective employee representation.

A recent European study found that share plans are introduced in the United Kingdom without union agreement in over 90 per cent of cases (Kalmi et al., 2006). By contrast, in Germany nearly 40 per cent of plans were introduced with the agreement of a works council. A similar pattern can be observed for employee involvement in plan development more generally. In the United Kingdom in 71 per cent of cases employees had no involvement, compared with 30 per cent in Germany. In 78 per cent of cases overall (84 per cent in the United Kingdom), employees or their representatives have no involvement in the administration and management of the plan after its introduction. However, in some countries (France, for instance) unions have a significant role in the administration of the savings schemes that provide funds for employee share ownership. In 2002, four trade union confederations established an Inter-Union Employee Savings Committee to vet savings products being made available to employees (Pernot, 2004).

An interesting issue is the extent to which union presence or activity influences employee orientations towards the share ownership plan. Recent research by Kalmi et al. (2006) indicates that the presence of indirect forms of representation in the company – either unions or works councils – tends to lower participation rates in share ownership and share option plans. However, where there is participation of employees or their representatives in the development of the plan this has a positive effect on participation rates, especially in share purchase plans. Worker involvement may be perceived as providing employees with some protection against risk.

Although employee share ownership is rarely directly integrated into collective bargaining, it is widely feared in union circles that share ownership plans may be used to weaken or decentralise collective bargaining as noted above. This raises the question as to the relationship between share ownership plans and pay bargaining level. A recent study by Kalmi et al. (2007), using data from a large number of European countries, finds that share ownership plans are significantly less likely to be found where centralised collective bargaining is the main form of pay determination, and less likely to be found where there is a mixture of centralised and decentralised bargaining. The latter finding in particular tends to suggest that share ownership plans are not used to decentralise bargaining, and instead tend to be used where bargaining has already been decentralised.

In relation to union fears about pay substitution, there is little evidence that share plans function in this way. Indeed, the extant evidence indicates that share-based rewards supplement pay (Whadwani and Wall, 1990) and indeed that employee share ownership firms tend to be high wage firms (Pendleton, 1997a). In practice it is difficult for share ownership plans to be used as a pay substitute. First, because share ownership plans usually provide deferred rewards – often three to five years into the future – it is difficult for firms to convince employees to substitute shares for current pay. Second, because share ownership plans usually operate entirely separately from collective bargaining, it is typically difficult for firms to bargain shares for wages. This is not to say that this cannot happen. There are cases where share ownership plans form part of concession bargaining – as in the US airline industry (Gordon, 1999) and the UK bus industry in the 1990s (see Pendleton, 2001) – but these are relatively unusual cases and the magnitude of the share ownership plan is extensive: the firms become substantially or even majority employee owned. Other recent instances are the 'new economy' firms during the 'dot.com' boom in the early 2000s, where the prospect of large capital gains from flotation of small firms substituted for cash wages when these firms faced liquidity constraints (little money to pay wages because of as yet unrealised revenue streams) (Murphy, 2003).

Conclusions

This chapter has highlighted the growing interest in and use of employee share ownership plans in European countries. However, the use of share ownership plans varies considerably between countries. Share ownership plans are widespread in countries such as the United Kingdom and France, but are less common in the Mediterranean countries. These variations in incidence seem to be influenced by the extent of supportive legislation. In turn, the presence of legislation owes much to government views and policies about share ownership. As shown in the chapter, governments differ in the merits they attach to share ownership plans. However, the predominant perspective amongst governmental actors emphasises the role of share ownership plans in enhancing company performance via changes to employee attitudes and behaviour. European Union policies have also highlighted this aspect of employee share ownership and have emphasised its potential to enhance employee flexibility and creativity.

The chapter has considered the policies and perspectives of governments, employers, and trade unions. It is clear that there are marked divergences in views between countries, and between and within social actors, especially within the trade union movement. Some unions are strongly opposed to share ownership whereas others are more favourably inclined. Some employers and employer organisations are strongly in favour of employee share ownership, others are more cautious. Although some see the interests of labour and capital as fundamentally incompatible, for most actors much hinges on the perceived implications of share ownership for management, governance, employee representation, and industrial relations.

It is apparent that employee share ownership could have substantial implications for corporate governance. Governance theory tells us that those holding ownership stakes should have control as well as return rights. On this basis, it would be reasonable to expect that employee share-owners play an active role in corporate governance. They might, for instance, have representation on the company board of directors. Some trade unions have welcomed this possibility. Others, however, have cautioned against worker involvement in governance and management as it may conflict with trade unions' primary role of labour representation. Employers have generally been hostile to an extension of worker or union involvement in governance. On balance, the evidence indicates that share ownership plans do not lead to a transformation of governance practices. In general, the equity stakes held by employees in most plans are too small to enhance worker involvement in corporate governance.

As for industrial relations and collective bargaining, some unions have feared that share ownership plans will undermine existing institutions for worker representation and pay determination or will function to decentralise collective bargaining. The advocacy of share ownership by some employers for this reason has added to union anxieties in this respect. However, the evidence that share ownership plans have this effect is not compelling. There is some evidence that share ownership plans are more prevalent in unionised firms, at least in some countries. Where share ownership plans are present, they tend to function separately from other forms of employee involvement and representation. Whilst this means that the capacity of share plans to enhance employee involvement may be limited, it also means that the potential for share ownership to damage existing institutions of employee representation is restricted. As for collective bargaining, the evidence suggests that share ownership plans tend to be used where bargaining is decentralised rather than vice versa.

Finally, we return to the issue of risk. Clearly, linking part of employee rewards to company performance exposes workers to risk. In practice, this exposure seems to be limited. Participation in share ownership plans tends to be influenced by employees' capability to bear risk: participation is higher amongst higher income earners. Share ownership plans tend to function separately from core remuneration, with share plans adding to wages rather than substituting for them. As recommended in the EU principles, most governments place limits on the extent to which employees can be exposed to risk, usually by placing limits on the amount of shares that can attract tax benefits.

Overall, the balance of evidence from Europe suggests that share ownership plans are less harmful to union interests than is often feared. Equally, the evidence on the impact of share plans on company performance suggests that claims about their beneficial effects should not be overstated. However, the evidence is complex and incomplete, and it is difficult to generate definitive assessments. What is clear is that the effects of share ownership plans are highly dependent on the context in which they operate, and on the goals of those involved. For these reasons, there is considerable diversity in the practice of employee share ownership. In turn, this means that there will be considerable debate about the costs and benefits of employee share ownership for some time to come.

Note

1. Unpublished research by the author indicates that where companies operate both kinds of scheme, the SIP participation rate is about two-thirds of that in SAYE.

References

Agnew, J., Balduzzi, P., and Sunden, A. (2003) 'Portfolio Choice and Trading in a Large 401 (k) Plan', *American Economic Review*, 93, 193–215.

Allen, M., Tuselmann, H., El-Sa'id, H., and Windrum, P. (2007) 'Sectoral Collective Agreements: Remuneration Straitjackets for German Workplaces?', *Personnel Review*, 36, 963–977.

Angle, H. and Perry, J. (1986) 'Dual Commitment and Labor-Management Relationship Climates', *Academy of Management Journal*, 29, 1, 31–50.

Baddon, L., Hunter, L., Hyman, J., Leopold, J., and Ramsay, H. (1989) *People's Capitalism? A Critical Analysis of Profit-Sharing and Employee Share Ownership*, London: Routledge.

Benartzi, S. (2001) 'Excessive Extrapolation and the Allocation of 401(k) Accounts to Company Stock', *Journal of Finance*, 56, 1747–1764.

Biagi, M. and Tiraboschi, M. (2002) 'Financial Participation of Employees: The Italian Case' in Biagi, M. (ed.) *Quality of Work and Employee Involvement in Europe*, Kluwer Law International, The Hague.

Buschak, W. (2002) 'Financial Participation for Employees in the European Union – A Pragmatic View', *Transfer*, 8, 76–86.

Carpenter, J. (1998) 'The Exercise and Valuation of Executive Stock Options', *Journal of Financial Economics*, 48, 127–158.

Commission of the European Communities (2002) *Communication from the Commission to the Council, the European Parliament, the Economic and Social Committee and the Committee of the Regions: On a Framework for the Promotion of Employee Financial Participation*, Brussels: Commission of the European Communities, Com (2002) 364 Final.

Conyon, M. and Freeman, R. (2004) 'Shared Modes of Compensation and Firm Performance: UK Evidence' in Card, D., Blundell, R., and Freeman, R. (eds) *Seeking a Premier Economy: The Economic Effects of British Economic Reforms 1980–2000*, Chicago, IL: University of Chicago Press.

Degeorge, F., Jenter, D., Moel, A., and Tufano, P. (2004) 'Selling Company Shares to Reluctant Employees: France Telecom's Experience', *Journal of Financial Economics*, 71, 169–202.

Department of Work and Pensions (2006) *Family Resources Survey 2005–2006*, Sheffield: Department of Work and Pensions.

European Economic and Social Committee (2003) *Opinion of the European Economic and Social Committee on the Communication from the Commission to the Council, the European Parliament, the Economic and Social Committee and the Committee of the Regions on the Framework for the Promotion of Employee Financial Participation*, Brussels: European Economic and Social Committee, Com 2002 364 final.

Gordon, J. (1999) 'Employee Stock Ownership in Economic Transitions: The Case of United and the Airline Industry' in Blair, M. and Roe, M. (eds) *Employees and Corporate Governance*, Washington DC: Brookings Institution.

Huberman, G., Iyengar, S., and Jiang, W. (2003) 'Defined Contribution Pension Plans: Determinants of Participation and Contribution Rates', London: Birkbeck College, Pensions Institute, Discussion Paper.

Incomes Data Services (2007) *Share Incentive Plans*, London: Incomes Data Services, HR Study 840.

Kalmi, P., Pendleton, A., and Poutsma, E. (2006) 'The Relationship between Financial Participation and Other Forms of Employee Participation: New Survey Evidence from Europe', *Economic and Industrial Democracy*, 27, 637–667.

Kalmi, P., Pendleton, A., and Poutsma, E. (2007) 'Financial Participation, Unions and the Structure of Collective Bargaining' Paper presented to International Industrial Relations Association European Congress, Manchester, September.

Kruse, D. (1996) 'Why Do Firms Adopt Profit Sharing and Employee Ownership Plans?', *British Journal of Indusrial Relations*, 34, 515–538.

Liang, N. and Weisbenner, S. J. (2002) 'Investor Behaviour and the Purchase of Company Stock in 401(k) Plans – The Importance of Plan Design', Boston, MA: National Bureau of Economic Research, Working Paper 9131.

Lowitzsch, J. (2006) *The PEPPER III Report: Promotion of Employee Participation in Profits and Enterprise Results in the New Member and Candidate Countries of the European Union*, Berlin: Free University of Berlin.

Madrian, B. and Shea, D. (2001) 'The Power of Suggestion: Inertia in 401(k) Participation and Savings Behaviour', *Quarterly Journal of Economics*, 116, 1149–1187.

Muelbroek, L. (2002) 'Company Stock in Pension Plans: How Costly Is It?', Cambridge, MA: Harvard Business School, Working Paper.

Murphy, K. (2003) 'Stock-Based Pay in New Economy Firms', *Journal of Accounting and Economics*, 34, 129–147.

Oakeshott, R. (2000) *Jobs and Fairness: The Logic and Experience of Employee Ownership*, Norwich: Michael Russell.

Pendleton, A. (1997a) 'Characteristics of Workplaces with Financial Participation: Evidence from the WIRS', *Industrial Relations Journal*, 28, 103–119.

Pendleton, A. (1997b) 'Stakeholders as Shareholders: The Role of Employee Share Ownership' in Kelly, G., Kelly, D., and Gamble, A. (eds) *Stakeholder Capitalism*, Basingstoke: Macmillan.

Pendleton, A. (2001) *Employee Ownership, Participation, and Governance: A Study of ESOPs in the UK*, London: Routledge.

Pendleton, A. (2006a) 'Incentives, Monitoring, and Employee Share Plans: New Evidence and Interpretations', *Industrial Relations*, 45, 753–778.

Pendleton, A. (2006b) *Who Invests Too Much in Employer Stock, and Why Do They Do It? Some Evidence from UK Stock Ownership Plans,* York: York Management School, Working Paper 24.

Pendleton, A. (2007) 'The Study of Employee Share Ownership Using WERS: An Evaluation and Analysis of the 2004 Survey' in Whitfield, K. and Huxley, K. (eds) *Innovations in the 2004 Workplace Employment Relations Survey,* Cardiff: Cardiff University.

Pendleton, A. and Poutsma, E. (2004) *Financial Participation: The Role of Governments and Social Partners,* Dublin: European Foundation for the Improvement of Living and Working Conditions.

Pendleton, A., Poutsma, E., Ommeren, J. van, and Brewster, C. (2001) *Employee Share Ownership and Profit Sharing in the European Union,* Luxembourg: Office for Official Publications of the European Communities/European Foundation for the Improvement of Living and Working Conditions.

Pendleton, A., Poutsma, E., Ommeren, J. van, and Brewster, C. (2003) 'The Incidence and Determinants of Employee Share Ownership and Profit Sharing in Europe' in Kato, T. and Pliskin, J. (eds) *The Determinants of the Incidence and Effects of Participatory Organisations* (Advances of the Economic Analysis of Participatory and Labor Management, Volume 7), Oxford: Elsevier Science.

Pendleton, A., Robinson, A., and Wilson, N. (1995) 'Does Economic Democracy Weaken Unions? Recent Evidence from the UK Bus Industry', *Economic and Industrial Democracy,* 16, 577–604.

Pernot, J. (2004) 'Developments in Employee Savings Plans', www.eurofound.europa.eu/eiro/2004/05/feature/fr0405103f.htm

Pérotin, V. and Robinson, A. (2003) *Employee Participation in Profits and Ownership: A Review of Issues and Evidence,* Luxembourg: European Parliament.

Poole, M. (1988) 'Factors Influencing the Development of Employee Financial Participation in Contemporary Britain: Evidence from a National Survey', *British Journal of Industrial Relations,* 26, 21–36.

Poole, M. (1989) *The Origins of Economic Democracy: Profit Sharing and Employee Shareholding Schemes,* London: Routledge.

Poutsma, E. (2001) *Recent Trends in Employee Financial Participation in the European Union,* Dublin: European Foundation for the Improvement of Living and Working Conditions.

Poutsma, E., de Nijs, W., and Dooeward, H. (1999) 'Promotion of Employee Ownership and Profit Sharing in Europe', *Economic and Industrial Democracy,* 20, 171–196.

PricewaterhouseCoopers (2002) *Employee Stock Options in the EU and the USA: Final Report to the European Commission (DG Enterprise),* London: PricewaterhouseCoopers.

Rojot, J. (2002) 'Financial Participation in France' in Biagi, M. (ed.) *Quality of Work and Employee Involvement in Europe,* Kluwer Law International, The Hague.

Tiraboschi, M. (2002) 'Financial Participation, Quality of Work and the New Industrial Relations: The Italian Case in a Comparative Perspective' in Biagi, M. (ed.) *Quality of Work and Employee Involvement in Europe,* Kluwer Law International, The Hague.

Union of Industrial and Employers' Confederations (UNICE) (2002) *Financial Participation of Employees in the European Union: UNICE Position,* Brussels: UNICE.

Useem, M. and Gager, S. (1996) 'Employee Shareholders or Institutional Investors: When Corporate Managers Replace Their Stockholders', *Journal of Management Studies,* 33, 5, 613–631.

Whadwani, S. and Wall, M. (1990) 'The Effects of Profit Sharing on Employment, Wages, Stock Returns, and Productivity: Evidence from Micro-data', *Economic Journal,* 100, 1–17.

Part IV

Conclusions

Drawing the threads together

Susan Corby and Esmond Lindop

In the first chapter, we pointed out that this book makes no claim to homogeneity or analytical or conceptual integration. Indeed, we are of the view that this book's lack of uniformity is a source of its richness. After all, the subject of reward is multifaceted and draws on various academic disciplines: industrial relations, economics, and law, as does this book, and the contributors have different perspectives as they have a variety of backgrounds; most are academics, but some are consultants/advisers to government bodies and employers.

Nevertheless, although we are aware that any ordering into a common mould may be forced, there are some themes that cross-cut a number of chapters. So in this final chapter we seek to draw the threads together. We have identified five themes: the public sector/private sector divide; the influence of legislation and regulation on reward; the limits to individualism; the extent to which an organisation's reward practices reflect the institutions and values of the host country; and the problems of terminology. We review each in turn below before concluding by looking at total rewards, itself a concept that is not defined uniformly and which seeks to knit together both financial rewards (on which this book has focused) and non-financial rewards; so we end by asking if a total rewards approach resolves the tensions we identified in this book's first chapter and therefore represents the future of reward.

Themes

Public/private sector differences

Our first and most significant theme is the difference in reward practices between the public sector and the private sector, a theme that emerges loud and clear in a number of chapters. We would argue that in many respects this is not just a difference in degree. It is a different model.

Thus in Chapter 3 on employee voice on reward, the authors point out that pay review bodies, which recommend the pay and, in some cases, conditions of service for approaching two million people, are only to be found in the public sector. Moreover, essentially all the other public servants have their pay and conditions determined by collective bargaining, unlike the great majority of those working in the private sector. This is illustrated by the trade union membership statistics (Grainger and Crowther, 2007): union density was markedly higher in the public than the private sectors (58.8 per cent compared to 16.6 per cent) with collective agreement coverage three times greater.

Moreover, this divergence in employee voice has widened. For instance, the number of pay review bodies has increased; most recently when the Government established the prison service pay review body in 2001.[1] Similarly, Labour Force Survey figures show that between 1993 and 2006 trade union density declined in the public sector by less than 3 per cent, but in the private sector by over 5 per cent (Grainger and Crowther, 2007). Interestingly, as Chapter 3 noted, employee surveys (a non-institutionalised forms of individual employee voice), are more prevalent in the public, than the private sector (Kersley et al., 2006).

Chapter 4 also highlighted a public/private sector divide: a marked difference in grading structures and progression arrangements. Narrow banded structures, pay spines with incremental points, as well as progression usually based on service and over a long time, not performance, were more prevalent in the public sector, compared to the private sector. The private sector was much more likely to use a combination of individual pay, broad bands, and job families than the public sector. As a result, private sector organisations had fewer grades by broad occupational classification than the public sector. Another key difference with the private sector was that public sector employees were more likely to receive a progression payment *in addition* to an annual 'cost of living' adjustment rather than just one rolled-up payment, both when compared to employees in manufacturing and, in particular, when compared to employees in private sector services.

The public/private sector divide also featured in Chapter 5 on local pay and Chapter 8 on pay equity. As Chapter 5 makes clear, in most parts of the public sector there are national agreements and national pay scales, and, with the exception of London and the South East, pay is usually the same regardless of the area of the country in which the employee works. In the private sector, multi-site employers operating in a number of regions/localities have a looser pay framework which allows them to vary pay rates and/or allowances geographically as local labour market conditions dictate. The less flexible approach in the public sector can result in the overpayment of staff in some parts of the country, and underpayment in others, leading both to a misallocation of resources and variations in service delivery.

Chapter 8 points out that only the public sector has proactive duties to promote equality on grounds of gender, race, and disability. No such legal provision applies to the private sector. Furthermore, multiple equal pay claims have been a hallmark of the public sector, particularly local government and the National Health Service.

Perhaps the most marked difference between reward in the public and private sectors is to be found in Chapter 10 on pensions, with defined benefit provision being increasingly restricted to the public sector and defined contributions being a mainly private sector phenomenon. Also, this chapter provides evidence of a more general growing divide between the public and private sectors in terms of pension provision. Between 1991 and 2006, the number of members of private sector occupational pension schemes declined by over two million, while over the same period the number of members of public sector occupational pension schemes rose by nearly two million.

Less surprisingly perhaps, when we come to top pay there is also a distinct public sector/private sector divide. Chief executives in the private sector normally have long-term incentive plans which are share based and reflect total shareholder return, and perhaps share option schemes as well. Chief executives of public bodies cannot have share-based items as part of their reward package and, in any event, rewards from their incentive plans are nowhere near the magnitude offered to their peers in the private sector.

The differences between the public and private sectors flagged up in these chapters are, however, not the only ones. Job evaluation schemes are significantly more prevalent in the public sector than the private sector. A survey jointly carried out by the Chartered Institute of Personnel and Development (CIPD) and the Office of Manpower Economics found that 67 per cent of public sector bodies used job evaluation, compared to 17 per cent in private sector services and 20 per cent in manufacturing (CIPD, 2006).

There is a marked difference when we look at employment tribunal (ET) claims. The private sector accounted for 82 per cent, the public sector for 12 per cent, and the non-profit sector for 6 per cent of all ET cases in 2003 (Hayward et al., 2004). The strike rate, the number of working days lost per 1,000 employees, (which takes into account the size of the labour force), also shows a public/private sector divide: a strike rate of 111 in the public sector, compared to five in the private sector in 2006. As noted already in respect of some matters covered in this book, this divide has widened: in 1997 the strike rate was 14 in the public sector compared to eight in the private sector (Hale, 2007). Furthermore, there are differences in workforce characteristics. Public sector workers are more likely to be female, to work part-time, and to be older than employees in the private sector (Audit Commission, 2002).

Perhaps surprisingly, these public/private sector differences and the growing divide have essentially taken place at a time when the government has sought to make the public sector more, not less, like the private sector. Thus the government has sought to 'modernise' the public sector and make it less risk averse and more innovative, and to reform pay systems to make them more performance-related and responsive to local labour markets. See, for instance, Cabinet Office (1999).

Legislation and regulation

The second theme to be found in many chapters is the influence of legislation and regulation on reward. In 1954, Kahn-Freund observed that there was, perhaps, no major country in the world in which the law had played a less significant role in the relationship between employer and worker than in Great Britain. The picture today is very different: the law has a key role in determining reward and there is a raft of legislation on pay-related matters, for instance, deductions from wages, maternity and paternity pay and leave, hours of work, holidays, and sick pay.

In addition, there is legislation and regulation on areas covered in this book. Thus Chapter 7 explores the national minimum wage legislation and its impact on pay and employment. Introduced in 1999, this was the first legislation to provide an overall national pay floor in the United Kingdom. Chapter 8 shows how the legislation and case law on pay equity in respect of gender has grown, while more recently there has been legislation on age. Moreover, besides regulating and offering redress to victims of law breaking, the law has provided a spur to voluntary practices such as pay reviews and the shortening of service-related pay scales.

Chapter 9 shows how the Director's Remuneration Report Regulations 2002 shaped the rewards of the most senior executives. Chapter 10 explains how pensions legislation and regulation has shaped, and is shaping, employer provision of occupational pensions. Chapter 12 points out that government legislation and regulations, especially in respect of taxation, have facilitated and shaped employee share ownership plans, for instance encouraging Save-As-You-Earn plans and, more recently, Share Incentive Plans.

Much of this legislation stems from European directives and the United Kingdom is converging with other European countries by becoming more regulated on reward. Even where it does not stem directly from Europe, for instance the national minimum wage legislation, the United Kingdom is merely in line with practice in the majority of other European Union countries which are regulated in a comparable, though not identical, manner (Economist, 2007).

The limits to individualism

A trend in reward in the past two decades has been towards individualism, and, theoretically at least, the 'new pay' discussed in Chapter 1. This agenda focuses on rewarding the person and paying for his/her individual contribution. This theory has gone hand in hand with developments on the ground; a decline in collective bargaining, see Chapter 3, in the United Kingdom and the United States and the growth of personal contracts (Brown et al., 1998).

Several chapters in this book, however, note the limits to individualism. For instance, the conclusion in Chapter 11 on flexible benefits (where the individual chooses his/her individual benefits package amongst a range of options) is that there is little prospect for a further growth of flexible benefits schemes, in view of the potentially high transaction costs needed to make a scheme succeed both in terms of communicating with employees, as well as other administrative requirements. Chapter 6 finds that performance pay has not undermined collective bargaining, but instead resulted in its reframing. (We have to look elsewhere to explain the decline of unions in the private sector.) Chapter 8 shows how the equal pay laws, although framed on an individual basis, have been used by groups of workers putting in multiple claims.

On pay too, as Chapter 4 shows, broad-banded pay structures that allow for wide variations in pay between individual employees have become more fettered by devices such as so-called 'anchor points' or 'reference points' and pay zones. These limit the scope for pay variations between individuals and run counter to the wide degrees of variation upon which early proponents of broadbanding had based their theories. Similarly, Chapter 5 on local pay suggests that most multisite private sector employers operating in various workplaces across the United Kingdom continue to operate within national pay structures with only limited, and centrally controlled, scope for local pay variation using a framework which clearly identifies the conditions under which higher pay can be awarded in some localities. This clearly limits the discretion of local managers to vary the pay provided to individual employees.

Perhaps this limit to individualism is no surprise. Almost ten years ago Brown et al. (1998) showed that when collective bargaining was replaced by personal contracts there was, paradoxically, increased standardisation of non-pay terms and conditions and increased harmonisation of terms and conditions between managerial and non-managerial staff. In short, we may have passed the high water mark of the trend to individualism. The Workplace Employment Relations Survey found that collective bargaining coverage for workplaces with 25 or more employees fell by 3.3 per cent a year on average between 1990 and 1998, but only by 0.7 per cent a year on average between 1998 and 2004 (Kersley et al., 2006).

National and organisational factors

It is generally agreed that an organisation's reward policies are the result of many factors. Figure 13.1 encapsulates the key factors, although it does not pretend to be exhaustive.

The Chapters differ in their views about which of these factors are the most important. Some chapters emphasise the importance of national institutions, values, and legislation. Thus Chapter 6 on performance pay and collective bargaining, which looks at machinery equipment and banking in the United Kingdom, Austria,

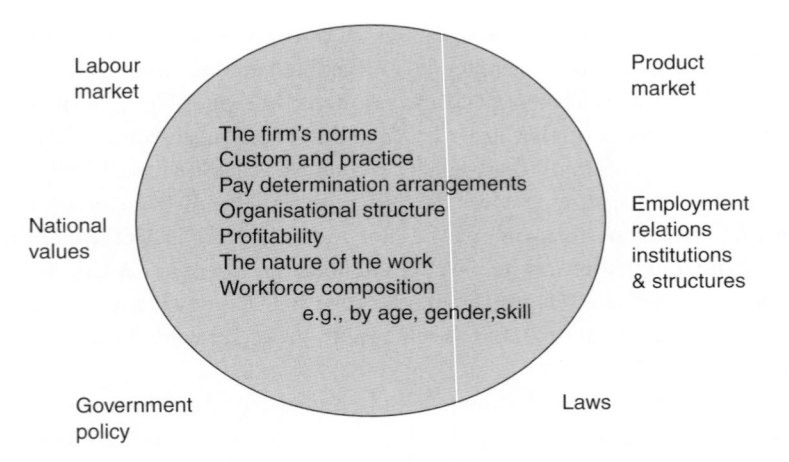

Labour
market

Product
market

The firm's norms
Custom and practice
Pay determination arrangements
Organisational structure
Profitability
The nature of the work
Workforce composition
e.g., by age, gender,skill

National
values

Employment
relations
institutions
& structures

Government
policy

Laws

Figure 13.1   National and organisational factors influencing reward

and Norway, is of the view that national employment relations institutions play a dominant role in shaping pay practices within the organisation. Chapter 10 notes the importance of national values in determining organisations' policies on pensions: whereas employers in the United Kingdom, the United States, and Australia have responded to increasing longevity by moving towards defined contribution arrangements, employers in Holland predominantly provide defined benefits schemes, following a career average approach. Chapter 12 on employee share ownership in Europe finds that the presence of supportive national legislation and the availability of tax concessions have had a strong influence on the incidence of share ownership plans at organisation level, a finding confirmed by further statistical analysis.

The strength of national institutions, laws, and values vis à vis an organisation's policy and practices on reward are not supported in other Chapters, however. They emphasise the importance of the firm's norms, which often have been imbibed from ideas, concepts, and practices imported from overseas. They make their own culture, rather than taking it from their immediate environment.

Thus, Chapter 1 shows how the new pay paradigm, which originated in the United States, has transcended national borders, having been transported to the United Kingdom by multinational companies and cross-border management consultancies. Similarly Chapter 11 shows how flexible benefits, originally a US concept, has been transported to UK-only organisations, while Chapter 2 on the pay strategies of multinationals suggests that HR managers of multinationals seek to implement pay strategies across national boundaries.

The research outlined in these Chapters is echoed in earlier research on Japanese companies such as Nissan, Toyota, and Sony, which established plants in the United Kingdom, and imported HR policies and practices from their home country to the United Kingdom. See, for instance, Oliver and Wilkinson (1992). More recently,

Stiles (2007) who looked at 30 multinational companies, concluded that although national variations in, for instance, employment legislation, governance structures, and the nature of the workforce are important, more important still for a multinational company's HR policies and practices was the organisation's own culture and values.

Perhaps the debate about which is more important – national factors versus organisational norms – is rather like the chicken versus egg debate in that no definite conclusion is possible, certainly at this juncture.

Terminology

Our fifth and final theme relates to terminology. In virtually all the chapters the terms used are often slippery. In some cases, they are terms of art which can be explained by definition, for instance 'performance pay schemes' (Chapter 6) or 'long-term incentive plans' (Chapter 9). Some terms seem designed to obfuscate, for example the new pay system in the National Health Service has 'gateways' in each grade and an individual's progression through the gateway depends on whether the relevant manager considers that the individual has acquired the necessary knowledge and skills (see Chapter 4). Anecdotally it seems that the term 'gateway' was used because the unions were unhappy with any term that embodied the words 'performance' or 'competency'. Elsewhere, both terms are increasingly wrapped in the more neutral concept of 'contribution'. This is the approach incorporated into the national framework agreement for UK universities.

Moreover, sometimes terms have more than one interpretation. For instance in Chapter 4, the author suggests that the phrase 'pay drift' is often confused with 'pay drive'. Sometimes terms are imprecise – newspapers are fond of the term 'inflation busting' but what exactly does that mean – or are defined in more ways than one. This is also the case with total reward (also termed total rewards) to which we turn in the next section.

Total reward?

Having looked at the themes across chapters, we now look at what might be the shape of reward in the future As we said in the first chapter, this book focuses solely on the financial aspects of reward but, of course, people do not work just for money. Financial rewards have to be seen alongside non-financial rewards; employees, in addition to their remuneration, want to learn and apply new skills and they want a workplace where they are respected and valued (Schuster and Zingheim, 2004); hence, the new approach to compensation termed 'total reward' or 'total rewards'. Thus total reward is more than a flexible benefits package (see Chapter 11); it includes the less tangible benefits of employment, such as career opportunities and appreciation, whether formally or informally, of employees' work.

The UK government has been particularly interested in the concept of total reward, both as part of its pay modernisation agenda, and for its contribution to assisting with public sector recruitment and retention. For instance, the Cabinet Office (2007) has published a total reward toolkit for the use of other public sector bodies. Amongst other things it says:

> The total reward strategy must identify how an organisation intends to position itself in the competitive employee market to achieve the fundamentals of people management:
>
> - recruitment
> - retention
> - development
> - motivation
>
> Both the remuneration aspect, (the pay and benefits), and the performance aspect, (the leadership of the employees), contribute to the success of these fundamentals.

The Cabinet Office also says that the total reward strategy must be communicated to employees so that they fully understand the value of their entire financial and non-financial reward package.

According to Kaplan (2005, p. 32) total rewards 'embraces everything employees value in their employment relationship' and is a 'holistic concept' that integrates four elements: compensation, benefits, development, and the work environment. The first two elements are transactional rewards, while the last two elements 'are relational rewards and are associated with the emotional aspects of an employment relationship' (Kaplan, 2005: p. 33). These four categories of reward are not definitive, however. For instance, WorldatWork (2006), a US organisation which subtitles itself 'The Total Rewards Association', claims that a total rewards strategy combines five elements: compensation, benefits, work-life balance, performance and recognition, and development and career opportunities.

Like 'new pay', total rewards originated in the United States (Industrial Relations Services, 2003) and it is perhaps no coincidence that the concept of total rewards arose at the time of the Internet and dot.com boom. Organisations saw total rewards as a way of providing them with competitive advantage when people with certain skills were much in demand, which in turn led to a boom in new and exotic benefits such as the provision of concierge services and 'duvet days'. Its popularity since then perhaps owes something to the fact that organisations, faced with financial constraints, are seeking a way of rewarding employees by providing them with non-pay benefits, while at the same time only modestly increasing remuneration. This certainly formed part of the evidence given by government departments in 2007 to the six public sector pay review bodies, where they were asked to take into account the existence of factors such as a defined benefit pension scheme, flexible working, and job security in reaching their recommendations on base pay.

Intuitively, a total rewards approach makes sense. At the start of this book, we discussed the tensions underlying reward: a total rewards model seeks to resolve the overarching tension between economics and social psychology. Other tensions, however, remain. Thus on the one hand total rewards and a holistic approach are championed as best practice (for instance, Pfau and Kay, 2002; Kaplan, 2005). On the other hand, organisations have to follow a best fit approach and implement reward policies that are aligned with their business strategy. See, for instance, Gross and Friedman (2004), Zingheim and Schuster (2001). Similarly, on the one hand a total rewards approach is designed to give the organisation a labour market advantage in respect of the individual the organisation wishes to recruit and retain. On the other hand, comparisons with significant others play a crucial role in respect of monetary rewards (Gratton, 2004) and arguably non-monetary rewards do not offset a felt discrepancy in monetary rewards.

In other words, the tensions between the labour market and equity and between best fit and best practice are not fully resolved by a total rewards approach, while the tension between rewarding the job and rewarding the person are seemingly ignored as many of the proponents of total rewards include some form of performance pay. See, for instance, Pfau and Kay (2002) and WorldatWork (2006).

We noted in the first chapter how ideas and approaches are spread by consultants. A total rewards policy is no exception. There is much prescriptive writing on total rewards and such writing is by consultants, for instance Kaplan (2005) who at the time of writing was managing principal of Diamond Consulting Group; Pfau and Kay (2002) who were then national practice leaders of Watson Wyatt Worldwide; Poster and Scanella (2001) who were respectively a principal and a director in the New York office of Unifi Network, a subsidiary of PricewaterhouseCoopers; Kochanski and Ledford (2001) both with Sibson Consulting, Gross and Friedman (2004) both consultants with Mercer in the United States, and Zingheim and Schuster (2001) partners in the pay and rewards consulting firm of Schuster-Zingheim and Associates.

Yet although there is prescription by consultants, we have been unable to locate any academic studies evaluating total rewards. We are not alone. Medcof and Rumpel (2007, p. 66) of McMaster University, Canada who conducted a literature review, 'found no studies that rigorously evaluated the efficacy of any implemented Total Rewards programs'; and they argue that to date a broadly accepted theoretical base for total rewards has not been presented. While a future edition of this book, therefore, might include chapters on training and development and the work environment, any further rethinking of reward is, at this juncture, premature and conceptually and empirically reward for the moment at least, remains focused on pay and benefits.

Note

1. Statutory Instrument 1161.

References

Audit Commission (2002) *Recruitment and Retention: A Public Service Workforce for the Twenty First Century*, London: Audit Commission.

Brown, W., Deakin, S., Hudson, M., Pratten, C., and Ryan, P. (1998) *The Individualisation of Employment Contracts in Britain*, Research Paper, London: Department of Trade and Industry.

Cabinet Office (1999) *Modernising Government*, CM 4310, London: Stationery Office.

Cabinet Office (2007) www.swyddfa-cabinet.gov.uk/workforcematters/pay_and_rewards/total_rewards [accessed 25.11. 2007]

Chartered Institute of Personnel and Development (CIPD) (2006) Reward Management. Annual survey report, London: CIPD.

Economist (2007) 'How Low Can You Go', *The Economist*, 8–14 December, 46–48.

Grainger, H. and Crowther, M. (2007) Trade Union Membership 2006, London: Department of Trade and Industry.

Gratton, L. (2004) 'More than Money', *People Management*, 29 January, 23.

Gross, S. and Friedman, H. (2004) 'Holistic Approach Better Supports Business Success', *Benefits Quarterly*, third quarter, 7–12.

Hale, D. (2007) 'Labour Disputes in 2006', *Economic & Labour Market Review*, 1, 6, June, 25–36.

Hayward, B., Peters, M., Rousseau, N., and Seeds, K. (2004) *Findings from the Survey of Employment Tribunal Applications*, 2003, London: Department of Trade and Industry.

Industrial Relations Services (2003) 'Totally Rewarding', *IRS Employment Review*, 782, 15 August, 34–36.

Kahn-Freund, O. (1954) 'The Legal Framework' in Flanders, A. and Clegg, H. (eds) *The System of Industrial Relations in Britain*, Oxford: Blackwell.

Kaplan, S. L. (2005) 'Total Rewards in Action: Developing a Total Rewards Strategy', *Benefits and Compensation Digest*, August, 32–37.

Kersley, B., Alpin, C., Forth, J., Bryson, A., Bewley, H., Dix, G., and Oxenbridge, S. (2006) *Inside the Workplace: Findings from the 2004 Workplace Employment Relations Survey*, London: Routledge.

Kochanski, J. and Ledford, G. (2001) '"How to Keep Me" – Retaining Technical Professionals', *Research Technology Management*, May–June, 31–38.

Medcof, J. and Rumpel, S. (2007) 'High Technology Workers and Total Rewards', *The Journal of High Technology Management Research*, 18, 1, 59–72.

Oliver, N. and Wilkinson, B. (1992) *The Japanization of British Industry*, 2nd ed., Oxford: Blackwells.

Pfau, B. and Kay, I. (2002) 'The Five Key Elements of a Total Rewards and Accountability Orientation', *Benefits Quarterly*, third quarter, 7–15.

Poster, C. Z. and Scanella, J. (2001) 'Total Rewards in an iDeal World', *Benefits Quarterly*, third quarter, 23–28.

Schuster, J. and Zingheim, P. (2004) 'Total Rewards', *Executive Excellence*, 21, 1, January, 5.

Stiles, P. (2007) 'A World of Difference?', *People Management*, 15 November, 36–41.

WorldatWork (2006) www.worldatwork.org/waw/aboutus/html/aboutus-whatis.html

Zingheim, P. and Schuster, J. (2001) 'Winning the Talent Game: Total Rewards and the Better Workforce Deal', *Compensation & Benefits Management*, Summer, 33–39.

Index

bonuses – *continued*
  target-driven, 11
  trade union views, 110, 111, 115
  US strategy, 78
broad banded pay structures
  anchor points, 67, 251
  employee expectations, 78
  individual job ranges, 68
  job families, 67
  limits to scope, 67, 251
  move towards, 16, 62
  'new pay', 7, 61
  pay progression, 65–7, 70
  private sector, 16, 64, 72, 248
  public sector, 74
  reference points, 67, 251
  segments and zones, 67, 68, 251
bus industry, 240

Cable & Wireless, 176
Cadman case, 63
cafeteria benefits, 18, 29, 206
care homes, 130, 131
career families, 67–8
Chartered Institute of Personnel and
  Development (CIPD), 4, 22, 27, 62, 70–2
chief executive officers (CEOs), 157, 163, 170
Churchill, Winston, 122–3
cleaners, cleaning, 12, 51, 53, 54, 94, 129, 131
clothing and footwear, 131
collective bargaining
  in Austria, Norway and UK, 15, 17, 112–14
  changing pattern, 43–7
  coverage, 46 (Table 3.2), 133
  decline, 6, 16, 43–7, 56, 82, 103, 121, 250
  employee share ownership, 241
  employee voice, 41–2, 48–9 (Figure 3.1)
  incidence and coverage, 46 (Table 3.2)
  performance pay and, 15, 17, 102–4, 106, 114,
    116, 251
  private sector, 21, 121
  role, 121
  traditional, 5, 37, 41
communication channels, 55–6
community unions, 55
company councils, 48–9
competency-based progression, 68–9
Conservative
  government, 73, 123
  party, 124, 150, 152
consultants, 30, 252, 255
consultative committees, 49 (Figure 3.1)
contingency theory, 26, 29, 35
contribution-based progression, 69–70
cost-control, 105, 109

cost of living
  annual adjustments, 7, 73, 248
  guaranteed adjustments, 77
  local and regional variations, 16, 86–90, 93
    (Figure 5.2), 95, 97
  PPSs, 110

defined benefit pension arrangements, 17, 185,
  186, 188–90, 194, 196
defined contribution pension arrangements, 17,
  168, 184, 185, 189 (Figure 10.3), 194, 204
Denmark, employee share ownership, 230
  (Table 12.1)
dentists, 50, 91–2
Director's Remuneration Report Regulations,
  159, 168, 250
discrimination law, 77–8, 139, 141–5, 147–9, 150–4
doctors, 50, 91–2, 94, 95–7, 142
dual channel representation, 112–13, 114, 116

early retirement, 187
East London Communities Organisation
  (TELCO), 54
economics
  perspectives, 15, 212–13
  tension with social psychology theories, 10–12
    (Figure 1.1), 13, 255
education, local pay, 91
employee expectations, 78
employee share ownership, 18, 224–5, 240–2
  characteristics of plans, 225–7
  evidence on union presence and share
    ownership, 238–40
  examples of plans, 228–9
  government policies towards, 232–5
  incidence, 229–32 (Table 12.1)
  legislation and regulations, 229–30, 250
  participation rates, 231–2
  pay strategy case studies, 29
  taxation arrangements, 227, 230
  trade union perspectives, 235–8
employee surveys
  employee voice, 16, 41, 49 (Figure 3.1), 53–4,
    56, 248
  flexible benefits, 213, 215 (Table 11.2), 216
employee voice, 41–2, 55–6
  emergence of, 42–7
  new outlets and influences, 47–55
  public sector, 41, 50–3, 248
employers, pension provision, 202–3
employment tribunals
  equal pay, 141, 150–3
  legal aid issues, 139, 144, 152
  multiple equal pay claims, 150–1
  National Minimum Wage, 127, 153